DISADVANTAGED BY WHERE YOU LIVE?

Neighbourhood governance in contemporary urban policy

Ian Smith, Eileen Lepine and Marilyn Taylor

WITHDRAWN
UTSA LIBRARIES

First published in Great Britain in 2007 by

The Policy Press
University of Bristol
Fourth Floor
Beacon House
Queen's Road
Bristol BS8 1QU
UK

Tel +44 (0)117 331 4054
Fax +44 (0)117 331 4093
e-mail tpp-info@bristol.ac.uk
www.policypress.org.uk

© Ian Smith, Eileen Lepine and Marilyn Taylor 2007

British Library Cataloguing in Publication Data
A catalogue record for this book is available from the British Library.

Library of Congress Cataloging-in-Publication Data
A catalog record for this book has been requested.

ISBN 978 1 86134 894 4 paperback
ISBN 978 1 86134 895 1 hardcover

The right of Ian Smith, Eileen Lepine and Marilyn Taylor to be identified as
editors of this work has been asserted by them in accordance with the 1988
Copyright, Designs and Patents Act.

All rights reserved: no part of this publication may be reproduced, stored in
a retrieval system, or transmitted in any form or by any means, electronic,
mechanical, photocopying, recording, or otherwise without the prior
permission of The Policy Press.

The statements and opinions contained within this publication are solely
those of the editors and contributors and not of The University of Bristol or
The Policy Press. The University of Bristol and The Policy Press disclaim
responsibility for any injury to persons or property resulting from any material
published in this publication.

The Policy Press works to counter discrimination on grounds of gender, race,
disability, age and sexuality.

Cover design by Qube Design Associates, Bristol.
Front cover: image kindly supplied by Getty Images.
Printed and bound in Great Britain by Hobbs the Printers Ltd, Southampton.

Library
University of Texas
at San Antonio

Contents

List of tables and figures

Tables

Figures

Acknowledgements

This book draws on a wide range of research carried out with partners both within and beyond the Cities Research Centre. We would like to take this opportunity to thank Professor Murray Stewart, under whose leadership much of this work began. We would also like to acknowledge the assistance and contribution of our research partners elsewhere in this endeavour: academic institutions, regeneration professionals and especially the agencies and communities whose experience is recorded here. However, the views expressed and any weaknesses contained within this volume are all our own.

Part of the research on which Chapters Six, Nine and Ten are based was carried out by the authors as members of the Phase One New Deal for Communities national evaluation team 2001-05, which was coordinated by the Centre for Regional, Economic and Social Research at Sheffield Hallam University and funded by what was then the Office of the Deputy Prime Minister. Phase One of the National Evaluation culminated in the interim evaluation that was published as NRU Research Report 17 (CRESR, 2005). Chapters Six and Nine also draw on the work of the national evaluation of the Neighbourhood Management Pathfinder Programme, also funded by the ODPM and coordinated by SQW (SQW, 2004, 2006). It should be stressed that the views included in each chapter are the views of the authors and not those of the Department for Communities and Local Government or indeed either evaluation team more widely.

Chapter Seven is an adaptation of Purdue (2005), published by Taylor & Francis Ltd (www.tandf.co.uk/journals). It has been adapted with permission from the publisher.

References

CRESR (Centre for Regional, Economic and Social Research) (2005) *New Deal for Communities 2001-2005: An Interim Evaluation*, Research Report 17, London: ODPM.

Purdue, D. (2005) 'Community leadership cycles and the consolidation of neighbourhood coalitions in the new local governance', *Public Management Review*, vol 7, no 2, pp 247-66.

SQW (2004) *Neighbourhood Management Pathfinder Programme National Evaluation*, London: ODPM/NRU.

SQW (2006) *Neighbourhood Management: At the Turning Point?*, Research Report 23, London: ODPM/NRU.

Notes on the contributors

Rob Atkinson is Professor of Urban Policy in the Cities Research Centre at the University of the West of England (UWE), Bristol. His research focuses on cross-national work on urban regeneration, urban governance, community participation in urban regeneration partnerships, urban social exclusion and European urban and spatial policy. He has worked on a range of research projects such as the New Deal for Communities (NDC) national evaluation, European Union (EU) 5th and 6th Framework and COST. He is vice-president of the European Urban Research Association Executive Committee and also sits on the EUROCITIES Urban Policy Research Working Group.

Yasminah Beebeejaun is a lecturer in spatial planning at the University of Manchester. Her research focuses on the construction of ethnicity within the planning process and the implications this has for equality. She is a member of the Royal Town Planning Institute Equal Opportunities (Race) Panel and a Trustee of the Women's Design Service, a charity established to promote gender equality in the built environment.

Laurence Carmichael is a researcher in the Cities Research Centre, UWE. She has been involved in a number of European-funded projects including Participation, Leadership and Urban Sustainability (PLUS) and Governance for Sustainability (G-FORS). She is interested in the role of the local level in multi-level governance, comparative urban politics and policies. She is a member of the European Urban Research Association's governing board and has also been a local executive councillor.

Laura Evans is a researcher in the Cities Research Centre, UWE. Her research interests lie in urban governance, local government and sustainable development and in particular in how sustainable development can be delivered through local governance. The focus of her work in the Centre is evaluating policy specifically around modernising local government. She has been involved in a number of national evaluations including the evaluation of the power of well-being, the evaluation of local Public Service Agreements, the evaluation of Local Area Agreements and the evaluation of community strategies in Wales.

Lucy Grimshaw is a researcher in the Cities Research Centre, UWE. Her research interests include evaluation (on which she also delivers a distance learning programme), area-based initiatives, urban regeneration, partnership working and gender. She is currently studying for a PhD on gender and regeneration organisations. She has worked on the national evaluations of the New Deal for Communities and Local Area Agreements and on Economic and Social Research Council (ESRC)-funded research on the democratic anchorage of governance networks in three European countries.

Joanna Howard is a researcher in the Cities Research Centre, UWE. Before joining the Centre, she worked for an international non-governmental organisation for six years in Central America, as trainer, project manager and programme manager. Her research interests include community participation, empowerment and democracy and particularly comparisons between the North and South. She has published work on local strategic partnerships and community involvement and is currently working on an ESRC-funded international project – Non-governmental Actors in New Governance Spaces: Navigating the Tensions.

Eileen Lepine is a researcher in the Cities Research Centre, UWE, which she joined in 2002; previously she had worked for many years in the public sector in diverse roles, which included community development and neighbourhood management. Her research interests include urban governance, local government and skills and learning for regeneration and sustainable development. She has worked on the national evaluation teams for New Deal for Communities and Local Area Agreements and the EU-funded Urban Matrix project – Knowledge Transfer for Sustainable Development.

Derrick Purdue is a Senior Research Fellow in the Cities Research Centre, UWE. His research interests include social movements, community engagement and urban governance. He is author of *Anti-Genetix* (2000), editor of *Civil Societies and Social Movements* (2007) and has had articles published in several academic journals, including *Urban Studies, Sociological Review, Environment and Planning, Public Money and Management* and the *Community Development Journal*.

Ian Smith is Director of the Cities Research Centre, UWE. His research interests include the nature of neighbourhood governance, the impact of cultural projects on urban regeneration, the use of evaluation methods and quantitative spatial analysis. He has worked as part of the Phase One of the national evaluation of the NDC programme. He has chaired the Evaluation Reference Group of the Bristol Strategic Partnership and has advised the South West RDA on urban issues.

Helen Sullivan is Professor of Urban Governance at the Cities Research Centre, UWE. Her interests include collaboration, citizenship and the role of local government in the new governance. She has published widely on the potential and the limits of neighbourhood governance.

David Sweeting is a researcher in the Cities Research Centre, UWE. His research interests are mainly in the area of local government studies, especially comparatively, and he specialises in local political leadership. He has worked on the evaluation of Neighbourhood Management Pathfinders. His most recent journal article, 'Political leadership and local democracy: drawing a map', written with Michael Haus, was published in 2006 in *Political Studies*.

Marilyn Taylor is Professor of Urban Governance and Regeneration at the Cities Research Centre, UWE. She has been involved in research on community development, the voluntary and community sector, partnerships and neighbourhood renewal for many years and is the author of *Public Policy in the Community* (Palgrave, 2003).

ONE

Introduction: of neighbourhoods and governance

Eileen Lepine, Ian Smith, Helen Sullivan and Marilyn Taylor

Introduction

In 1997, a New Labour administration came to power. Its manifesto promised to 'help build strong families and strong communities, and lay the foundations of a modern welfare state in pensions and community care' (Labour Party, 1997, p 5), as well as cleaning up politics and decentralising power through the restoration of 'good local government' (1997, p 29). There was, after all, such a thing as society – not just families and individuals[1] – and some of New Labour's aims for the revival of society were to be pursued through a neighbourhood connection.

For successive New Labour administrations the neighbourhood has appeared as a significant focus for policy making and public service delivery. The neighbourhood has been part of a number of policy initiatives that have been concerned with tackling disadvantage, improving service delivery, renewing democracy, engaging citizens, reinvigorating civil society and creating sustainable communities. By 2003, for some commentators at least, it was apparent that there were important changes underway in the substance and style of policy:

> Six years ago, it would have been hard to imagine the extent to which people living and working in neighbourhoods would be involved in informing policy, as secondees within government departments and regional offices, as members of first the Policy Action Teams and now the Community Forum, and as representatives of local strategic partnerships and a range of other local initiatives. (Taylor, 2003a, p 190)

Under the third New Labour administration, in 2005/06, the involvement of the neighbourhood in such new forms of governance appeared set to increase. In the proposals under discussion for what was then called 'double devolution', power and influence were to flow from local government, but on condition that they continued to flow beyond it, to citizens and to neighbourhoods. These proposals have since been developed further in the Local Government White Paper published in October 2006 (CLG, 2006) in which the term double devolution does not appear. There appears to be some ambivalence about the place of the neighbourhood in its proposals and this will be discussed further. However, even if the specific focus on the neighbourhood that characterised the later years of the Office of the Deputy Prime Minister (for example, ODPM/HO, 2005) fades, the evidence of history suggests that it will recur. As Lowndes and Sullivan (forthcoming, 2008) have argued, although there is no constitutional commitment to decentralisation and there have been contradictory trends for both market-oriented and government-centred solutions, there is a 'frequent, if intermittent, interest in the potential of the neighbourhood as a site for governance, service delivery, and/or regeneration'.

In this book we are concerned with questions about the nature, purpose and potential or actual impact, of developments in neighbourhood governance – defined broadly as 'arrangements for collective decision making and/or public service delivery at the sub local authority level' (Lowndes and Sullivan, forthcoming, 2008). Both 'neighbourhood' and 'governance' are slippery terms, used descriptively and normatively by policy makers and academics and the ways in which both terms are defined and deployed are considered in more detail in Chapter Two. At this point the following elaboration of key terms is offered:

- Neighbourhoods are understood here as complex, dynamic, multidimensional and subjective constructs, with identities and governance capacities that go beyond preconceived geographical or administrative boundaries.
- Governance is understood here as the combination of rules, processes and structures in operation to secure 'ordered rule' (Rhodes, 1997) in complex and fragmented societies, including the determination of key policy goals, and the design and delivery of related policies, programmes and services.

Drawing on evidence from the post-war period in the UK as well as contemporary accounts from a range of European countries, this book explores why the neighbourhood is perpetually attractive to policy makers. It elaborates the dominant rationales that underpin key policy initiatives and discusses the ways in which the policies and practices of neighbourhood governance have adapted to broader contextual changes, such as the emergence of multi-level governance. Focusing specifically on the New Labour programme in England, it sets out to understand what is asked of neighbourhood governance by a range of stakeholders, including politicians, officials and various 'publics'. It examines whether and how such aspirations are realised in practice, through the development of neighbourhood-based initiatives and programmes, bespoke governance structures and processes, and/or new ways of making and delivering services. It also explores the tensions and 'trade-offs' that occur in the policy and practice of neighbourhood governance, in order to contribute to ongoing debates about the utility of the neighbourhood as a governance vehicle and to illuminate broader discussions of governance challenges for the future. In pursuing these objectives, it also offers insights into New Labour's approach in and beyond the neighbourhood.

This chapter provides the context for the book, offering an overview of the development of neighbourhood policy in the UK and an introduction to a decade of New Labour policy on neighbourhoods. This book is primarily concerned with how neighbourhood governance manifests itself in disadvantaged neighbourhoods. This in part reflects its evidence base of research that has been concerned mainly with these neighbourhoods. It also recognises that concern with disadvantaged neighbourhoods has been a central focus of New Labour policy. However, it should not be taken to imply that the neighbourhood is not significant beyond such areas; and some aspects of the policy agendas that are outlined (such as Sustainable Communities and exhortations to active citizenship) have plainly had a wider relevance. This introduction to key policies is followed by a further exploration of the idea and practice of neighbourhood governance, which frames the key issues and themes we will be pursuing throughout the book. A brief introduction to each of the chapters is then given. This points to some of the key themes emerging from these contributions – themes that are explored further in Chapter Two and in the concluding chapter.

Neighbourhood policy in the UK

In the UK, policy makers have been drawn to the neighbourhood as an arena for policy action since the 1960s. While New Labour has demonstrated particular enthusiasm for the neighbourhood, many of its programmes have antecedents in the policies of other post-war governments. Alleviating poverty and stimulating regeneration through targeted neighbourhood action are both longstanding objectives of urban policy. In the 1960s and 1970s this found expression through programmes to 'improve' housing stock and to rebuild 'community' in the wake of major slum clearance and redevelopment programmes. Neighbourhood combined with a community development approach in time-limited programmes to improve service coordination and build community capacity. Also evident among some programmes of the period was an emphasis on tapping into community resources at a neighbourhood level as a means of providing particular services.

These programmes and the many that have followed them have in part been a response to concerns about a spatial polarisation of disadvantage in the wake of important demographic, economic, technological and social changes, which have touched all levels of (urban) society and government (for further discussion of the European response, see Chapter Three). Targeted approaches have been criticised for excluding poor people who do not live in poor areas from support and for failing to take sufficient account of the fact that the root causes of disadvantage may lie in wider processes of economic and social change beyond the neighbourhood (Bradford and Robson, 1995). Nonetheless, governments have persisted with these programmes. While doubts remain over the exact causal processes involved in, and the relative importance of, the 'neighbourhood effect' there is widespread recognition of the importance of 'poverty of place' in determining people's quality of life and life chances (for example, Andersen, 2003; Fitzpatrick, 2004; Vranken, 2005).

In addition, there has been a fluctuating awareness that persistent inequality and poverty in neighbourhoods may not be explained by individual and collective pathology, but instead may be the result of the actions of unresponsive and uncoordinated public service organisations (Sullivan and Skelcher, 2002). Consequently, by the late 20th century, central government's regeneration initiatives were seeking better coordination and service improvements through a more cross-cutting approach. Neighbourhood-based programmes such as City Challenge and later the Single Regeneration Budget, for example, covered employment, education, crime, health and the environment as well as community development. In addition to this broader focus there was some awareness among programme designers that meeting the needs of the most disadvantaged neighbourhoods required longer-term change to mainstream service delivery in addition to short-term injections of attention and resources. Regeneration programmes also incorporated a wider range of interests in their implementation, affording prominent roles first to private sector bodies and then to neighbourhood communities themselves, although both with varying degrees of success (Bailey et al, 1995).

Meanwhile, other policy developments focused on neighbourhoods as sources of community governance. This approach to governing sought to address the complexity, fragmentation and remoteness from the public of the prevailing system, by combining network organisation and a citizen orientation (Sullivan, 2001; McLaverty, 2002). This highlights another aspect of neighbourhood policy, present since the 1960s, which links the relative proximity and intimacy of interactions between citizens, service providers and decision makers at the neighbourhood level with improved participation and greater responsiveness, and enhanced democracy (Dahl and Tufte, 1973).

Since 1997, neighbourhoods have been at the heart of the mainstream Urban Policy agenda across the UK. Arguably, however, it is in England that attention on the neighbourhood has been most intense with a constant flow of initiatives emerging from Whitehall since New Labour took office and it is England that is the central focus of this book. The neighbourhood connection has been pursued in various policy arenas, each associated with particular initiatives. Some of these are introduced here, before being discussed in greater detail in later chapters; a glossary at the end of the book also provides information about them.

In the *National Strategy for Neighbourhood Renewal* (SEU, 2001), developed during New Labour's first term, neighbourhoods appeared as a site in which to tackle disadvantage. Most of the programmes associated with the strategy (such as New Deal for Communities and the Neighbourhood Renewal Fund) have had a strong focus on narrowing the gap between deprived neighbourhoods and the rest of the country. Joined-up service delivery and community engagement have also been significant in the strategy. The intention was to place communities at the heart of key initiatives, through their engagement both in the governance of these initiatives and through strategies intended to regenerate community life and citizenship.

The vision for *civil renewal* set out by the then Home Secretary, David Blunkett MP in lectures in 2003 and 2004 connected particularly with neighbourhoods as a space in which to revitalise citizenship. Active citizens, able to define and address key problems and stronger communities – community groups with the capacity to agree and deliver shared solutions – were to work in partnership with public bodies willing and able to work with local people. Later, *Together We Can* (Home Office, 2005) set out a plan to enable people to engage with public bodies and influence the decisions that affected their communities.

The Local Government Modernisation Agenda (LGMA) also identified neighbourhoods as spaces within which to engage citizens in service improvement and to stimulate democratic renewal. Part of a wider agenda for *Modernising Government* (Cabinet Office, 1999) the LGMA has involved more than 20 policy initiatives designed to modernise and improve performance in local government. In this context, citizens have also appeared in part as users or consumers of services and local authorities have been urged to involve them through a range of mechanisms, including area-based forums. A neighbourhood governance connection has been particularly relevant to some of these initiatives, including community strategies, Local Strategic Partnerships (LSPs) and Local Area Agreements (LAAs).

In the Sustainable Communities agenda, neighbourhoods have appeared as places to be produced, in which citizens can gain access to housing and a decent quality of life and that will attract people because of 'opportunity and sustainable growth' (Urban Task Force, 1999, p 25). The sustainable communities plan launched in 2003, following the Urban Task Force (1998-99), and the Urban White Paper (DETR, 2000) set out a long-term programme of action that aimed to tackle issues of sustainable growth and housing supply, particularly in the South East; to encourage regional economic development; and to address areas of low demand and run-down neighbourhoods.

Similar policies and programmes can be found in Scotland and Wales and the programmes in all three countries also operate alongside European initiatives focusing on disadvantaged neighbourhoods, such as the URBAN and Objective 1 programmes. In Scotland, policy for regeneration is contained within a social justice framework and implemented through a nationwide community planning policy, which provides a framework for citizen involvement and also includes special funding mechanisms for targeted neighbourhoods. There is no statutory obligation to involve communities at local authority level (as in England, through LSPs), but there is a duty to engage citizens at the sub-authority level. Welsh regeneration policy also centres upon a concern with social justice and the Communities First programme targets funds at 132 neighbourhoods and 10 communities of interest. Communities are expected to play a key role in the cross-sectoral, sub-local partnerships that support this programme, and community empowerment and capacity development are key objectives. This emphasis is much stronger in Wales than in the other home nations and the Communities First programme has been less prescriptive or target driven than the equivalent programmes in England and, to some extent, Scotland.

In each of the policy areas referred to here, neighbourhood governance can be associated (to a greater or lesser extent, depending on the central focus of policy or programme) with:

*   managing physical and economic development;
*   service improvement;
*   democratic renewal; and
*   socialisation and citizenship.

The particular purposes of neighbourhood governance expressed in these policy agendas are complex and interrelated (and are explored in more detail in Chapter Two). It is a combination of service improvement, democratic renewal and social cohesion through socialisation and citizenship that defines the 'New Localism' agenda (see Aspden and Birch, 2005). 'New localism' is also associated with arguments for increased flexibility at local government level, in recognition of the limits of the centrally driven performance management that has been a key feature of New Labour policy (Lowndes and Sullivan, forthcoming, 2008).

The New Localism agenda has been part of the context for the 2006 Local Government White Paper (CLG, 2006). Its proposals for neighbourhood governance will be developed further in implementation, but an initial reading suggests that neighbourhoods continue to be seen not only as an effective and efficient level for service delivery but also as a level at which citizens can hold services to account through mechanisms for scrutiny and challenge. Ambiguity remains, however, as to the significance of neighbourhoods and neighbourhood governance to future policy and such questions will be considered further in the concluding chapter.

The next section of this chapter introduces some of the key academic debates on the nature of governing and being governed that have informed this book and to which it contributes.

Making sense of neighbourhood governance

Contemporary attention on the neighbourhood has coincided with the emergence of new governance arrangements in many western democracies. These have developed in response to major political, economic and social shifts, including globalisation, Europeanisation, urbanisation and changes to the composition, orientation and sophistication of citizens (Denters and Rose, 2005). These developments are associated with policy drivers (such as those considered in the previous section), which are based on a 'new conventional wisdom' about how cities work (see Gordon and Buck, 2005). In ever more complex and dynamic economies and societies they provide a means by which concerns about competitiveness, cohesion and sustainability can be addressed, through changing the public and private division of labour and locating 'the appropriate administrative scale at which to formulate and implement industrial, social and infrastructural policies' (Gordon and Buck, 2005, p 13). This 'new governance' is characterised by an upward movement of authority to global institutions and a downscaling of responsibilities to the sub-national level (Brenner, 2004, p 3). It is also marked by the engagement of institutions and actors drawn from the private, voluntary and community sectors in the processes of decision making, delivery and resource allocation (Pierre and Peters, 2000; Kooiman, 2003).

For some commentators these developments represent a shift from *hierarchical* modes of governance (preoccupied with vertical relationships and the dominance of governmental authority), via *market* forms (based on competition and contracts), through to *network* forms (built on trust and a sense of common purpose between partner agencies) (Rhodes, 1997). Others disagree with this assessment claiming that, in nation states, governments retain sufficient influence over legal, financial and policy levers to ensure that governance takes place 'in the shadow of hierarchy' (Jessop, 1997, p 5). Nonetheless, there is general acknowledgement that governing now does occur in a wider range of spheres and includes a broader range of actors than previously.

Arrangements for collective decision making and/or public service delivery at a sub-local government or neighbourhood level have an important part to play in new governance arrangements, as regeneration is pursued through neighbourhood partnerships, for example, or service improvement is sought through forms of neighbourhood management. The neighbourhood therefore offers an opportunity to explore the changing boundary between state and civil society, identified by Bevir and Rhodes (2003) as a key characteristic of governance. Indeed Kearns and Parkinson suggest that 'the neighbourhood forms the foundation upon which the other levels of governance must depend' (2001, p 2108), since citizens' reactions to governance changes will be responded to through the filter of the neighbourhood lens and will be informed by individuals' perceptions of neighbourhood confidence (the trajectory the neighbourhood is making). Consequently, pessimism in the neighbourhood will translate into limited participation in local governance and vice versa (2001, p 2108).

Theories about 'network governance' (Rhodes, 1997; Stoker, 2004) pay particular attention to the potential role of the state in a complex and fragmented environment. Stoker (2000) argues that while the state's capacity to control may be diminished, new opportunities to influence through 'steering' have become available, which involve:

> government learning a different 'operating code' which rests less on its authority to make decisions and instead builds on its capacity to create the conditions for positive–sum partnerships and setting or changing the rules of the game to encourage what are perceived as beneficial outcomes. (Stoker, 2000, p 98)

New Labour has pushed this shift to a 'different operating code' locally, for example through its (albeit rather inconsistent) emphasis on local government's 'community leadership' role in relation to both strategic planning and neighbourhood-based activity (Sullivan, 2007).

Various tensions are associated with network governance. Power dependence within networks assumes a need to share, exchange or pool resources premised on a mixture of mutual benefit, trust and reciprocity. However, in practice, exchanges may be unbalanced reflecting the differential bases of power and authority of different stakeholders. For example, while some consider the focus on local government leadership to be an important acknowledgement of the contribution of locally elected members to neighbourhood governance (Sullivan and Howard, 2005), others are concerned that it reinforces local government's tendency to dominate and so 'crowd out' other stakeholders, in particular the public. There are also costs associated with involvement in networks, which the National Evaluations of LSPs (ODPM/DfT, 2006) and of Community Participation Programmes (ODPM, 2005) suggest have a particular impact on community and voluntary sector organisations.

Governing through networks also poses important challenges for accountability (Sullivan, 2003). Parry and Moran (1994) consider networks the burial ground of accountability, as they disguise and confuse lines of accountability. Others argue that we simply need to develop our conceptions of accountability so that they are appropriate to the new governance. For example, Considine (2002, p 23) argues for the development of horizontal rather than vertical accountability relationships, based on a 'culture of responsibility' rather than a 'line of accountability', located in agency rather than organisations and manifest in routines as opposed to formal rules. In practice, any developments in this direction within neighbourhood governance arrangements have tended to be negated by the development of performance-oriented upwards accountability to central government (Sullivan, 2003; see also Chapter Ten, this volume).

A 'new politics' has accompanied the rescaling of governance, which eschews conventional party-based activity to operate through new kinds of political agency and organisation, making connections between international concerns and their impact on local communities. This presents important challenges to national and local government, whose claims to authority and legitimacy rest in no small part on the degree to which they are identified as democratically representative institutions. Newman (2005) argues that these developments have generated new opportunities for citizens to participate directly in the co-production of particular policy outcomes that matter to them (often at the level of the neighbourhood), through networks created by the state for the purpose of improved system effectiveness or via citizen-led networks operating outside conventional political systems and structures. Cornwall (2004, p 2) identifies the former as 'invited spaces' into which citizens enter at the behest of the state and the latter as 'popular spaces ... arenas in which people come together at their own instigation'. These developments represent a particular challenge to 'state-centric' or 'top-down' approaches to neighbourhood governance, which have frequently sought to make a connection to community and civil society, through local leaders or wider resident or public involvement (and sometimes through the intermediary of the voluntary and community sector).

The concern with citizen participation, acknowledged as an important feature of new forms of governance, is clearly influenced by normative arguments about the appropriate role of citizens in society. The communitarian view that the development of appropriate governance arrangements must begin with a consideration of the rights and responsibilities of citizens and the bonds that arise from collective action within communities (Etzioni, 1995) has been particularly important in the discourses of New Labour. From this perspective, self-help, social capital and community building are identified as important building blocks of 'successful' or 'inclusive' communities and neighbourhoods (Tam, 1998). The role of the state is to provide support to these activities and to develop governing and service delivery structures and processes that are decentralised and responsive. The civil renewal agenda espoused by David Blunkett (2003) reflected these values and critically proposed that collective action within and between different communities would help to foster stronger and more cohesive communities.

While New Labour's interpretation of communitarianism has been roundly criticised as being 'conditional, morally prescriptive, conservative and individual ... rather than ... redistributional, socio-economic, progressive and corporate communitarianism' (Driver and Martell, 1997, in Taylor, 2003b, p 40), the work of communitarian theorists has renewed attention on the extent to which citizens should expect and/or aspire to play more active roles in governing themselves and securing their own well-being and the ways in which the operation of the state can facilitate/hinder this. What remains unresolved in communitarian prescriptions is the potential for tensions between communities (of geography, interest or identity) to generate conflict and exclusion, rather than consensus and inclusion, and for differential capacities and resources within communities to support the dominance of some over others.

An alternative perspective on the new governance in general and its manifestation in neighbourhoods in particular is provided by governmentality theory (Foucault, 1979). This draws attention to the possibility that the development of forms of power beyond the state may, in practice, maximise its effectiveness as, while new forms of governance may be:

> innovative and often promising in terms of delivering improved collective services and ... contain germs of ideas that may permit greater openness, inclusion and empowerment of hitherto excluded or marginalised social groups ... there are equally strong processes at work pointing in the direction of a greater autocratic governmentality and an impoverished practice of political citizenship. (Swyngedouw, 2005, p 1993)

Here the spatialisation of relations of power can be understood not as devolution but as a new technology for centralised control with government spreading its tentacles down to neighbourhood (and indeed individual) level. Thus, Rose (1999, p 175) argues that 'community is the new site of governance' and that the 'community discourse' has hijacked a 'language of resistance and transformed it into an expert discourse and professional vocation'. Communities, he argues, have become zones to be investigated, mapped, classified, documented and interpreted.

Research provides some support for this view. For example, evidence on participation suggests that many community representatives in partnerships still feel on the margins of power (Taylor, 2003b; Lowndes and Sullivan, 2004), bearing the responsibilities of the state but without the means to fulfil these new expectations (Atkinson, 2003). However, new governance spaces at neighbourhood level do offer opportunities that citizens can exploit and 'opportunities for the articulation and implementation of alternative agendas' (Raco, 2003, p 79). State strategies are subject to challenge and contestation and often generate new sources of agency for citizens to act on their own terms (Barnes et al, 2007; Taylor, 2007).

In combination the different aspects of the new governance can be argued to have created room for the emergence of neighbourhood governance as an important component of a multi-level and multi-actor environment (Lowndes and Sullivan, forthcoming, 2008). But what forms can neighbourhood governance take and what will influence its shape and nature in practice? It is suggested here that the emergence of neighbourhood governance can be understood in terms of *sites*, *spaces* or *spheres*, each with distinctive characteristics but also with potentially overlapping rules, structures and processes. These are constructions that draw on observable, empirical phenomena, may not be found in their entirety in 'the real world', but offer a lens through which to view developments in neighbourhood governance. They are designed to reflect particular aspects of neighbourhood governance thereby helping to 'bring conceptual order to messy realities, [and] enabling the investigation of variation within and between institutional alternatives' (Lowndes and Sullivan, forthcoming, 2008).

A site of governance

Here the neighbourhood is a defined spatial territory within which policies are enacted and services delivered. However, claims to collective decision making are diluted by the fact that the key levers of power, resources and influence are external to the neighbourhood and remain relatively impervious to neighbourhood influence. The identification of the neighbourhood is itself a feature of administrative and/or professional convenience, rather than a reflection of service user or resident identity. Political representation will be situated at the ward level, but with no executive powers attached although the scrutiny function may be contained within a locally elected member's role. While policies may be enacted in such neighbourhoods for the expressed purpose of 'improvement', resident and user perceptions may reflect a strategy of 'containment', that is, managing poverty and inequality through tailor-made programmes that are separate and distinct from the mainstream.

A governance space

Here the neighbourhood is defined in multiple ways and there may be clear differentiation between those governance institutions that are created and owned by the state and those that are created and owned by the private, voluntary and community sectors (as suggested by Cornwall's [2004] definition of 'invited' and 'popular' spaces, cited earlier). The amount of financial, political and managerial/professional power that is devolved will vary by policy or service area and will be contingent on national policy and local strategic frameworks. For state agencies the emphasis may be on drawing on neighbourhood identities to help make decisions about how resources are allocated and how 'joined-up' action may be secured between relevant providers. For private, voluntary and community sector bodies the emphasis may be on representing the views of particular interests to these 'top-down' bodies and/or making claims to design and deliver programmes, projects and services, either in partnership with public bodies or as freestanding providers. Locally elected members are a core part of the state-owned neighbourhood institutions but also have a role as a bridge between these and those of the private, voluntary and community sectors.

A governance sphere

The emphasis here is on collective decision making through the operation of neighbourhood networks and to this end financial, political and managerial/professional power is devolved to the relevant neighbourhood institution. Again, the neighbourhood is defined in multiple ways to reflect the interests of different stakeholders, but in each case it is situated in a set of relationships with other spheres of governance, be they local, sub-regional, regional, national or supra-national. There are physical manifestations of neighbourhood governance but these may be within the control of any/all of the public, private, voluntary and community sectors. Services and policy initiatives are designed and delivered in a variety of ways and co-production is prioritised. Locally elected members play a key role in facilitating exchanges where necessary between networks, both horizontally and vertically.

Neighbourhoods and neighbourhood governance have been longstanding features of the urban policy landscape and academic discourse for over 30 years. New Labour has embraced both concepts in a variety of policy settings and in Chapter Eleven the three lenses of site, space and sphere will be applied to the deployment of these terms since 1997. The evidence relating to the interrogation of the concepts is set out in the chapters of this volume. These chapters are summarised in the next section.

Chapter summaries

Chapter Two, 'Theories of "neighbourhood" in urban policy', examines the different theories of 'neighbourhood' that have informed the development of public policy. It considers also the shift in academic focus over time from an emphasis on neighbourhoods as a set of physical entities to neighbourhoods as socially constructed objects imbued with meaning by residents. The normative neighbourhood discourse in current UK policy (and especially in England) brings together a number of policy strands from civil renewal, community engagement and consumerism, to democratisation and decentralisation. Sullivan and Taylor flesh out the policy world that has been outlined earlier and the challenges that it poses, reminding us that neighbourhoods are complex, multidimensional and dynamic.

Chapter Three, 'Neighbourhood as a new focus for action in the urban policies of West European states', sets developments in UK urban policy in a European context. Atkinson and Carmichael examine a growing focus on neighbourhoods, which has been closely related to a concern with social exclusion within European societies and with a growing recognition that it is taking distinct spatial forms in danger of becoming deeply embedded in those societies. The chapter compares area-based responses in England, France and Denmark and the differing national contexts that have shaped them.

In Chapter Four, 'Under construction – the city-region and the neighbourhood: new actors in a system of multi-level governance?', Atkinson examines the functions of and linkages between neighbourhood governance and broader sets of governance arrangements. Under the growing pressure of globalisation and the apparent decline of the nation state, the city-region (or metropolitan region) has increasingly been defined as the natural focus for economic development policies while the neighbourhood has become a key arena for a range of more 'socially oriented' policies associated with disadvantaged areas related to urban regeneration, service delivery and policing. Both are forms of territorial governance under construction emerging in an already complex governance environment.

Chapter Five, 'More local than local government: the relationship between local government and the neighbourhood agenda', considers the particular relationship between local government and neighbourhood governance. Lepine and Sullivan draw on evidence from old and new approaches to decentralisation below the local government level. The chapter explores the motivations that have been at work and the gains that have been sought through connection to the neighbourhood. In doing so, it looks not only at the issues of design and performance of good governance, but also at the changing discourse of governance and the processes of argument, acceptance and change in our ideas about what is to be done (administrative 'doctrines' after Hood and Jackson, 1991).

In Chapter Six, 'Neighbourhoods, democracy and citizenship', Howard and Sweeting explore the realities of neighbourhood governance and examine tensions between forms of democracy through an analysis of key programmes in the government's Neighbourhood Renewal agenda. The current emphasis on neighbourhood governance promises to reconfigure local democracy and the neighbourhood level is presented as having the potential for widespread citizen participation and engagement. Government asserts that 'neighbourhood arrangements must be consistent with local representative democracy' (ODPM/HO, 2005, p 16), but government prescription remains ambiguous on the nature of democracy in neighbourhoods.

In Chapter Seven, 'Community leadership cycles and neighbourhood governance', Purdue outlines the process by which community leaders engage with regeneration partnerships through leadership coalitions. He describes a cycle of leadership, which operates differently in areas with different histories of community activity, and considers how far leaders relate to their wider constituency and how they deal with issues of succession. Purdue uses Hirschman's conceptual framework of exit, voice and loyalty to explore the way in which leaders negotiate partnerships at different points in the leadership cycle, and discusses how far community leaders actually become part of local leadership coalitions rather than being left on the margins.

Chapter Eight, 'Neighbourhood governance and diversity: the diverse neighbourhood', takes on the problematic issue of diverse communities within neighbourhood governance. The chapter recognises the potential of neighbourhood governance to respond to diversity but rejects easy assumptions about its capacity to do so. It notes and challenges the tendency to see equalities questions as answered through the representation of particular groups and suggests that homogenising assumptions about groups lead to a failure to understand neighbourhood dynamics and recognise complex, multiple identities.

Chapter Nine, 'Mainstreaming and neighbourhood governance: the importance of process, power and partnership', considers the importance of engaging core mainstream service providers within neighbourhood partnerships as the preferred mechanism for getting resources to neighbourhood renewal. One central element of contemporary urban regeneration is that exceptional funding is not enough on its own to tackle area-based disadvantage. The chapter plots the state of mainstream agency engagement in neighbourhood renewal and considers the degree to which this demonstrates the limitations of neighbourhood governance to act. Smith, Howard and Evans thus ask the question of whether mainstreaming is an effective agenda for the delivery of the neighbourhood management of core public services.

Chapter Ten, 'Evaluation, knowledge and learning in neighbourhood governance: the case of the New Deal for Communities', explores the relationship of knowledge and policy through the explicit processes by which knowledge has been generated. Here, Grimshaw and Smith are particularly interested in the impact of knowledge generation on the activities of New Deal for Communities partnerships. This impact is explored in relation to two potential interpretations of how knowledge is turned into learning. The first interpretation is based on the notion of communicative theory and the collaborative approach to the co-production of policy implementation. The second interpretation is based on governmentality theory whereby a dominant discourse imposes learning on less powerful parties. The control of the framework through which knowledge is generated and validated is seen as a key resource in neighbourhood renewal. The outcome is that the strong centralising tendencies in knowledge-generating activities such as performance management and nationally funded evaluation research tend to drown out local voices and local priorities.

Chapter Eleven, 'The future of neighbourhoods in urban policy', brings together the key insights from these contributions in a further examination of the tensions inherent in governance. Lepine, Smith and Taylor argue that neighbourhood governance is not a simple solution to such tensions but one of the arenas in which they are played out. While it is possible to learn important lessons from the evidence about 'what works', which should inform future developments in neighbourhood governance, it is not possible to frame discussions of governance in purely technical or managerial terms; rhetoric and reality are at work in the policy process, and essentially political choices are not reducible to a technical or value-neutral discourse.

Note
[1] As asserted by Margaret Thatcher in an interview with *Woman's Own*, 23 September 1987.

References
Andersen, H.S. (2003) *Urban Sores: On the Interaction Between Segregation, Urban Decay and Deprived Neighbourhoods*, Aldershot: Ashgate.

Aspden, J. and Birch, D. (2005) *New Localism – Citizen Engagement, Neighbourhoods and Public Services: Evidence from Local Government*, London: ODPM.

Atkinson, R. (2003) 'Addressing social exclusion through community involvement in urban regeneration', in R. Imrie and M. Raco (eds) *Urban Policy, Community, Citizenship and Rights*, Bristol: The Policy Press, pp 101-19.

Bailey, N., Barker, A. and MacDonald, K. (1995) *Partnership Agencies in British Urban Policy*, London: UCL Press.

Barnes, M., Newman, J. and Sullivan, H. (2007) *Power, Participation and Political Renewal: Case Studies in Public Participation*, Bristol: The Policy Press.

Bevir, M. A. W. and Rhodes, R. (2003) *Interpreting British Governance*, London: Routledge.

Blunkett, D. (2003) *Civil Renewal: A New Agenda*, The CSV Edith Kahn Memorial Lecture, 11 June.

Blunkett, D. (2004) *Active Citizens, Strong Communities: Building Civil Renewal*, The Scarman Trust Forum Lecture, 11 December.

Bradford, M. and Robson, B. (1995) 'An evaluation of urban policy', in R. Hambleton and H. Thomas (eds) *Urban Policy Evaluation: Challenge and Change*, London: Paul Chapman, pp 37-54.

Brenner, N. (2004) *New State Spaces: Urban Governance and the Rescaling of Statehood*, Oxford: Oxford University Press.

Cabinet Office (1999) *Modernising Government*, Cm 4310, London: The Stationery Office.

CLG (Communities and Local Government) (2006) *Strong and Prosperous Communities: The Local Government White Paper*, Cm 6939-I, London: The Stationery Office.

Considine, M. (2002) 'The end of the line? Accountable governance in the age of networks, partnerships, and joined-up service', *Governance: An International Journal of Policy, Administration, and Institutions*, vol 15, no 1, pp 21-40.

Cornwall, A. (2004) 'New democratic spaces? The politics and dynamics of institutionalised participation', in A. Cornwall and V. Coelho (eds) *New Democratic Spaces?*, Institute of Development Studies Bulletin, vol 35, no 2, pp 1-10.

Dahl, R. A. and Tufte, E. R. (1973) *Size and Democracy*, Stanford, CA: Stanford University Press.

Denters, B. and Rose, L. E. (2005) 'Local governance in the third millennium: a brave new world?', in B. Denters and L. E. Rose (eds) *Comparing Local Governance*, Basingstoke: Palgrave, pp 1-11.

DETR (Department of the Environment, Transport and the Regions) (2000) *Our Towns and Cities: The Future*, White Paper, Cm 4911, London: The Stationery Office.

Driver, S. and Martell, L. (1997) 'New Labour's communtarianisms', *Critical Social Policy*, vol 17, no 3, pp 27-46.

Etzioni, A. (1995) *The Spirit of Community: Rights, Responsibilities and the Communitarian Agenda*, London: Fontana.

Fitzpatrick, S. (2004) 'Poverty of place', Keynote address given at the Joseph Rowntree Foundation Centenary Conference, 'Poverty of Place: Policies for Tomorrow', University of York, 14 December.

Foucault, M. (1979) 'On governmentality', *Ideology and Consciousness*, no 6, pp 5-21.

Gordon, I. and Buck, N. (2005) 'Introduction: cities in the new conventional wisdom', in N. Buck, I. Gordon, A. Harding and I. Turok (eds) *Changing Cities: Rethinking Competitiveness, Cohesion and Governance*, Houndmills: Palgrave Macmillan, pp 1-24.

Home Office (2005) *Together We Can, Action Plan, Parts I and II*, London: Civil Renewal Unit, Home Office.

Hood, C. and Jackson, M. (1991) *Administrative Argument*, Aldershot: Dartmouth.

Jessop, B. (1997) *Governance and Metagovernance: On Reflexivity, Requisite Variety and Requisite Irony*, Lancaster: Department of Sociology, Lancaster University, at www.comp.lancs.ac.uk/sociology/papers/Jessop-Governance-and-Metagovernace.pdf [URL correct as of October 2006].

Jessop, B. (1998) 'The rise of governance and the risks of failure: the case of economic development', *International Social Science Journal*, vol 50, no 155, pp 29-45.

Kearns, A. and Parkinson, M. (2001) 'The significance of neighbourhood', *Urban Studies*, vol 38, no 12, pp 2103-10.

Kooiman, J. (2003) *Governing As Governance*, London: Sage Publications.

Labour Party (1997) *New Labour, Because Britain Deserves Better*, Labour Party Manifesto, General Election 1997, London: The Labour Party.

Lowndes, V. and Sullivan, H. (2004) 'Like a horse and carriage or a fish on a bicycle: how well do local partnerships and public participation go together?', *Local Government Studies*, vol 30, no 1, pp 51-73.

Lowndes, V. and Sullivan, H. (forthcoming, 2008) 'How low can you go? Rationales and challenges for neighbourhood governance', *Public Administration*.

McLaverty, P. (ed) (2002) *Public Participation and Innovations in Community Governance*, Aldershot: Ashgate.

Newman, J. (2005) 'Introduction', in J. Newman (ed) *Remaking Governance: Policy, Politics and the Public Sphere*, Bristol: The Policy Press, pp 1-17.

ODPM (Office of the Deputy Prime Minister) (2005) *Making Connections: An Evaluation of the Community Participation Programmes*, Neighbourhood Renewal Unit, Research Report 15, London: ODPM.

ODPM/DfT (Office of the Deputy Prime Minister/Department for Transport) (2006) *National Evaluation of LSPs: Formative evaluation and Action Research Programme, 2002-2005*, Warwick Business School/ Liverpool John Moores/OPM/UWE, London: ODPM.

ODPM/HO (Office of the Deputy Prime Minister/Home Office) (2005) *Citizen Engagement and Public Services: Why Neighbourhoods Matter*, London: ODPM.

Parry, G. and Moran, M. (1994) *Democracy and Democratization*, London: Routledge.

Pierre, J. and Peters, G. B. (2000) *Governance, Politics and the State*, New York: Macmillan.

Raco, M. (2003) 'Governmentality, subject-building and the discourses and practices of devolution in the UK', *Transactions of the Institute for British Geography*, vol 28, no 1, pp 75-95.

Rhodes, R. (1997) *Understanding Governance: Policy Networks, Governance, Reflexivity and Accountability*, Maidenhead: Open University Press.

Rose, N. (1999) *Powers of Freedom Reframing Political Thought*, Cambridge: Cambridge University Press.

SEU (Social Exclusion Unit) (2001) *A New Commitment to Neighbourhood Renewal: National Strategy Action Plan*, London: SEU.

Stoker, G. (2000) *The New Politics of British Local Governance*, Oxford: Macmillan.

Stoker, G. (2004) *Transforming Local Governance: From Thatcherism to New Labour*, Basingstoke: Palgrave Macmillan.

Sullivan, H. (2001) 'Modernisation, democratisation and community governance', *Local Government Studies*, vol 27, no 3, pp 1-24.

Sullivan, H. (2003) 'New forms of local accountability: coming to terms with "many hands"?', *Policy & Politics*, vol 31, no 3, pp 353-69.

Sullivan, H. (2007) 'Interpreting community leadership in English local government', *Policy & Politics*, vol 53, no 1, pp 141-61.

Sullivan, H. and Howard, J. (2005) *Below the Local Strategic Partnerships*, Issues Paper, National Evaluation of Local Strategic Partnerships, London: ODPM.

Sullivan, H. and Skelcher, C. (2002) *Working across Boundaries: Collaboration in Public Services*, Basingstoke: Palgrave.

Swyngedouw, E. (2005) 'Governance innovation and the citizen: the Janus face of governance-beyond-the-state', *Urban Studies*, vol 42, no 11, pp 1991-2006.

Tam, H. (1998) *Communitarianism*, London: Palgrave Macmillan.

Taylor, M. (2003a) 'Neighbourhood governance: Holy Grail or poisoned chalice?', *Local Economy*, vol 18, no 3, pp 190-5.

Taylor, M. (2003b) *Public Policy in the Community*, London: Palgrave.

Taylor, M. (2007) 'Community participation in the real world: opportunities and pitfalls in new governance spaces', *Urban Studies*, vol 44, no 2, pp 297-317.

Urban Task Force (1999) *Towards an Urban Renaissance: Final Report of the Urban Task Force chaired by Lord Rogers of Riverside*, London: E&FN Spon.

Vranken, J. (2005) 'Changing forms of solidarity: urban development programs in Europe', in Y. Kazepov (ed) *Cities of Europe: Changing Context, Local Arrangements and the Challenge to Urban Cohesion*, Oxford: Blackwell.

TWO

Theories of 'neighbourhood' in urban policy

Helen Sullivan and Marilyn Taylor

Introduction: definitions and debates

The concept of 'neighbourhood' has become increasingly powerful in urban policy and academic discourse. This is illustrated in England both by the targeting of policies at neighbourhood level and also by investment in the production and dissemination of meaningful neighbourhood-level data and the dedication of academic centres and think tanks to the study of neighbourhoods. However, the concept itself remains contested, its use accompanied by ongoing debates about definition and constitution as well as any contribution to the achievement of key policy goals.

Kearns and Parkinson (2001, p 2103) encapsulate the state of the contemporary debate in their declaration that 'there is no single, generalisable interpretation of the neighbourhood'; rather, neighbourhoods are complex and multidimensional and dynamic and their construction depends on the nature of the interactions between individuals and their environments. This academic position is supported by recent policy statements in England, which seek to mobilise support for the role of neighbourhoods in local governance, while at the same time acknowledging that:

> [w]hat people perceive as their neighbourhood depends on a range of circumstances including, for example, the geography of the area, the make-up of the local community, senses of identity and belonging. People's perceptions of their neighbourhood will also depend on whether they live in a rural, suburban or urban area. It may be that people regard an area as their neighbourhood for certain issues or events and a different area as their neighbourhood for other purposes. For example, a single street may be the neighbourhood when people are addressing issues of safety,

such as street lighting or neighbourhood watch. Equally, a much wider area may be seen as the neighbourhood when considering, for example, the contribution a school could make to the life of the locality. Thus neighbourhoods will be essentially self-defined by the people who live in them. (ODPM/HO, 2005, paras 34–35)

Whitehead (2003) offers a rather different interpretation of this apparent policy flexibility. He draws on Marxian interpretations as well as those of Lefebvre to propose the significance of the 'politics of scale' and the social, economic, political and ecological processes through which these scales are (re)produced for the idea of 'neighbourhood' in the 21st century. He argues that the re-emergence of neighbourhood in English public policy is as a 'set of practices – or *neighbourhood actions* – based upon a set of preconceived ethical norms and discursive utterances' (Whitehead, 2003, p 280). In support of his argument Whitehead reviews New Labour's 'neighbourhood' social programmes to reveal the variety of sites that are constituted as 'neighbourhoods' for the purposes of public policy. This suggests to him that 'the neighbourhood is providing the British government with a supple scale within which a flexible geography of state interventions can be legitimated and realised' (p 280).

These different contributions all draw attention to the fact that in practice 'neighbourhoods' will be defined in multiple and often competing ways by different agents (Barnes et al, 2007). Often the bases of these definitions pertain to the particular purposes that agents seek to ascribe to neighbourhoods. Forrest and Kearns' (2001) typology – neighbourhood as *community, context, commodity or consumption niche* – helps reveal these different purposes.

When neighbourhood is equated with *community*, the common identity, interests and collective practices of individuals sharing a (small) bounded area are emphasised. Policy makers often lay claim to the imagery of neighbourhood as community in rhetorical appeals to a past time of community cohesion, contentedness and control. By contrast, residents and community groups may lay claim to the neighbourhood as community as a means of establishing their identity with decision makers, demarcating a sphere of influence (that excludes as well as includes) and resisting the imposition of policy agendas. Often critiqued by academics keen to debate the impact of the 'new governance' on urban living in terms of the 'time–space compression' and related matters of mobility, speed and flows that transcend geographical scales (see Harvey, 1989; Massey, 2005), the 'neighbourhood as community' construction is supported by others like Vaiou and Lykogianni (2006) who argue that most urban citizens inhabit neighbourhoods where the 'everyday', the 'domestic' and the small scale are dominant concerns.

Neighbourhood as *context* focuses attention on the conditions and circumstances that prevail in a given neighbourhood, the infrastructure and quality of service provision, the quality of life of residents, their access to and interaction beyond the neighbourhood, and how these factors affect the life chances of those living in the neighbourhood. Understanding neighbourhoods in this way provides policy makers and service providers with a means of classifying neighbourhoods (for example, as deprived or affluent) and with a rationale for targeting specific interventions. From the 'bottom up', local organisations may also make use of the idea of neighbourhood as context for the purposes of accessing funds and delineating areas of activity.

Understanding neighbourhoods as *commodities or consumption niches* allows for the segmentation of urban areas into marketable units, each offering rather different qualities for different consuming audiences. Private sector interests including property developers and service providers will highlight particular qualities (aspirational, secure, vibrant, family-friendly) in order to market 'lifestyle choices' in residential schemes. Potential residents meanwhile may seek out neighbourhoods whose residential profile and cost offers them status and security (Suttles, 1972).

While accepting the inherent complexity and dynamics of neighbourhoods, it is still possible to identify a number of key elements common to any definition. These are concerned with geography, with the neighbourhood as a social construction, with the significance of attachment and with the lived experience of neighbourhood.

Geography

Urban planners' early work considered neighbourhoods as collections of particular physical entities such as schools, shops, health and recreation centres and much of the delivery of the welfare state was likewise designed around these sites, but the significance afforded to geography has declined. Lowndes and Sullivan (forthcoming, 2008) capture the contemporary relationship between neighbourhood and geography, noting that 'geography is now a necessary – but not sufficient – element of any definition of neighbourhood'. Nonetheless, it remains a means of distinguishing between 'community' and 'neighbourhood' as 'a 'community' may not have a geographic border but a neighbourhood does, even if that border is understood differently by different people

– or even by the same people in relation to different activities and relationships, and at different stages in their life course' (Lowndes and Sullivan, forthcoming, 2008). The significance of geography is also acknowledged in recent discussions of neighbourhood governance. For example, the Young Foundation proposes that neighbourhoods may be defined as: streets and blocks of about 50-300 people, where association, informal social control and mutual aid are key governance tools; 'home neighbourhoods' or 'proximity neighbourhoods' of around 500-2,000 people, bringing together a few blocks – an appropriate scale for neighbourhood warden schemes, for example; and public or strategic neighbourhoods of 4,000-15,000 people where more structured governance starts to make sense (Hilder, 2005).

Social construction

Another key element in neighbourhood definitions is that of neighbourhoods as social constructions, bereft of significance as collections of physical entities until they are imbued with value by citizens (Jacobs, 1994). Healey (1998) articulates this value as being rooted in the neighbourhood as an 'everyday life-world' in which social relations are produced and reproduced. The neighbourhood is:

> a key living space through which people get access to material and social resources, across which they pass to reach other opportunities and which symbolises aspects of the identity of those living there, to themselves and to outsiders. (Healey, 1998, p 69)

Brower's (1996) criteria for 'good neighbourhoods' considers value across three dimensions: physical environment (ambience), choicefulness (of lifestyles) and social interaction (engagement). Ambience refers to the qualities of urban environments, such as density, diversity and vitality that help generate a particular identity or character for a neighbourhood. The value of such attributes is not universal, however, and their appeal is likely to be contingent upon the preferences of particular sections of the population. Likewise, 'choicefulness' of lifestyles is also likely to appeal more to some sections of the population than others. What is interesting about the 'choicefulness' dimension as emphasised by Kearns and Parkinson (2001) is that it can also mean the availability of choice to individuals about where they live, coupled with a perception that their neighbourhood is likely to appeal to others.

Attachment and interaction

Neighbourhood constitution is contingent upon human *attachment and interaction* and the utility of available resources to act as vehicles for self and community expression (Brower's third dimension). 'Dwelling in nearness' (Casey, 1977) facilitates an intimacy of human relationships that can provide psychosocial benefits to individuals, fostering identity and belonging (Kearns and Parkinson, 2001) and can also help generate a collective identity that may be of use in providing resistance to the homogenising effects of (global) capitalism (Harvey, 1973). Jacobs' (1994) conceptualisation of 'social seams' – spaces in neighbourhoods in which interaction between different ethnic and racial groups is sewn together through schools, churches or cultural and social events – provides another source of connectivity in diverse neighbourhoods where different communities may otherwise live 'parallel lives'.

In recent years social capital has emerged as an important concept for understanding how individuals and communities interact with and remain connected to each other. Robert Putnam (1993) has claimed that communities and societies that are rich in social capital are more likely to have healthy democracies, while others cite evidence of social capital as the basis for social cohesion and improved outcomes (Halpern, 2005). Putnam (1993, p 35) defines social capital as the 'features of social organisation such as networks, norms and trust that facilitate co-ordination and co-operation for mutual benefit'. While these attributes are not intrinsically connected to neighbourhoods, many studies of social capital have a neighbourhood dimension and policy makers have become increasingly drawn to the idea of supporting the building or increase of levels of social capital as a means of tackling neighbourhood deprivation and exclusion (Taylor, 2006).

Forrest and Kearns (2001) argue, however, that while the components of social capital may be important in facilitating connections and cooperation between residents in neighbourhoods, there is insufficient evidence of how social capital functions across a variety of neighbourhood types to justify the policy rush to 'build' social capital in deprived areas. Drawing on the findings of a range of social capital theorists, they argue that social capital is insufficient of itself; it needs to be accompanied by other factors such as resources and opportunities if it is to realise the potential that policy makers claim for it. Without these other elements social capital may in fact have a limited impact, enabling individuals and communities to 'cope' but not enabling them to 'overcome' (Forrest and Kearns, 2001, p 2141). With other social capital theorists – notably Bourdieu (1986) – they also draw attention to the 'closed' nature of social capital, when defined as a property of individuals. In this analysis, people who realise their capital through their networks of social capital do so precisely because others are excluded (namely, the old school tie) and social capital is as likely as other forms of capital to reproduce socioeconomic inequalities.

The refinement of social capital theory to distinguish three types of social capital – bonding, bridging and linking – addresses some of these concerns (Putnam, 2000, p 413; Woolcock, 2001; Gilchrist, 2004, p 6). These distinctions emphasise the need not only to build bonding social ties within communities but also bridging social ties between different social groups and linking ties beyond peer boundaries, which cut across status and similarity. The latter in particular allow people to exert influence and reach resources outside their normal circles.

Experiential

Neighbourhoods are experienced in different ways by individuals depending on a variety of factors including age, gender, ethnicity, social mobility and connectedness (see later discussion) (Chaskin, 1997). The experiences of neighbourhoods as places are also informed by and inform individuals' sense of place, what Davies and Herbert (1993) refer to as their 'conceptual identity'. The 'cognitive' strand of this pertains to how neighbourhoods are identified and named, while the 'affective' strand refers to the attitudes that individuals have about their neighbourhoods and the value that they attach to them. Davies and Herbert concede that defining and measuring these 'affective' dimensions is difficult, but is nonetheless 'of central importance in understanding neighbourhoods and place-communities as social constructs with social identities' (Davies and Herbert, 1993, p 2175). Healey (1998, p 69) argues that 'the social experience that develops in places where those in particularly difficult circumstances find themselves concentrated adds to the difficulties people already experience'. Parkes et al (2002) find that residents in less affluent areas are more sensitive to unfriendliness and crime. Current survey evidence also suggests that neighbourliness is less likely where there is overdependence on the neighbourhood context (Bridge et al, 2004).

Lowndes and Sullivan (forthcoming, 2008) highlight several key features of neighbourhoods that reflect the elements discussed here. Neighbourhoods have geographic boundaries, the meaning and value of which are socially constructed; fulfil basic needs such as shopping, healthcare, housing and education; act as sources of predictable encounters; facilitate connections and interactions with others; and help to support/shape the development of individual and collective identities.

Neighbourhoods are valuable to citizens if these key features provide positive comfort and support, but there is no guarantee that they will. Individuals' relationship with and experience of the neighbourhood is contingent on a variety of factors. The subjective, even dialectical, nature of the neighbourhood experience poses an important dilemma for policy makers who seek to determine what are 'successful' and 'unsuccessful' neighbourhoods. Neighbourhoods are simultaneously places of inclusion and exclusion: there are residents who benefit from the prevailing circumstances and those who suffer as a consequence of them. For example, street gangs may experience a sense of pride in the neighbourhoods they have made 'no go' areas, while their neighbours feel vulnerable and marginalised. Or, while newcomers enjoy rising property values and new amenities, long-term residents in gentrifying neighbourhoods may feel like 'strangers' as they see their traditional way of life disappearing.

Because of such mediating factors, it is important to note that neighbourhoods are not the only sources of support. Very often individuals will access and secure support from outside their neighbourhood, via social networks linked to employment, leisure or other activities, which may be more important to individuals than their residential connections. For some, support will be available both within and beyond the neighbourhood, while others will be forced by a lack of connectedness with the neighbourhood to seek support from further afield (Kearns and Parkinson, 2001). This may be particularly important for minority ethnic communities and other marginalised groups. Thus Forrest and Kearns (1999) show how wider minority ethnic networks across the cities they studied reinforced and supplemented neighbourhood ties. This underlines the need to understand neighbourhoods as part of a wider set of interconnected elements that may include the city, the region, the nation and beyond.

While neighbourhoods are clearly experienced differently, it is still possible to compare more or less 'healthy' neighbourhoods. Residents of flourishing neighbourhoods live there out of choice and have pride in the area. Residents of struggling neighbourhoods may feel trapped by an inactive housing market; they may experience a sense of insecurity that is masked by the perceived need to control 'turf', echoing Suttles' (1972) identification of 'defended neighbourhoods'. Flourishing neighbourhoods tend to have better-managed local environments and higher-quality public services. Such neighbourhoods tend to be multifunctional areas, with a diversity of lifestyles and a capacity for bridging as well as bonding social capital. Neighbourhoods characterised by inactive housing markets and welfare dependency may be sites of strong bonding social capital. Here acts of neighbouring may be very important to residents in helping them to cope with their difficult circumstances (Forrest and Kearns, 2001). However, these residents may lack the bridging social capital that is associated with dynamic and productive localities and enables individuals to reach beyond the neighbourhood for support (Taylor, 2006; Halpern, 2005; Bull and Jones, 2006). Bonding social capital can be oppressive to those within and exclusive to others; it can also entrench behaviours that further cut people off from the wider world.

Neighbourhood and neighbourhood governance in English public policy

Just as the constitution of neighbourhood is a matter of considerable debate, so too is the value of policy intervention at this level. Chaskin's (1997) discussion of neighbourhoods is helpful here. He contrasts the 'ecological perspective' of the city and its constituent neighbourhoods as 'the product of natural processes of selection and competition' (p 524), the interaction of which leads to the 'reconfiguration' of the urban landscape over time, with the 'political economy' paradigm, within which such processes are not 'natural' but 'mechanical and manipulable' (p 530), permeable to the actions of governments, developers and companies among others. The former perspective suggests a lifecycle for cities and neighbourhoods that is independent of and impermeable to government action, while the latter affords governments and others some agency. What remains uncertain, however, is how well governments understand what makes 'successful' neighbourhoods, and their efficacy in taking action to help transform the 'unsuccessful'.

As Chapter One demonstrated, neighbourhood is assuming greater significance in policy at the present time, based on the view first that the services people care about are experienced very locally and second that there is a need to 'harness people's interest in the issues that affect their daily lives' (ODPM/HO, 2005, p 9). Policy statements use neighbourhood normatively as a signifier of identity and common focus to those who live there, implying neighbourliness and social ties between its residents. They may make assumptions also about the capacity of neighbourhoods and communities to act as agents to maintain or change their circumstances, as in recent policy statements referring to 'new opportunities for neighbourhoods' (ODPM/HO, 2005, p 1), and in the Local Government White Paper, with its references to mechanisms such as neighbourhood charters and the Community Call for Action (CLG, 2006).

In policy terms therefore, both neighbourhood and neighbourhood governance carry with them a complex set of associated ideas, overlapping and often used interchangeably. To understand their application, it is necessary to unpack the assumptions that come with the neighbourhood label and their implications for policy, as well as the tensions and dilemmas that the label may mask. As Chapter One indicated, it is possible to suggest four dimensions to the use of neighbourhood and neighbourhood governance in policy: the management of physical and economic development, service improvement, democratic renewal and citizenship/socialisation.

The neighbourhood and urban development

The first dimension sees neighbourhood development and governance as a means of managing growth and giving some form of order to a very large scale and long process of urban development, differentiating markets for segregated societies and achieving sustainability (Madanipour, 2005).

The use of neighbourhood to give some form of order – indeed, a human face – to development has a long track record. In the 1940s and 1950s, post-war new towns were built around neighbourhoods with associated neighbourhood facilities – shops, pubs and community centres and sometimes churches – that were expected to act as 'social seams' (Jacobs, 1994). Some 60 years later, interest in the idea of neighbourhood 'hubs', which provide a visible and functional focus for neighbourhood identity has returned to this theme (Hilder, 2005). This package of ideas can be expected to have considerable significance for the large-scale housing market renewal policies of the early 21st century. Meanwhile, it could be argued that the increasing focus on the role of local governance in 'place-making' also contributes to this theme.

The use of neighbourhood as a form of market differentiation raises significant problems for current policy. There can be little doubt that choice of neighbourhood is a powerful factor in people's identity. As we have seen, both Suttles (1972) and Brower (1996) emphasise the importance of what Brower called 'choicefulness' in choosing a neighbourhood to live in – as Suttles argues, one of the main ways of guaranteeing status and safety is by buying into an area where the character of fellow residents is assured by the cost of living there. However, the segregation that this causes has been a source of concern to social commentators and policy makers at least since Disraeli's famous warning about the 'two nations' that Britain had become in the mid-19th century. It is arguable that it is precisely the operation of the market in housing that has created the pockets of place- and tenure-based deprivation that are exercising the minds of politicians today.

One response to this in current policy is to encourage the development of mixed communities in order to introduce greater tenure – and hence social – diversity to social housing estates that are characterised by multiple deprivation. The evidence on the effectiveness of the mixed communities' strategy is as yet unclear – indeed, it is likely to be several years before it can be meaningfully evaluated (see Cheshire, 2006). Atkinson (2005) suggests that it is less likely to be effective where owner-occupation is introduced to very deprived mono-tenure neighbourhoods than when a mixed community is built from scratch. There is certainly a conventional wisdom, however, that a mixed community policy can be effective in tackling stigmatisation (see SEU, 2000). Meanwhile, considerable tensions remain between these government-led deconcentration policies on the one hand, and the tendency to enclave development in the market on the other.

Insofar as neighbourhood is the vehicle for market differentiation, the growing divide between affluent and disadvantaged neighbourhoods might be seen as representing a major threat to sustainability – indeed, the focus on place-based disadvantage in policy is in part a response to the real and feared social disorder that erupts from time to time. However, neighbourhood governance offers an important tool for encouraging sustainability in the broadest sense of the term. In the Sustainable Communities agenda, neighbourhoods have appeared as places to be produced, in which citizens can gain access to housing and a decent quality of life and that will attract people because of 'opportunity and sustainable growth' (Urban Task Force, 1999, p 25). As Chapter One argued, the proximity and intimacy of interactions at this level also offers the opportunity for both community and citizen empowerment that many commentators see as critical to sustainability and for the generation of new and more sustainable norms of behaviour in relation to the environment.

The neighbourhood and service delivery

The failure of services to meet the needs of the most disadvantaged neighbourhoods has been a central theme in New Labour policy. Focusing on the neighbourhood is seen as a way of making the system work better (Sullivan, 2002; Taylor, 2003). It represents a more 'local' or 'in touch' scale of delivery for making services both more responsive and efficient (Smith, 1985), especially over issues that are seen by government as 'close to home', for example 'how safe the streets are, how clean the environment is, whether residents can physically access local services, how good local schools are and what opportunities there are for young people' (ODPM/HO, 2005, p 8). The neighbourhood can act as a focus for joining up services and making them more accountable and relevant to the imagined and real needs of local populations (Raco, 2003), literally through co-locating services in a neighbourhood office and structurally by developing joined-up or holistic responses to problems experienced locally through better coordination, pooled information, joint planning and, in theory at least, pooled budgets. In England, Neighbourhood Management Pathfinders have tested out this idea in practice. While initially introduced in the most disadvantaged neighbourhoods as part of the National Strategy for Neighbourhood Renewal, neighbourhood management is now being promoted in the 2006 Local Government White Paper (CLG, 2006) on a much wider scale.

The neighbourhood and democracy

The third dimension to the use of neighbourhood – and particularly neighbourhood governance – in policy relates to the 'democratic deficit': the need, with falling voting figures and levels of trust in government institutions, to modernise not only the administration but also the political structure of government in order to underpin the legitimacy of state action in an increasingly complex society. New Labour's 'new localism' has introduced a wide range of reforms into local government (see Chapter One), some specifically concerned with improving the relationship between the citizen and local decision makers. These have included separating the executive and scrutiny processes of local government and 'streamlining' executive decision making.

Resident participation has been a key feature of neighbourhood renewal programmes, with an expectation that residents will be involved at board level as well as in a variety of other ways. Neighbourhood structures or arrangements are also being encouraged more widely in the Local Government White Paper (CLG, 2006) as one way of mediating between the individual citizen and the strategic decision making of the local authority. The neighbourhood focus is based on both the assumption that people will be motivated to act on issues of daily concern and the belief that residents' knowledge can enhance the decision-making process. Local authorities have for some time had the freedom to establish area committees (committees that function at a sub-local level with executive decision-making powers), or area forums (consultative bodies with an advisory role) as part of the new political management system. The 2006 White Paper also proposes the extension and updating of the parish council system (parish councils being the most local tier of elected government in England with the power to set a precept). The community 'champion' or 'leader' role of the local ward councillor has also been reinforced as part of this reform programme.

These reforms to local government build on a long tradition among English local authorities of experimenting with decentralisation schemes for a variety of purposes, usually including increased and enhanced public participation in local decision making (see, for example, Burns et al, 1994; Hambleton et al, 1996; Carley et al, 2000; Sullivan et al, 2001). Unlike most other neighbourhood policies, these local schemes tend to be universal in their application rather than targeted. They are explored in further detail in Chapter Five.

The neighbourhood, active citizenship and socialisation

The fourth dimension to neighbourhood policy relates to the mobilisation of the citizen. While the 2006 Local Government White Paper places an emphasis on the role of the ward councillor as the 'community leader' or advocate at neighbourhood level (CLG, 2006), there is still a recognition that enhanced democracy needs to be built on active citizenship at local level. As Chapter One indicated, this has been a major theme in policies such as civil renewal, which have focused on 'active citizens', individuals who recognise the importance of self-discipline and family life, and who are prepared to take on the obligations of citizenship, through individual and collective action (Barnes et al, 2007). The citizenship dimension may also be elaborated to include neighbourhood as a 'unit of socialisation'. Much policy interest in, first, the communitarian approach and, more recently, social capital has been instrumental, seeking to tap relational resources as a means to meet welfare, economic, democratic and service delivery ends. However, social capital and community cohesion are also valued as public goods or 'ends' in their own right, facilitating integration, sustainability, resilience and hence the health of society as a whole.

The assumption here is that it is the lack of social or 'community' ties (social capital) rather than the system of democracy that is in need of repair. The neighbourhood is seen as an appropriate site within which to recreate these ties and associated moral responsibilities that are felt to have been lost, whether it be as a result of physical redevelopment (in the 1960s and 1970s), the individualism of the market, economic decline or, in the eyes of some commentators, the development of an underclass separate from the mores of mainstream society (Murray, 1990). It is worth remarking, however, that, while the need for social capital is particularly strongly advocated for disadvantaged communities, there is no strong evidence that bonding social capital is stronger in more affluent communities. Indeed, research on gated communities suggests that residents there do not necessarily interact with their neighbours (Atkinson, 2005).

Policy challenges

This chapter has described the overlapping ways in which neighbourhood is both understood and used within policy. But a neighbourhood focus is not without its tensions. The implementation of neighbourhood governance, in particular, raises a number of important questions, which are outlined here and addressed more fully in subsequent chapters.

Targeting or reinforcing exclusion?

Until recently, the neighbourhood discourse has been applied mainly to disadvantaged neighbourhoods and, under New Labour, has been closely associated with the policy focus on social exclusion (see Chapter One). As Murie and Musterd argue (2004), the focus on neighbourhood draws attention not only to the concentration of disadvantage but also the compound nature of disadvantage, its persistence over time and its resistance to existing or traditional solutions.

Targeted policies are concerned with the need to 'narrow the gap between the most deprived neighbourhoods and the rest of the country' (SEU, 2001, p 8). An assumption underlying these policies is that certain neighbourhoods lack the inherent capacity or social capital to compete and that, for a variety of reasons, they are not able to attract the levels of service delivery, political attention and choice available elsewhere. They therefore need capacity building, community (or social capital) development, improved service delivery and economic investment in order to improve their life chances.

It is certainly open to debate whether focusing on particular neighbourhoods is an efficient way of addressing disadvantage, as many of the most disadvantaged in society live outside those neighbourhoods that have the highest Index of Multiple Deprivation scores. It is also open to question whether targeting the most disadvantaged areas is a politically viable solution to inequality and social exclusion and whether the electorate will support this long term. In this respect, the fact that policy interest in neighbourhoods is moving away from targeted approaches may be seen as positive.

There are a number of inherent pitfalls within targeting. In a society where most people relate to each other in different ways and in different dimensions, approaches focused solely on disadvantaged neighbourhoods could be building a trap rather than a route out of disadvantage (Taylor, 2003). Targeting encourages neighbourhoods to parade their disadvantage and focus on their problems in order to succeed in the funding marketplace, rather than building on strengths and assets. Related to this, targeted policies tend to focus on deficits and solutions *within* the neighbourhood, ignoring the fact that many of the problems experienced at the neighbourhood level have their causes in wider socioeconomic forces. Murie and Musterd (2004) remind us that the neighbourhood is not always the key factor in exclusion – the ability to cope at this level may be determined at national, regional and sub-regional levels. Targeted neighbourhood policies need therefore to be embedded within multi-level governance (see Chapter Four).

Similarly, policies that focus on the neighbourhood also risk focusing on bonding at the expense of bridging and linking social capital. Friedrichs (2002, p 102) remarks that 'in poverty neighbourhoods, the action spaces and social networks of most residents seem to be limited to the local area' and that this is especially pertinent for those neighbourhoods where poverty is a long-term condition.

Targeting also raises questions about the preparedness of government to tolerate differences and potential inequity between neighbourhoods in terms of access to resources and the 'what' and 'how' of service provision. One of the arguments for devolution is the greater potential of localities and neighbourhoods to respond to their specific and diverse needs. However, for some (for example, Walker, 2002), the fact that neighbourhood control may result in diverse and potentially unequal outcomes – a postcode lottery – is a key obstacle to supporting significant devolution to the neighbourhood level. This issue continues to preoccupy policy makers anxious to establish which decisions can safely be made at the neighbourhood level, and which need to remain within the purview of local or even central government:

> Central Government has a vital role to play in securing minimum standards ... and driving improvement in priority areas. But these central priorities must be carefully focused

... [and] ... should not inhibit innovative local solutions. (CLG, 2006, p 114)

A rather different line of argument focuses on the issue of citizens' choice about whether or not they engage in neighbourhood-based decision making and service delivery. The emphasis on community participation in the National Strategy for Neighbourhood Renewal has given rise to debate about how equitable it is to expect residents in the most disadvantaged neighbourhoods to participate in order to get better services when the rest of society does not have to go to these lengths. By focusing intervention *within* disadvantaged neighbourhoods, critics suggest that such policies are 'responsibilising' the most excluded residents – expecting them to manage their own exclusion (Taylor, 2002, p 125), an argument that is pursued in Chapter Four. A common complaint about much New Labour policy towards neighbourhoods is that it expects the greatest expression of citizenship (through taking responsibility for neighbourhood revitalisation) from those least equipped (in terms of time and resources) to deliver it (Taylor, 2003).

Cohesion and diversity

As this chapter has already argued, the appeal to neighbourhood is often made precisely on the basis that it allows a reformulation of the relationship between the state and the diversity within society. At the same time, however, criticism has also been levelled at neighbourhood policy on the basis that it exacerbates rather than addresses inequalities among diverse populations resident *within* neighbourhoods (Lowndes and Stoker, 1992a, 1992b; Burns et al, 1994). In a communitarian analysis, neighbourhoods are seen as sources of strong singular values and identities. However, neighbourhoods are not the homogenous communities that communitarian rhetoric assumes, and devolution may result in perceived 'outsiders' or those who are different from the dominant groups in any neighbourhood being considered a threat to the prevailing social solidarity. As a result they may be marginalised or excluded from access to neighbourhood decision making and may not be able to benefit from the service responsiveness identified as one of the key benefits of neighbourhood governance. In a multiracial society where minority ethnic groups remain disproportionately represented among the poorest and community cohesion is often fragile, such criticisms need to be addressed if neighbourhood governance is to be viable. These issues are discussed further in Chapters Eight and Eleven.

Efficiency and system capacity

The appropriate scope and scale of neighbourhood governance remains a key area for debate. While citizens *may* desire greater control over decisions and delivery of services at the neighbourhood level, factors such as economies of scale and inadequate infrastructure often result in decision making and service delivery being located one or more steps removed from the neighbourhood where 'system capacity' is greater. Indeed, it could be argued that the new localism runs counter to the efficiency agenda promoted by the Gershon review (Gershon, 2004).

Such issues of scale and capacity were highlighted in earlier experiments in devolving decision making and service delivery in England that were criticised for not having sufficient system capacity for efficient management or fairness in service delivery (Lowndes and Stoker, 1992a, 1992b; Burns et al, 1994). These antecedents are discussed further in Chapter Five. On the other hand, technological developments and changes in management techniques may now mean that service commissioning and decision making are no longer reliant on the physical replication of public service organisations at the local level. A great deal could therefore be accomplished through the operation of neighbourhood networks interacting with service providers who may be located at the district level or beyond.

Linked to the issue of system capacity is the competence of local citizens, elected representatives and other leaders, and officials working in the neighbourhood. Key questions include whether they have the necessary skills, attributes and resources to govern effectively, where support to develop the relevant competences might come from, who will fund such support and for how long it might be needed. As the earlier discussion of diversity has suggested, the skills and resources to deal with the inevitable differences that will emerge from time to time, within communities, between communities and between communities and power-holders are particularly important. The closeness of these conflicts to people's everyday lives can have serious consequences. This places a considerable responsibility on elected members and frontline workers at neighbourhood level, as well as community representatives. But these key players also have to balance immediate local interests with both wider concerns and longer-term considerations. While their nearness to local communities means that they are likely to interact frequently with them, feel strong bonds of attachment and responsibility to them and therefore to try and respond to expressed aspirations, this will often conflict with organisational imperatives and create considerable tensions that, again, existing systems are rarely equipped to manage.

Representative versus participatory democracy

Attempts to encourage active citizen involvement at a local level have always raised complex issues about how new forms of engagement fit with traditional democratic arrangements. The resistance to engaging communities in new forms of governance that is documented in a range of research stems at least in part from a belief that it is the local councillor who is formally elected to represent the 'community' and that this is where ultimate legitimacy lies. Indeed, some commentators see the central government drive for community engagement as being 'a means of disciplining out of touch and self-interested politicians and professionals' (Lowndes and Sullivan, 2004, p 55). On the other hand, the growing emphasis on the community leadership role of the local authority and local councillor suggests a different story. Indeed, the 2006 Local Government White Paper (CLG, 2006) clearly places the elected local authority and the ward councillor at the centre of its proposals for reform, with participatory mechanisms a resource for more formal representative democratic mechanisms and the ward councillor as the channel through which the community voice is mediated. While it does require local authorities to 'show that they are ready to make a fundamental change in attitudes and culture, engaging with citizens and working with their partners in new ways' (CLG, 2006, p 5), the extent to which this resolves the tensions between representative and participatory democracy is an issue that will be discussed further in Chapters Six and Eleven.

Conclusion

This chapter has demonstrated the complexity of the neighbourhood concept and the many assumptions that underpin the interest in the neighbourhood and neighbourhood governance on the part of policy makers. The persistent policy challenges introduced here are discussed further in Chapters Three to Ten, which examine the evidence pertaining to neighbourhood governance, and in Chapter Eleven, which reconsiders the central tensions of the neighbourhood governance debate in the light of that evidence.

References

Atkinson, R. (2005) *Neighbourhoods and the Impacts of Social Mix: Crime, Tenure Diversification and Assisted Mobility*, CNR Paper 29, Bristol: Centre for Neighbourhood Research.

Barnes, M., Newman, J. and Sullivan, H. (2007) *Power, Participation and Political Renewal: Case Studies in Public Participation*, Bristol: The Policy Press.

Bourdieu, P. (1986) 'The forms of capital', in J. Richardson (ed) *Handbook of Theory and Research for the Sociology of Education*, New York: Greenwood Press, pp 241-58.

Bridge, G., Forrest, R. and Holland, E. (2004) *Neighbouring: A Review of the Evidence*, CNR Paper 24, Bristol: Centre for Neighbourhood Research.

Brower, S. (1996) *Good Neighbourhoods*, Westport, CT and London: Praeger.

Bull, A. and Jones, B. (2006) 'Governance and social capital in urban regeneration', *Urban Studies*, vol 43, no 4, pp 767-86.

Burns, D., Hambleton, R. and Hoggett, P. (1994) *The Politics of Decentralisation: Revitalising Local Democracy*, Basingstoke and London: Macmillan.

Carley, M., Chapman, M., Hastings, A., Kirk, K. and Young, R. (2000) *Urban Regeneration through Partnership: A Study in Nine Urban Regions in England, Scotland and Wales*, Bristol: The Policy Press.

Casey, E. (1997) *The Fate of Place: A Philosophical History*, Berkeley, CA: University of California Press.

Chaskin, R. J. (1997) 'Perspectives on neighbourhood and community: a review of the literature', *Social Service Review*, December, pp 521-47.

Cheshire, P. C. (2006) 'Resurgent cities, urban myths and policy hubris: what we need to know', *Urban Studies*, vol 43, no 8, pp 1231-46.

CLG (Communities and Local Government) (2006) *Strong and Prosperous Communities: The Local Government White Paper*, Cm 6939-I, London: The Stationery Office.

Davies, W. K. D. and Herbert, D. T. (1993) *Communities within Cities: An Urban Social Geography*, London: Bellhaven Press.

Forrest, R. and Kearns, A. (1999) *Joined-up Places? Social Cohesion and Neighbourhood Regeneration*, York: Joseph Rowntree Foundation.

Forrest, R. and Kearns, A. (2001) 'Social cohesion, social capital and the neighbourhood', *Urban Studies*, vol 38, no 12, pp 2125-43.

Friedrichs, J. (2002) 'Response: contrasting US and European findings on poverty neighbourhoods', *Housing Studies*, vol 17, no 1, pp 101-4.

Gershon, P. (2004) *Releasing Resources for the Frontline: Independent Review of Public Sector Efficiency*, London: HMSO.

Gilchrist, A. (2004) *The Well-Connected Community*, Bristol: The Policy Press.

Halpern, D. (2005) *Social Capital*, Cambridge: Polity.

Hambleton, R., Hoggett, P. and Razzaque, K. (1996) *Freedom within Boundaries: Developing Effective Approaches to Decentralisation*, Luton: LGMB.

Harvey, D. (1973) *Social Justice and the City*, London: Edward Arnold.

Harvey, D. (1989) *The Condition of Postmodernity*, Oxford: Basil Blackwell.

Healey, P. (1998) 'Institutionalist theory, social exclusion and governance', in A. Madanipour, G. Cars and J. Allen (eds) *Social Exclusion in European Cities*, London: Jessica Kingsley, pp 53-74.

Hilder, P. (2005) *Seeing the Wood for the Trees: The Evolving Landscape for Neighbourhood Arrangements*, London: The Young Foundation.

Jacobs, J. (1994) *The Death and Life of Great American Cities*, Harmondsworth: Penguin Books (first published 1961).

Kearns, A. and Parkinson, M. (2001) 'The significance of neighbourhood', *Urban Studies*, vol 38, no 12, pp 2103-10.

Lowndes, V. and Stoker, G. (1992a) 'An evaluation of neighbourhood decentralisation: part one', *Policy & Politics*, vol 20, no 1, pp 47-61.

Lowndes, V. and Stoker, G. (1992b) 'An evaluation of neighbourhood decentralisation: part two', *Policy & Politics*, vol 20, no 2, pp 143-52.

Lowndes, V. and Sullivan, H. (2004) 'Like a horse and carriage or a fish on a bicycle: how well do local partnerships and public participation go together?', *Local Government Studies*, vol 30, no 1, pp 51-73.

Lowndes, V. and Sullivan, H. (forthcoming, 2008) 'How low can you go? Rationales and challenges for neighbourhood governance', *Public Administration*.

Madanipour, A. (2005) 'Urban development and governance through neighbourhoods', Paper presented at the European Consortium for Political Research, 3rd ECPR Conference, Budapest, 8-10 September.

Massey, D. (2005) *For Space*, London, Sage Publications.

Murie, A. and Musterd, S. (2004) 'Social exclusion and opportunity structures in European cities and neighbourhoods', *Urban Studies*, vol 41, no 8, pp 1441-59.

Murray, C. (1990) *The Emerging British Underclass*, Choice in Welfare Series No 2, London: IEA Health and Welfare Unit.

ODPM/HO (Office of the Deputy Prime Minister/Home Office) (2005) *Citizen Engagement and Public Services: Why Neighbourhoods Matter*, London: ODPM/HO.

Parkes, A., Kearns, A. and Atkinson, R. (2002) 'What makes people dissatisfied with their neighbourhoods?', *Urban Studies*, vol 39, no 13, pp 2413-38.

Putnam, R. D. (1993) *Making Democracy Work: Civic Traditions in Modern Italy*, Princeton, NJ: Princeton University Press.

Putnam, R. D. (2000) *Bowling Alone: The Collapse and Revival of American Community*, New York: Simon and Schuster.

Raco, M. (2003) 'Governmentality, subject-building and the discourses and practices of devolution in the UK', *Transactions of the Institute for British Geography*, vol 28, no 1, pp 75-95.

SEU (Social Exclusion Unit) (2001) *A New Commitment to Neighbourhood Renewal: National Strategy Action Plan*, London: SEU.

Smith, B. (1985) *Decentralisation: The Territorial Dimension of the State*, London: George Allen and Unwin.

Sullivan, H. (2002) 'Modernisation, neighbourhood management and social inclusion', *Public Management Review*, vol 4, no 4, pp 505-28.

Sullivan, H., Root, A., Moran, D. and Smith, M. (2001) *Area Committees and Neighbourhood Management: Increasing Democratic Participation and Social Inclusion*, London: Local Government Information Unit.

Suttles, G. (1972) *The Social Construction of Community*, Chicago, IL: University of Chicago Press.

Taylor, M. (2002) 'The new public management and social exclusion: cause or response', in K. McLaughlin, S. Osborne and E. Ferlie (eds) *New Public Management: Current Trends and Future Prospects*, London: Routledge, pp 109-28.

Taylor, M. (2003) *Public Policy in the Community*, London: Palgrave Macmillan.

Taylor, M. (2006) 'The nature of community organizing: social capital and community leadership', in R. Cnaan and C. Milofsky (eds) *Handbook on Community Movements and Local Organizations*, New York: Springer, pp 329-45.

Urban Task Force (1999) *Towards an Urban Renaissance*, The Report of the Urban Task Force chaired by Lord Rogers of Riverside, London: E&FN Spon.

Vaiou, D. and Lykogianni, R. (2006) 'Women, neighbourhoods and everyday life', *Urban Studies*, vol 43, no 4, pp 731-43.

Walker, D. (2002) *In Praise of Centralism: A Critique of the New Localism*, London: Catalyst, www.catalystforum.org.uk [URL correct as of February 2007].

Whitehead, M. (2003) 'Love thy neighbourhood: rethinking the politics of scale and Walsall's struggle for neighbourhood democracy', *Environment and Planning A*, vol 35, no 2, pp 277-300.

Woolcock, M. (2001) 'The place of social capital in understanding social and research outcomes', *Isuma, Canadian Journal of Policy Research*, vol 2, no 1, pp 1-17.

THREE

Neighbourhood as a new focus for action in the urban policies of West European states

Rob Atkinson and Laurence Carmichael

Introduction

Concern about social exclusion in European societies has led to a growing emphasis, across Europe, on neighbourhoods and particularly on 'neighbourhoods in crisis' (*quartiers en crise*). These are the areas deemed to require 'special' forms of intervention, usually in the form of area-based initiatives (ABIs). Such concerns have been related to a strong focus on social exclusion/social inclusion (and associated notions such as insertion and integration) within European societies and with a growing recognition that developments are taking distinct spatial forms that are in danger of becoming deeply embedded. In most West European countries, especially in their cities, the economic developments of the past 10 to 15 years have been expressed in a growth of inequalities between social groups and the development of 'excluded spaces' and racial tensions (see Madanipour et al, 1998). In many ways, society, and urban areas in particular, has become more unequal, segmented and less cohesive (see Musterd and Ostendorf, 1998).

The emergence of problem areas or *quartiers en crise* in a fragmented urban landscape has triggered a renewal of an old debate on the origins of urban social problems. Are they triggered mainly through spatial processes (for example, neighbourhood effects) or are urban problems embedded in society in general (see Andersen and van Kempen, 2001)? Whatever the cause, there is a widespread acknowledgement that spatial inequalities in urban areas are growing, with consequences for the social and economic dimensions of life for many urban dwellers and that differences within cities are also more acute. City residents may all live in the same city but do not share the same environment and their quality of life and opportunities will often be strongly influenced by the neighbourhood in which they live. Furthermore, while it is recognised that neighbourhoods, whether poor or affluent, can function as important sites of social cohesion, disparities between poor and rich neighbourhoods within a city can affect cohesion at the urban and inter-community level (see Kearns and Forrest, 2000).

In this context, policy makers have had to adapt existing policies, and in some instances develop new ones, to face up to the realities of increasingly heterogeneous cities. The European Union (EU) and most West European states have developed some form of urban policy (see, for example, van den Berg et al, 1998) and a renewed emphasis has been put on the use of neighbourhood-focused ABIs throughout the EU (see Parkinson, 1998; Atkinson, 2000). The renewed emphasis on localised intervention (through ABIs) has, to some extent, contributed to a sense of 'democratic renewal', through community participation and resident involvement at the neighbourhood level in particular. This chapter explores this trend in relation to neighbourhood-based urban interventions in three European countries: France, Denmark and England. Through the comparisons made, it considers the ways in which the wider governance context affects the operation and meaning of neighbourhood governance and neighbourhood-level programmes. The essential argument here is that different European contexts are producing policy interventions that, although superficially similar, are underpinned and therefore shaped by very different social and political processes and that this, inevitably, affects the nature of participation, from its weakest form (information) to stronger forms (handing over resources and control to neighbourhood communities).

It is necessary to be cautious, as neighbourhood means different things in different countries and it is simplistic to generalise national trends to the whole of Europe. Every European state has different state traditions within which welfare is provided, through different institutional mixes between state, market and family, and the scale of participation at the neighbourhood level will depend, in part, on national attitudes to pluralist democratic arrangements. However, this should not deter us from developing comparative analyses of local governance as these allow us to identify causal mechanisms and drivers of political, economic and social change at the urban level (Pierre, 2005).

Case studies of neighbourhood-based urban policy

This chapter outlines the contexts for, the nature of and the social and political processes underpinning the application of one neighbourhood-level programme in each of France, Denmark and England. The particular focus of interest is twofold. First, it sets out the ways in which these programmes have identified the problems addressed, selected neighbourhoods for intervention and gone about tackling the problems. Second, given that resident participation has been identified in all three programmes as part of their respective solutions to place-based disadvantage, it explores both the expectations and the manifestations of community involvement.

The three countries under the spotlight here demonstrate different contexts for neighbourhood-based urban policy because of their differing political traditions and differing local government structures. Given that neighbourhood interventions are a form of welfare policy the focus of the comparisons made here is on welfare state models, the degree to which it is seen as legitimate for the state to intervene and the status of local government (see Table 3.1).

Table 3.1 sets out some of the key characteristics of the three state contexts. Each of these nations has been categorised using a simple three-way typology outlined by Kazepov (2005 – developed from the work of Esping-Andersen, 1990) in which three basic welfare regimes are identified based on the differing roles of the market, the family and the state: the liberal, the conservative and the social-democratic.

Table 3.1: Nature of the state and local government in France, Denmark and England

	France	Denmark	England
Welfare state model	Conservative	Social-democratic	Liberal
Dominant position on role of state	State has right to act in the *'intérêt général'* of all (ie, beyond the scope of standing legislation)	State has right to act in the general interest but strong consensus between state and local government on social action	State action limited to what Parliament defines – state represents threat to freedom
Status of local government	Constitutionally protected as part of unitary republican state	Constitutionally protected as one of three autonomous administrative levels	Limited by statute and doctrine – not constitutionally protected

Kazepov (2005, p 15) distinguishes the three regimes 'by different relations of dependence/independence from the market in relation to meeting one's own needs and by specific outcomes in terms of social stratification and inequality'. Under this schema, England is characterised as a *liberal* regime with a high dependency on market mechanisms for the delivery of public services and a relative willingness to accept inequality. France is characterised as a *conservative* regime, taking an intermediary position in relation to market dependence for the provision of public services between the liberal and the social-democratic. Under such a conservative regime, the political tendency is to maintain the status quo in relation to inequality. Finally, Denmark is classified as a *social-democratic* regime where dependence on market mechanisms is lowest and there is a strong emphasis on universalism, social solidarity and redistribution.

However, in outlining the context for neighbourhood-level programmes, we must add to this simplifying typology an understanding of the dominant position on the relationship between the state and 'civil society'. In France there is general recognition that the state 'has an inherent power to act' (Laborde, 2000, p 546), as if it were the representative of the *intérêt général* ('general interest').[1] Here we have a top-down, statist republican tradition that emphasises the state as the 'representative of the nation' and has an underlying focus on economic development and (national) social cohesion. Hence, groups and organisations in civil society that seek to represent *particular* interests can be seen as threatening the solidarity of civil society as a whole and to the state's right, from national to local level, to define and seek to secure that solidarity.

The Danish state is also recognised as having a legitimate right to intervene in society in the pursuit of the 'general interest'. This emerges, however, out of a strong labour movement and a desire for social consensus and societal solidarity, aided by a small and relatively homogeneous population. It is counterbalanced by a strong localism, embedded in Danish political traditions. Thus in Danish democracy, local government has an important place and is responsible for the delivery of public services.

The English context is markedly different since, while the state's role in pursuing objectives that further 'societal interests' is by no means denied, there is unwillingness to accord the state the same scope of action as in France and Denmark in defining and seeking solidarity and social policy. There is a longstanding English tradition, reinforced since 1979, that the state represents a threat to freedom and thus there is greater willingness to countenance activities that promote autonomous actions by bodies in civil society. Moreover, in urban policy, and social policy since 1979, there have been a variety of attempts to ensure that non-state bodies (for example, voluntary organisations, community/resident groups, religious groups and so on) play a greater role, in partnership with the state, in the provision of services, notably through the policy of privatisation and the weakening of local authorities.

Since one might expect local government to play a prominent role in the implementation of urban policy, the final part of this description of context focuses on local government structure. Table 3.2 outlines the general structure of regional and local government within the three countries. Within both France and Denmark, the existence of local government is constitutionally protected. In France, local government is part of the single indivisible state. In Denmark, local government is one of three constitutional, autonomous, administrative and political levels. However, in England, local government is not constitutionally protected but is a creature of Parliament and statutes and doctrines (for example, *ultra vires*) restrict its role.

Table 3.3 outlines the size of the lowest-tier local government units in the three countries in relation to population numbers. In England, where local authorities are relatively large, a neighbourhood is often idealised as a community of around 5,000 people. France, on the other hand, has a local government structure of neighbourhood representation through 34,000 *communes*, each of which has an elected mayor if little else. The Danish situation sits between the two. In both Denmark and England local authorities administer key welfare state functions, although within England these functions have been increasingly under the financial control of central government since 1979. French

Table 3.2: Regional and local government/administration in France, Denmark and England, 1997-2006

	France	Denmark	England
Population	60.2 million	5.4 million	49.6 million
Regional units	22 regions	0	10 regions
Upper-level local authorities	96 départements	13 amter	34 counties
Lower-tier local authorities	36,551 communes	271 kommuner	239 districts/boroughs
Local authorities combining lower and upper tier	1 (Paris) covering 3% population	3 (including Copenhagen) covering 12% population	115 unitary authorities covering 53% population

Table 3.3: Size of lower-tier local government units in France, Denmark and England, 1997-2006

Number of lower- and unitary-tier authorities with population of:	France	Denmark	England
0-5,000 persons	34,812	16	1
5-10,000 persons	898	114	1
10-20,000 persons	445	78	0
Over 20,000 persons	396	66	352

communes demonstrate a very diverse range of capacities to play a role in the delivery of welfare services and the suite of competence taken on is proportional to their population base. Where the *commune* does not have the capacity to take on local government competence, the administrative role is taken on by central government on behalf of the *commune*.

Neighbourhood-level programmes in France, Denmark and England

Having set out the contexts for urban policy in our three countries, the next stage is to outline the nature of ABIs to be found in each of them. Three area-based programmes covering a similar time period are examined here. These programmes are the *Grands Projets de Ville* (GPV) in France, the *Kvarterløft* programme in Denmark and the New Deal for Communities (NDC) programme in England. Table 3.4 sets out the key characteristics of each programme.

In England the use of area-based targeting dates back to the 1960s and 1970s whereas in France ABIs first emerged in the 1980s. Denmark has the shortest history of using ABIs for social regeneration, with its initial list of 500 problem estates only set out in 1994. Area-based initiatives in both England and France have had a strong association with the need to avoid or respond to social unrest. In England, the threat of social unrest due to immigration in the late 1960s and actual rioting in the 1980s was a spur for urban policy. In France it was the rioting of the late 1970s and early 1980s that initially sparked a concern with neighbourhood-level problems. More recently, the Danish approach has come to be dominated by concerns about concentrations of immigrants.

All the programmes set out in Table 3.4 are based on neighbourhood areas, although there is some variation over the size of area that has been covered by each of the local programmes. The English and Danish areas are of similar size while the French GPV programme tends to

Table 3.4: Neighbourhood-level regeneration programmes in France, Denmark and England

	France	Denmark	England
Programme name	*Grands Projets de Ville* (GPV)	*Kvarterløft*	New Deal for Communities (NDC)
Coordinating framework	*Contrats de Ville* (CDV)	Urban Development Programme	National Strategy for Neighbourhood Renewal
Period of programme	2000-06	1997-2007	1999-2010
Population size of targeted areas	6,500-220,000 residents	1,000-16,000 residents	5,000-24,000 residents
Number of targeted areas	48 (in mainland France)	7 (1997-2001) (5 more added 2001-07)	39
Funding per local programme (per annum per area)	3.7million Euros	2 million Euros	8.2 million Euros
Key objectives	Improve built environment, improve transport links, economic development. Social aspects of better access to employment, education, public services and community safety	Improve social mix in disadvantaged neighbourhoods. Improve built environment, traffic flows and economic development. Social dimension includes integrating immigrants and marginalised groups	Reduce polarisation between most disadvantaged and other areas. Concentrate on housing and physical environment, access to employment, education, health and community safety

cover wider areas, often including tens of thousands of people across different communes within an urban area. The level of funding available per annum per area has been of a similar order of magnitude (between 2 and 8 million Euros per annum).

Each of the neighbourhood-level programmes has been part of a particular, national urban policy framework. Thus, in the case of France the framework for the GPVs was the *contrats de ville* between central government and each of the 160 urban 'agglomerations' with populations of over 50,000 residents. These agglomerations could be represented either by the most significant urban *commune* or by groupings of communes acting together. In either case, the *contrats de ville* detailed the resources central government would direct towards the area. As such, *contrats de ville* are nested both within the five-yearly National Plan and the strategic regional *Contrat de Plan*. In the case of Denmark, the coordinating framework came through the Urban Committee, which brought together six central government ministries. In England, the NDC programme has been coordinated through the National Strategy for Neighbourhood Renewal and the central government department responsible for this. In theory, coordination between the NDC programme and the other programme strands of the National Strategy for Neighbourhood Renewal (for details, see Chapter One) has been achieved through Local Strategic Partnerships that have been set up at local government level; in practice, this has not always happened.

All three programmes have had an expectation of resident involvement but it is in the detail of resident participation that we can see the cultural influence of the national context as it has affected what is observed and what is expected of resident participation. Table 3.5 fleshes out some aspects of neighbourhood governance in these three programmes, focusing on institutional arrangements for the selection process for neighbourhoods and the management of neighbourhood-level programmes and on resident participation in the implementation of the local programmes.

The selection process in France was very much ad hoc in nature, based on factors thought to be relevant by the local and central state. The *préfet de région* (state representative authority in the region) set the areas for intervention and mayors decided which neighbourhoods within their *commune* would benefit from *contrats de ville*. Within the GPV programme, locally elected members (such as the local mayors) selected neighbourhoods to be included (in the context of the *contrats de ville*) in negotiation with local and regional *préfets*.

Table 3.5: Neighbourhood-level governance in French, Danish and English regeneration programmes

	France	Denmark	England
Programme name	*Grands Projets de Ville* (GPV)	*Kvarterløft*	New Deal for Communities (NDC)
Selection process for neighbourhoods	Agreement between local mayors and central government	Bidding mechanism	Combination bidding/selection – one area permitted to bid from most disadvantaged local authority areas
Institutional form of local management	Partnership between local mayors and state in multi-agency executive group and steering group (*comité de pilotage*)	Independent partnership. Executive group of agency stakeholders (local and central government) – some residents on steering committees	Independent partnership governed by board including local stakeholders (local government one of several)
Involvement of residents in initiation and early planning	Yes – tendency to consultation	Yes – residents are involved in setting up projects	Yes – some evidence of deliberative process and involvement in projects
Involvement of residents in outcome delivery	No	Mainly around communication	Some examples of ongoing resident engagement

Within the *Kvarterløft* programme there was a far more explicit bidding process for projects and selection of target neighbourhoods. Starting with a list of 500 disadvantaged areas, prospective *Kvarterløft* areas put in their case for inclusion in the programme. The selection criteria adopted by the Urban Committee included quantitative, socioeconomic indicators, as well as qualitative assessments of each proposal. An interesting aspect, compared to the selection process in both France and England, was the requirement to identify not just social exclusion or racial tensions in the neighbourhoods but positive factors, such as social networks, the quality of the built environment or of open spaces. However, the general framework and the basis of participation were still driven by central government, as it provided the major financial resources and the initial list of 'crisis neighbourhoods'.

The NDC programme operated in a similar fashion to the *Kvarterløft* programme in that central government used a set of indicators (the Index of Multiple Deprivation or IMD) to establish the 88 most disadvantaged local authority areas in England. It was the job of each of these local authorities to coordinate a single bid from their areas and thus create the list from which central government selected the NDC areas.

The basic institutional structures for running these local neighbourhood programmes show some similarities across the three countries. All have been run by partnerships between key public agencies, which had a stake in the neighbourhoods but which rely to varying degrees on the human, organisational and financial resources of central and local government. In France, the implementation of the GPV programme required the setting up of a partnership of local stakeholders and residents although by 2002 only three out of 50 GPV programmes had direct resident representation on their steering committees (*comités de pilotage*) and none had representation on their executive management groups (*groupement d'intérêt public* or GIP) (DIV, 2002). Similarly in Denmark, local *Kvarterløft* programmes were managed by an independent management group, although all projects required the approval of the local authority. In addition to the management committee there were steering groups that included representation from resident groups. In England NDC programmes have been run by partnership boards that combine the executive and steering group functions (in addition there are also groups that steer individual projects and oversee thematic work). These boards have representation from the key public service agencies in the area (local government is only one of many) and by 2005 34 out of 39 NDC areas had elections for resident representatives on NDC boards. In 2005 local residents constituted a majority on 24 out of 39 boards (CRESR, 2005, p 25). However, in 38 out of 39 NDC areas the local authority remained the 'accountable body' for the partnership such that the local authority was legally liable for the use of public money in NDC areas by NDC partnerships.

The logic of the French context dictates a high level of involvement from locally elected members (in particular local mayors), since the *communes* are seen as the most democratic level of government (Desjardins, 2006). The GPV programme emerged from within the agencies of the state to which local elected councillors have a great deal of access (Kirszbaum, 2002, p 2). In France, there is no equivalent to the English concept of community participation. However, in recent years there has been an emphasis on specific forms of resident participation. There would appear to be at least an emerging and implicit proposition that the purpose of resident participation has been to address social fractures not addressed by the existing system of representative democracy. However, in the French context, such participation presents challenges both to the nature of the representative democracy and to the way public services are produced.

Participation mechanisms have increased in France over the past 20 years, especially since the 1995 local elections. However, they have largely taken ad hoc forms associated with specific aims, means and results rather than developing within a coherent framework (Blondiaux, 1999). It was only in the 1990s that community participation *à la française* (perhaps more accurately described as community consultation) was given a legal recognition. The intention of the GPV programme was that, from the beginning, its design should be resident led. GPVs were to combine actions that had an 'immediate impact' on the daily lives of residents in the targeted neighbourhoods, with more long-term sustainable objectives.

The degree to which resident engagement within French urban policy initiatives has extended beyond mere consultation is open to question. In reviewing resident participation in the setting up of *contrats de ville*, Cavallier (1999) has indicated that this has largely been a rhetorical device that has achieved little in practice since it was first introduced in the early 1980s. Others have identified a number of limiting factors. Individual reluctance to participate in a complex policy process still remains, building residents' capacity is time consuming and viewed as 'expensive' and difficult to achieve, as one local study demonstrates (GIE Villes et Quartiers, 2000). Practitioners remain to be convinced of the link between public services and efficiency and need to understand their new role in the system (Foret, 2000). Mayors need to adapt their leadership role and skills to give a stronger voice to neighbourhood forms of representation that directly represent the community and bypass traditional representative channels (see Mabileau et al, 1989; Paoletti, 1999). The same is true for state representatives on the local level (*sous-préfets* for urban affairs) who have the duty to explain resident participation principles and methods. Their methods have been developed in a traditional representative system and it is often difficult for them to embrace resident participation, to understand its advantages and to implement it (DIV, 1999).

The approach of the *Kvarterløft* programme to resident participation was built on a traditional Danish 'consensus-oriented' decision-making model. The programme included housing renovation and new buildings, public space renovation and management, and the development of neighbourhood services and facilities (job centre, sports and cultural facilities). Citizen participation was intended to help create sustainable neighbourhoods, both in terms of institutions and social policy. There was resident and stakeholder (for example, local businesses, schools) participation, through public meetings, workshops and working groups, from the early stages of the policy, setting priorities for projects to answer specific needs, through design, implementation and project management. However, plans drawn up after the initial planning stage still needed to be approved by the local authority. Agreements of cooperation (contracts) between the Ministry and mayors of the cities were signed and were subject to annual renegotiation.

One of the most significant outcomes of the *Kvarterløft* programme was that in some municipalities more permanent forms of cooperation were established between local authorities and elected tenants' boards on the estates. However, in others there was little change in the overall strategy of local authorities and cooperation with the estates remained at a low level. Moreover, social activities on the estates were directed at all tenants and as a result tended to bypass more marginalised groups, particularly immigrants, even though these groups were intended to be the main target of the programme (Kristensen, 2001).

A number of issues appear to have been crucial to the *Kvarterløft* programme including moving to a more integrated approach, the key role of professional project managers and, last but not least, community participation. In many of the *Kvarterløft* projects, community participation may be judged to have been a success as considerable numbers of local people participated in consultation and planning activities. In the case of Copenhagen, one important tool that helped create a sense of belonging and empowerment was good communication, in particular through newspapers distributed in the areas where projects were implemented. Funding for these newspapers was built into the projects themselves (Corcoran and Thake, 2003).

However, generally speaking, many local people still viewed their interaction with the local municipal administration as something of a mystery. Not surprisingly, large parts of the local population did not participate in any activities and were unaware that a *Kvarterløft* project was taking place in their neighbourhood. Community involvement appears to have been limited to the 'usual suspects' with only a very small number maintaining their engagement over the life of each project. Also, while there was an explicit intention to introduce more democracy into urban policy, the legitimacy of the active citizens taking part in decision making could also be questioned since they were not elected (Atkinson and Larsen, 2000).

In England, within the NDC programme, multi-sectoral regeneration partnerships, involving the public, private, voluntary and community sectors, have been central to the elaboration and implementation of local programmes. There was a strong expectation that 'the local community [would be] at the heart of the programme' (CRESR, 2005, p iii) and in particular that there would be an emphasis on engaging and supporting black and minority ethnic communities. Within this it was accepted that:

> community engagement embraces a wide range of activities
> including consultation with residents, boosting community
> infrastructure, involvement of residents in partnerships and
> as board members, and direct involvement in devising and
> running projects. (CRESR, 2005, p iii)

The patterns of resident involvement mirror those of the *Kvarterløft* programme with a relatively limited engagement in NDC activities by the majority of the population and a smaller group of dedicated activists working as board members, project workers and volunteers. On average, after four years of the programme, some 22% of funding had been dedicated to community development (around £100 million) and 79% of residents had heard of the NDC programme. However, of those who had heard of the NDC programme, only 19% had been involved in activities organised by the NDC partnership (CRESR, 2005). As in Denmark, it is reasonable to assume that only a fraction of those residents who had been involved in activities organised by the NDC would take the even more hands-on role of managing projects or sitting on boards and working groups.

The interim evaluation of the NDC programme, at its mid-point in 2005, identified three processes that had encouraged community engagement in NDC areas. First, it was important for partnerships to deliver 'visible and well-branded projects which meet local needs' (CRESR, 2005, p 66). Second, partnerships needed to take a wide-ranging approach to consultation and involvement and be seen to respond to consultation. Third, partnerships needed good communications with residents. The interim evaluation also identified barriers to engagement as: the perception of NDC partnerships as cliques; the entrenched attitudes of residents to public service agencies; a transient population; problems where the concentration on engagement with black and minority ethnic communities undermines a concern with other diversity groups; and finally the institutional history of the area, especially where there is a limited infrastructure of community groups and a history of failed regeneration projects (CRESR, 2005, p 67). Overall, early evaluation evidence for the NDC scheme suggests that the residents in NDC areas at the mid-point of their schemes did not feel more able to influence decisions in their areas. However, over the same period (2002-04) residents were more likely to say that they felt part of their community.

Comparative perspective on involvement, governance and context

All three programmes discussed here share the common aim of solving urban social problems through area-based policies, partnership structures and, at least rhetorically, resident and tenant participation. However, below the level of such broad aims, which are a reaction to a common set of socioeconomic drivers (spatial polarisation of disadvantage, immigration, concerns about social order), superficially similar programmes are underpinned by different political philosophies and differing contexts. They all aim at building citizen capacity at the neighbourhood level in a way that can either be seen to challenge or in a way that offers to complement 'traditional' forms of representative democracy. However, the differing traditions through which the relationship between the state and civil society are articulated either impede or facilitate this process.

As discussed earlier in this chapter, the very act of engaging with people (communities) in specific neighbourhoods and providing them with the opportunity to express themselves represented a significant challenge to the French Republican ethos, in a political context where people are usually 'briefed' rather than engaged in a process of dialogue and co-decision making. It appears that French urban policy will have to overcome ideological and practical problems before it can develop a clear neighbourhood focus and an associated notion of resident participation. However, while progress in France may have been relatively slow, and 'subterranean', compared to the UK, it should be acknowledged that legitimating the taking into account of local, territorially based, points of view is a philosophically significant change in French state political culture. Indirectly and incrementally this may lead to a process of wider change. Thus, it could be argued that due to the largely pragmatic and ad hoc nature of local initiatives in France, and in spite of the limiting factors identified earlier, neighbourhood-based resident involvement could evolve from rhetorical statements to more effective forms of participation. When resident participation is underpinned by the idea of 'sharing power', it can then be argued, following Donzelot (1995), that participation is moving away from its original intention of involving people in dealing with the deficiencies of the institutions they engage with towards something more constructive and empowering.

In Denmark, the 'place-based' approach of neighbourhoods potentially comes into conflict with a welfare regime based around 'people-based' policies that seek to guarantee equality of access and services to all. On the other hand, Denmark, with its longer tradition of 'direct' engagement with citizens, has had less difficulty in justifying neighbourhood-based approaches that require the development of new forms of representation although Larsen (2001, cited in Etherington, 2003, p 13) indicates that individual schemes have found this problematic. As discussed earlier, there have been some emerging examples of more permanent forms of engagement. However, representatives elected through more traditional democratic means (that is, councillors) have still found it difficult to come to terms with the idea of neighbourhood-/community-based forms of representation, which potentially challenge their position. More recently, however, as noted earlier, neighbourhoods with concentrations of immigrants have come to dominate the Danish approach. The problems of these areas have been redefined primarily in terms of their inhabitants' non-integration in Danish society with the blame being laid at the door of immigrant communities.

English urban policy has been much less concerned about the wider implications of area-based approaches and demonstrates a greater willingness to accept the involvement of non-state actors. Arguably, therefore, it provides the most developed examples of neighbourhood/community participation, but also most vividly illustrates the problems that may be faced (see Atkinson, 2005). The English turn to local (neighbourhood) citizen participation is part of a wider approach to modernising central and local government that aims to change the way in which public services are delivered through the 'empowerment' of local people who will put pressure on delivery agencies to change their mode(s) of operation. Arguably, it is also part of an even wider agenda – that of 'responsibilisation' – which seeks to govern through new territories and means (the neighbourhood and the community). This can be seen to operate through the inculcation of people, particularly in deprived neighbourhoods, with new (individual) citizen rights and responsibilities in order to make them responsible for their future and bring about changes in their behaviour (that is, to make them active and responsible citizens – on this, see also the discussion of governmentality in Chapter One).

Thus, we can see that within the three countries, superficially similar area-based programmes are underpinned by very different sets of political philosophies. It is differences in the underlying philosophies that shape the nature of the debate on the use and effectiveness of ABIs in these countries. But we can also understand the interplay of context and the delivery of these programmes in terms of the opportunity structures for neighbourhood governance and neighbourhood-based programmes in these countries. For example, the nature of the engagement of local government with area-based programmes varies in the three countries depending on the scale and competence of local government. In England where local authority areas are very large in comparison to neighbourhoods, local authorities are seen more as a coordinating agency and the conventional wisdom sees elected councillors as distant. However, in France where local authorities are very small in comparison to neighbourhoods, there is the issue of getting lower-tier authorities to work together and the idea of using locally elected councillors to represent neighbourhoods. The notion of scale leads to different perceptions of the 'democratic deficit' but a simple comparison of political participation in England and France illustrates that this is not only a scale issue. Thus, although in France lower-tier authorities are smaller and theoretically 'closer' to citizens, Garbaye (2005) has shown that the nature of local politics in France has made it more difficult for black and minority ethnic communities to achieve local power than has been the case in England. Thus, the challenge for neighbourhood governance in addressing any democratic deficit is not just about being the right size but also about being permeable enough.

However, although one may see a continuum of involvement across the three cases examined here, in none of them is there significant evidence of new forms of neighbourhood governance evolving into co-management and co-decision-making processes at either a local level or a more strategic level. There are common tensions to be resolved. In both England and Denmark, for example, the issue of who it is that community representatives can claim to represent has often been raised. Equally there are common tensions where traditional activists often feel bypassed by new developments such as those examined here. At the same time, a range of groups are largely invisible (for example, minority ethnic communities have often been particularly underrepresented in *Kvarterløft*).

There is also often an inherent assumption within area-based programmes that one of the things needed to improve neighbourhoods is a better 'social mix' of people and tenures; once the 'right mix' is achieved the area will change. However, this also carries the assumption that the problems these neighbourhoods experience have their origins within the neighbourhoods, or at best that the public services provided to these areas are failing to addresses their problems. There may be little attempt to link the problems of these neighbourhoods to wider forces originating at the urban and national (and even global) level. Instead, the assumption is that by changing the behaviour of those living within these neighbourhoods, by developing the appropriate forms of social capital, the problems can be solved.

The past evidence from across Europe on this issue is not particularly positive. For instance, one overview of community participation in Europe concluded:

> We found that most public authorities, whilst approving of community involvement in theory, had little notion of what it entailed in practice, and few policies to support it. Its fragility and extreme patchiness on the ground was clearly related to this general lack of recognition. (Chanan, 1997, p 39)

The cases discussed here suggest that significant efforts have been made to overcome such problems, in programmes developed over the past 10 years, but that they tend to persist. As Chapters Seven and Eight illustrate, communities are not coherent, identifiable bodies with a single set of interests. Conflicts of interest frequently exist within neighbourhoods and the communities that make them up, thereby making it difficult to identify and articulate a coherent series of proposals that partnerships can address. Recent UK research (Getimis et al, 2006) has also shown that neighbourhood partnerships (in two UK cities) did create opportunities for direct participation in governance, but that relatively few citizens actually participated, and those who did were already active in other networks and organisations and so already participated in governance in some way. In order for social inclusion initiatives to reach the most excluded groups, it appears that long-term community development work is required to encourage marginalised groups (especially young people and minority ethnic groups) to participate. The situation elsewhere in Europe is no different and significant sectors of the community remain outside the consultation/ empowerment processes (see Bull and Jones, 2006; Keil, 2006).

The introduction of the neighbourhood and community, however constituted, into partnerships offers both opportunities and threats to governance. Increased community involvement can aid the legitimisation of government interventions in an area, as well as playing an integrative role in terms of combating social exclusion and increasing social cohesion. However, it can also produce resistance to particular forms of development, calls for increased social expenditure that cannot be met from regeneration budgets and demands for more democratic control of projects. Moreover, communities, particularly deprived ones, do not necessarily have an existing capacity to organise themselves, nor the resources that would allow them to participate in partnerships as equal partners.

Neighbourhood is clearly a focus for urban policy in different European countries. Neighbourhood regeneration aims to build durable institutional and community capacity across cities, but to achieve this requires the investment of significant resources over a considerable period of time and the willingness of other partners to support this, both financially and in terms of the development of community infrastructure (of knowledge, confidence and self-organising abilities). In the programmes outlined in this chapter, efforts have been made to address the challenges of community engagement based on different national contexts. Yet it is equally clear that as 'old' challenges are tackled 'new' ones emerge where new and innovative forms of community participation have too often been subordinated to forms of accountability and management required to win and retain external financing. Any new focus is likely to bring new tensions in its wake.

Note
[1] As opposed to the Anglo-Saxon 'public interest' that empirically aggregates particular interests in a utilitarian way, the '*intérêt général*' refers to a greater, rational principle, which everybody is supposed to agree with in building society.

References

Andersen, H. T. and van Kempen, R. (2001) 'Social fragmentation, social exclusion and urban governance: an introduction', in H. T. Andersen and R. van Kempen (eds) *Governing European Cities: Social Fragmentation, Social Exclusion and Urban Governance*, Aldershot: Ashgate, pp 1-18.

Atkinson, R. (2000) 'Combating social exclusion in Europe: the new urban policy challenge', *Urban Studies*, vol 37, no 5/6, pp 1037-55.

Atkinson, R. (2005) 'Urban regeneration partnerships and community participation: lessons from England', in O. Dilek, O. Pinar and T. Sirmar (eds) *Istanbul 2004 International Urban Regeneration Symposium*, Istanbul: Yayin Tarihi, pp 119-29.

Atkinson, R. and Larsen, J. N. (2000) 'The developing EU urban policy: lessons from Kvarterloft and SRB', Paper presented at the 'Cities in the Region' conference, Department of Regional & Urban Planning, University College Dublin, 14-15 April, (unpublished).

Blondiaux, L. (1999) 'Représenter, délibérer ou gouverner? Les assises politiques fragiles de la démocratie participative de quartier', in *La démocratie locale, représentation, participation et espace public*, CRAPS/CURAPP, Paris: Presses Universitaires de France, pp 367-404.

Cavallier, G. (1999) *Nouvelles recommandations pour la négociation des contrats de ville 2000-2006*, Rapport final du groupe de travail interministériel et interpartenaires sur la définition des contrats de ville du XIIème Plan, Paris: Ministère de la Ville.

Chanan, G. (1997) *Active Citizenship and Community Involvement: Getting to the Roots*, Dublin: European Foundation for the Improvement of Living and Working Conditions.

Corcoran, M. and Thake, C. (2003) *Partnership, Urban Regeneration and the European City: A Community Participation Perspective*, EU project ENTRUST report (www.ensure.org/entrust).

CRESR (Centre for Regional, Economic and Social Research) (2005) *New Deal for Communities 2001-2005: An Interim Evaluation*, Research Report 17, London: ODPM.

Desjardins, X. (2006) 'Intercommunalité et décentralisation', *Géographie Cités – Paris I*.

DIV (Délégation Interministérielle à la Ville) (1999) 'Compte-rendu du séminaire de formation destiné aux Sou-Préfets chargés de mission pour la politique de la ville', 5-6 October.

DIV (2002) 'Deuxième rencontre nationale des grands projets de ville, 29 January – Répertoire des GPV'.

Donzelot, J. (1995) 'Participation: de la consultation à l'implication', *Informations sociales*, no 43, pp 21-32.

Esping-Andersen, G. (1990) *The Three Worlds of Welfare Capitalism*, Cambridge: Polity.

Etherington, D. (2003) *Welfare Reforms, Local Government and the Politics of Social Inclusion: Lessons from Denmark's Labour Market and Area Regeneration Programmes*, Research Paper 4/03, Roskilde: Department of Social Sciences, Roskilde University, Denmark.

Foret, C. (2000) 'De la "participation des habitants" au débat public: refonder la démocratie', *Les Cahiers du CRDSU*, no 26, March.

Garbaye, R. (2005) *Getting into Local Power: The Politics of Ethnic Minorities in British and French Cities*, Oxford: Blackwell Publishing.

Getimis, P., Heinelt, H. and Sweeting, D. (eds) (2006) *Leadership and Participation: Searching for Sustainability in European Cities*, London: Routledge.

GIE Villes et Quartiers (2000) 'La Gestion urbaine territorialisée en relation avec les opérations de renouvellement urbain: méthodes et repères', September, GIE Villes et quartiers/CREPAH/Partenaires Development, avec l'appui de M. Krosrokhavar, EHESS.

Jones, B. and Bull, A.C. (2006) 'Governance through civil society? An Anglo-Italian comparison of democratic renewal and local regeneration', *Journal of Civil Society*, vol 2, no 2, pp 89-110.

Kazepov, Y. (2005) 'Cities of Europe: changing contexts, local arrangements and the challenge to social cohesion', in Y. Kazepov (ed) *Cities of Europe: Changing Context, Local Arrangements and the Challenge to Urban Cohesion*, Oxford: Blackwell, pp 3-42.

Kearns, A. and Forrest, R. (2000) 'Social cohesion and multilevel urban governance', *Urban Studies*, vol 37, no 5-6, pp 995-1017.

Keil, A. (2006) 'New urban governance processes on the level of neighbourhoods', *European Planning Studies*, vol 14, no 3, pp 365-64.

Kirszbaum, T. (2002) *Le traitement preferential des quartiers pauvres: les grands projets de ville au miroir de l'expérience américaine des empowerment zones*, Etude réalisée pour le compte du Plan Urbanisme Construction Architecture (PUCA) et du Fonds d'Action et de Soutien pour l'intégration et la Lutte contre les Discriminations (FASILD), December.

Kristensen, H. (2001) 'Urban policies and programmes against social exclusion and fragmentation: Danish experiences', in H. T. Andersen and R. van Kempen (eds) *Governing European Cities: Social Fragmentation, Social Exclusion and Urban Governance*, Aldershot: Ashgate, pp 234-54.

Laborde, C. (2000) 'The concept of the state in British and French political thought', *Political Studies*, vol 48, no 3, pp 540-57.

Mabileau, A., Moyser, G., Parry, G. and Quantin, P. (1989) *Local Politics and Participation in Britain and France*, Cambridge: Cambridge University Press.

Madanipour, A., Cars, G. and Allen, J. (eds) (1998) *Social Exclusion in European Cities: Processes, Experiences and Responses*, London: Jessica Kingsley.

Musterd, S. and Ostendorf, W. (eds) (1998) *Urban Segregation and the Welfare State: Inequality and Exclusion in Western Cities*, London: Routledge.

Paoletti, M. (1999) 'La démocratie locale française, spécifités et alignement', in *La démocratie locale, représentation, participation et espace public*, CRAPS/CURAPP, Paris: Presses Universitaires de France, pp 45-61.

Parkinson, M. (1998) *Combating Social Exclusion: Lessons from Area-based Programmes in Europe*, Bristol: The Policy Press.

Pierre, J. (2005) 'Comparative urban governance: uncovering complex causalities', *Urban Affairs Review*, vol 40, no 4, pp 446-62.

van den Berg, L., Braun, E. and van der Meer, J. (eds) (1998) *National Urban Policies in the European Union*, Aldershot: Ashgate.

FOUR

Under construction – the city-region and the neighbourhood: new actors in a system of multi-level governance?

Rob Atkinson

Introduction

In recent years the notions of city-region and neighbourhood have gained growing prominence in both policy and academic fields; in a sense both are increasingly seen as 'natural units' for analysis and policy focus in terms of addressing a range of problems facing urban areas. This emphasis on the city-region is by no means a trend unique to the UK. Across Europe, under the growing pressure of globalisation and the apparent decline of the nation state, the city-region (or metropolitan region) has increasingly been defined as the natural focus for economic development policies (see Le Galès, 2002, pp 156-9). Cities are now widely viewed as the 'motors of economic growth' (see CEC, 1997, 1998; Atkinson, 2001) and the search for 'urban competitiveness' has become the new 'holy grail' of city development. Over a somewhat longer period across Europe the neighbourhood has become a key arena for a range of more 'socially oriented' policies (see also Chapter Three). The neighbourhood is if anything an even more longstanding and widely used notion in both policy and academic work and has increasingly been assumed to have significance for (urban) policy (Kearns and Parkinson, 2001).

In terms of this chapter, what is important is that one of the crucial ways in which the city-region and the neighbourhood are to be linked, if at all, will be through the form(s) of multi-level governance developed within the city-region (on debates over governance see Kooiman, 1993; Rhodes, 1995, 1997; Stoker, 1998; MacLeod and Goodwin, 1999; Pierre, 2000). More recently this has also included debates over how to link both economic development (or competitiveness) and social cohesion (or social integration) (see Boddy, 2002) and how, and to what extent, different forms of governance can promote such links (see Ache, 2000). At the same time, linked to debates over governance, there has also been a renewed emphasis on citizen and community participation within the neighbourhood (Miliband, 2005a). Thus, in part, the link between the city-region and the neighbourhood is implicitly made in terms of multi-level governance and how the different levels of governance within a city-region can operate efficiently and effectively to govern and promote economic development while ensuring that the organisations/ institutions and formal and informal networks that constitute this system of multi-level governance are transparent, accountable and open to wider participation. Thus, this chapter will focus on the situation in England and seek to outline some of the attempts to build links between the city-region and the neighbourhood that are currently under development, bearing in mind that these are ongoing and lack a clear sense of what it is they are seeking to achieve.

Why the city-region?

Over the last 20-30 years several large urban areas have developed strategic metropolitan (or city-regional) partnerships that aim to work across traditional administrative boundaries in order to address the problems facing urban areas. In part this reflects the recognition that it is necessary to adopt a strategic and concerted approach to the problems facing a city-region. Also there has been something of a 'new fashion' across Europe for the development of such an approach based on the desire to replicate the 'success' stories of several European cities (for example Barcelona) (see Salet et al, 2003, for examples of these across Europe). In England major cities such as Birmingham, Liverpool and Manchester, and smaller cities such as Bristol, have developed various forms of city-region (or metropolitan) partnerships (see Murie et al, 2003 – Birmingham; Harding et al, 2004 – Liverpool and Manchester; Boddy et al, 2004 – Bristol). Moreover, this new prominence for city-regions has also been connected to their role in the development of a 'knowledge-based' (regional) economy and the apparent need to ensure that a certain quality of life is available in order to attract and retain key knowledge workers (Florida, 2000, 2002). The city, as a collective actor, has been allocated a key role in these developments.

In political terms the issue, and role, of city-regions has moved up the political agenda. For instance, David Miliband, the former Minister for Communities and Local Government, made it clear that cities (or city-regions) were to be viewed as the 'locomotives of economic and social progress' in the UK (Miliband, 2005a, p 1; see also Core Cities

Working Group, 2004; CLG, 2006, ch 4; ODPM, 2006a, 2006b). In 2006 Ruth Kelly, the Secretary of State at the Department for Communities and Local Government, emphasised this new status of city-regions by clearly stating that:

> [I]t is city regions – that is the wider economy of cities – that have generally led regional growth in the last decade.... If we are to compete as a nation we must have cities that can hold their own on the global stage ... and getting governance over the right spatial area is essential. Many ... challenges cut across local authority areas, suggesting that some key decisions need to be taken across the city region. Indeed empirical analysis across EU cities suggests that a better fit between administrative boundaries and the real, underlying economic geography, strengthens economic performance across the city-region. (Kelly, 2006)

Kelly's speech implied that for a select band of cities (for example those associated with the Core Cities Group and the Northern Way) there could be a reorganisation of local government's administrative boundaries to bring them into line with the city-regions' economic boundaries.

These proposals were given further backing by the Local Government White Paper (CLG, 2006, ch 4), which made the case for realigning some local authority boundaries with functional urban economic areas and stronger strategic (political) leadership in city-regions to meet the economic challenges facing cities. The White Paper stated:

> The boundaries of individual local authorities are often drawn much more tightly than functional economic areas. This can pose challenges for tightly-bounded ... councils.... This is critical to considering the full economic benefits or core costs of different decisions and can limit the likelihood of optimal economic outcomes from investment. (CLG, 2006, p 78)

It is interesting to note the extent to which the White Paper accepts neoclassical notions of economic development and the search for 'urban competitiveness' as the new 'holy grail' of city development. In this formulation, strategic leadership and 'stronger governance', with partnership at its core, are key catalysts in achieving urban competitiveness. Thus, the White Paper argued:

> The purpose of stronger governance is to provide clearer leadership on strategic issues that cut across existing local authority boundaries, establish a common purpose between partners, and work through challenges in a cooperative rather than competitive manner. Only through such arrangements can hard strategic decisions be made in the most effective way, and can the private sector and all investors rely with confidence on continuity and a robust business environment. (CLG, 2006, p 90)

What emerged from these arguments was a justification for city-regions based largely on an urban competitiveness rationale rather than one based on democratic accountability and closer relations with citizens. In a sense this potentially downgrades the importance accorded to the neighbourhood in terms of democratic renewal, participation and better service delivery. How the two forms will be reconciled is unclear, particularly as the links between city-region, urban governance, neighbourhood and citizens remain vague and there are no clear lines of accountability between citizen and decision making in this form of multi-level governance. One obvious link would be through the stronger political leadership advocated by the White Paper, but it is unclear just how this will operate. Another possibility is through Local Strategic Partnerships (LSPs) (see later). The White Paper (CLG, 2006, ch 4) does, however, offer an alternative to the creation of new administrative city-regions created by a redrawing of boundaries. This alternative could be through the use of Multi-area Agreements (MAAs) that would integrate the Local Area Agreements (LAAs) of contiguous local authorities within a designated city-region. The development of MAAs would be voluntary, allow for pooling of funds and have targets associated with them. The White Paper sees MAAs as not simply limited to large cities; they could also be developed by proximate places in unitary authorities or in two-tier areas. What remains unclear is how and by whom the decision would be made to opt for either a redrawing of boundaries or the use of MAAs. Much of the detail of how city-regions will be organised and governed appears to have been left to a report that will be delivered as part of the 2007 Comprehensive Spending Review. Given that this process will be dominated by the Treasury it is not unreasonable to assume that the 'urban competitiveness' rationale will drive the process.

The link between these emerging forms of city-region/urban governance and the neighbourhood and citizen remain implicit, given the lack of formal means for accountability of the system as a whole. Thus, there is a failure to address how one links strategic decision making at the city-region (or even local authority) level with neighbourhood and citizen wishes other than through traditional electoral mechanisms, which themselves may lack the ability to hold strategic decision makers to account. Nor has the issue of the legitimacy of city-region governance institutions/organisations received much attention, and the question of whom they are accountable to remains largely unresolved both in theory and practice. Given the government's emphasis on what it terms 'stronger leadership models, including directly elected executives, indirectly or directly elected mayors' (CLG, 2006, p 90) the need for transparency and accountability is vital. What we can say is that when considering these issues it is perhaps sensible to bear in mind that 'there is no necessary agreement about what comprises a City-Region nor a great deal of clarity about how the concept could – and even more important, why it should – be operationalised' (ODPM, 2006c, p 13). However, there does seem to be a minimum agreement that the city-region refers to something more than a city as administratively defined; at the very least it includes contiguous suburbs located in adjacent local authorities. Furthermore, there is also a growing recognition that surrounding smaller towns are part of the city-region. Indeed, it may be that a complex of proximate medium-sized (and even large) cities constitutes a city-region (or a polycentric metropolitan region).

Why the neighbourhood?

Increasingly the neighbourhood has taken on a dual status as a location in which deprivation can be tackled and as a potential space for democratic engagement. Moreover, since the late 1990s the term 'neighbourhood renewal' has tended to replace urban regeneration in the language of urban policy and the National Strategy for Neighbourhood Renewal (SEU, 1998, 2001) has largely shaped the current debate. However, the neighbourhood remains a rather vague term and notions of neighbourhood constantly overlap, and clash, with notions of community (or more correctly 'communities of place'), both referring to a local space within which people develop some sense of identity and attachment based around propinquity. There is no clear, or easy, means of differentiating between the two terms – indeed, there is a 'slipperiness' in terms of how they are used (see Chapter Two for more detail on these issues; see also Wilmott, 1989, pp 5-6; Taylor, 2003), with the two terms largely being used interchangeably in the language of policy. Nor is there clarity over the extent to which policy is aimed at the neighbourhood per se, the community(ies) within an area or both. Given these issues it is also worth reminding the reader that in the late 1960s and the first half of the 1970s, under the aegis of corporate management, there was a range of initiatives (such as the Community Development Project, Neighbourhoods Scheme and neighbourhood councils) that sought to focus on the neighbourhood and the community (see Simmie, 1974, pp 27-33; Cockburn, 1977; Atkinson and Moon, 1994, ch 3).

Despite their lengthy and widespread use we are no nearer to reaching any agreement on how to define what constitutes the neighbourhood or community (or city-region). In part this relates to the fact that all are dynamic notions, constantly changing, but we also need to recognise that the different starting points and approaches utilised will strongly influence the definition developed. If we then throw in the issue of identity (in affective and spatial terms) the situation becomes even more complex.

The neighbourhood and new localism

In recent years the 'new localism' has emerged as part of a drive:

> ... that is making services more locally accountable, devolving more power to local communities and, in the process, forging a modern relationship between the state, citizens and services. (Milburn, 2004)

The 'new localism' is part of the Local Government Modernisation Agenda that includes best value, local public service agreements and LAAs that it is hoped will produce the reforms and improvement in service delivery viewed as increasingly central to addressing the needs of urban areas and their constituent neighbourhoods. It also shares the assumption that local government as it currently exists is inadequate and will be unable to secure these objectives. Moreover, these changes are seen as a key element in the politics and practice of empowerment – the empowerment of citizens and neighbourhoods (see Miliband, 2006; see also Pratchett, 2004 for critique). Additionally, although not always in concert, government has sought to develop and promote local action at a more strategic level. There have been several developments that potentially impact on the way in which neighbourhoods could be linked into city-wide developments and potentially to the city-region.

A key element of this 'new localism' is an emphasis on increased citizen participation in determining priorities for service delivery, particularly at the neighbourhood level, and in setting overall priorities for the local authority (for example through the Community Strategy – see later). Increasingly, participation has been redefined to mean more than simple electoral participation, to include both more direct individual and collective forms of participation. In the latter sense, it is the community that is the central focus and this is most commonly associated with the neighbourhood. As David Miliband (2005b), the then Minister for Communities and Local Government, argued:

> At the heart of this renewal is the commitment to civic action that creates value for society – civic action that is done in the main at local rather than national level, civic action that takes root in a partnership of the public sector and private and voluntary sectors, civic action that is rooted in civic pride.

It is within the context of a developing system of multi-level governance and an emphasis on new forms of participation that the link between neighbourhood (and community) and the city-region is, provisionally, being constructed. We need to ask how, if at all, these links are being built and what the organisations and methods are that are being used to construct links between the city-region and the neighbourhood.

Neighbourhoods and partnerships

It is now widely accepted that partnerships, usually related to area-based initiatives (ABIs), are essential elements in the approach to tackling urban problems within neighbourhoods, in particular social exclusion (see Atkinson and Cope, 1997; Atkinson 1999a, 1999b, 2003a). These partnerships, along with the involvement of the community, and to a lesser extent the voluntary and community sector, represent something new in the urban arena. Furthermore, these new partnerships also represent an important part of the new forms of (urban) governance that have emerged over the last 10-15 years and form a growing component of the increasingly complex architecture of governance that characterises contemporary cities (see Stewart, 2003). In a sense, ABIs have been an important vehicle for the development and articulation of community views on the future of their neighbourhoods. But these developments have by no means been city-wide and there has often been little attempt to develop new forms of participation in areas lacking ABIs (although in some cases at the local authority level there have been experiments with participation methods such as citizen juries and referenda). The point is that to date relatively little has been done to put mechanisms in place that ensure all neighbourhoods in a city have the opportunity to develop and articulate collective neighbourhood views and to ensure that these can be brought together at a city-wide level other than through traditional local electoral mechanisms, which are increasingly viewed as inadequate. However, it may be argued that LSPs offer the possibility of developing new forms of participation and representation that go beyond the individual neighbourhood and relate to a more local authority-wide focus.

Developing a more strategic focus at the local level

Local Strategic Partnerships are intended to bring together a wide range of local participants to specifically address issues at a strategic level. As the guidance on LSPs states:

> The aspiration behind local strategic partnerships is that *all* local service providers should work with each other, the private sector and the broader local community to agree a holistic approach to solving problems with a common vision, agreed objectives, pooled expertise and agreed priorities for the allocation of resources. (DETR, 2000a, p 3)

They should 'provide a single overarching co-ordination framework within which other, more specific local partnerships can operate' (DETR, 2000a, p 6; see also CLG, 2006, ch 5). The development of a strategic view of a local authority's needs and how to address them is one of the key tasks of the LSP and here the community is one of the players involved. This implies the need to develop methods of involving all communities (of both place and interest) in the LSP and suggests one potential way in which neighbourhoods (or the communities within them) can be linked into strategic decision making through the processes of co-governance (see Johnson and Osborne, 2003). Local Strategic Partnerships are also expected to streamline the increasingly complex and confused situation that has developed at the local level through the growth of an overlapping network of partnerships and ABIs associated with the new governance system (see Stewart, 2003). Moreover, in areas in receipt of the Neighbourhood Renewal Fund, LSPs are responsible for agreeing the allocation of this funding in order to narrow the gap between the most disadvantaged neighbourhoods and the rest of their area through the elaboration of a Local Neighbourhood Renewal Strategy. However, LSPs do not seem to have displayed a great deal of interest in the neighbourhood level beyond those neighbourhoods that are already the object of regeneration initiatives. Even here such neighbourhoods are often not integrated into a strategic approach to address underlying problems of deprivation and social exclusion. As the ODPM (2004a, p 13) report on LSPs notes:

> Where LSPs have neighbourhood responsibilities we have not observed, except in the case of Leeds, any discussion of the city-wide policies which would underpin the development of an urban policy across the city as opposed to its priority neighbourhoods.

Thus, the situation as regards those neighbourhoods outside the 'regeneration loop' does not appear to have attracted a great deal of attention.

Although only the 88 local authorities in receipt of the Neighbourhood Renewal Fund were actually required to set up an LSP, by 2005 around 370 had been set up (ODPM, 2005, p 21). According to research carried out for the ODPM (2003, p 5) the vast majority of LSPs cover a single local authority area; only a very small number cross local authority boundaries. In essence the LSP is coterminous with the local authority administrative unit. In terms of this chapter what is of equal concern is the lack of resources that LSPs actually have to carry out their roles. This means that local authorities have largely been the driving force behind the establishment and development of LSPs, thereby increasing the possibility that they will be seen as 'creatures of local government'. In practice a great deal depends on the attitude of the local authority and how well established and active other sectors are in each city and their desire and capacity to engage with the LSP.

Nor is there a clear picture of how the regional tier of government has engaged with LSPs. The limited evidence available (ODPM, 2004a, p 11) suggests that while the Government Offices for the Regions (GOs) have engaged with and supported LSPs, a lack of resources has forced them to focus on those in the 88 Neighbourhood Renewal Fund areas. Even here one might presume that the majority of GO efforts are focused on supporting regeneration programmes through Local Neighbourhood Renewal Strategies. As regards the regional development agencies the level of engagement with LSPs seems to be at best patchy. While Regional Development Agencies have supported the development of sub-regional (economic) partnerships, many of these have not been coordinated, either spatially or functionally, with LSPs, thus causing confusion and a potential for conflict over what are the most appropriate units for planning and policy coordination. Furthermore, Regional Assemblies have also tended to create sub-regional fora for developing their Regional Spatial Strategies. This confusing and uncertain mix of institutions and networks makes it very difficult for those based at the neighbourhood level to participate.

A key factor here is the extent to which the capacity already exists for community and voluntary sector groups to engage with the LSP. Most representation of community and voluntary interests on LSPs takes place through umbrella organisations such as city-wide voluntary and community sector organisations and community partnerships, thus the link between neighbourhoods and LSPs will be indirect. Evidence to date suggests that 'many community groups ... are at best uncertain at worst suspicious or antagonistic towards what is seen as yet another initiative [LSPs] which may marginalize them' (ODPM, 2004a, p 20).

Even where pre-existing levels of capacity are high there may be doubts within the voluntary and community sector over the value of using precious and scarce time and resources to engage in yet another initiative. Community Participation Programmes (such as the Community Empowerment Fund) have helped ease this burden but it is worth noting that such initiatives have tended to be restricted to the 88 Neighbourhood Renewal Fund areas and have not been available to the vast majority of localities. While the barriers to community and voluntary sector groups engaging with LSPs may not be as serious as those related to regional government (see Harris et al, 2004) they should not be underestimated. Nor should the potential for conflict within and between the two sectors be underplayed.

Overall there appears to be a lack of clarity regarding how the LSP should function in a context characterised by a multiplicity of potentially conflicting interests and multi-level governance. Local Strategic Partnerships were intended to rationalise and simplify these local systems, providing them with greater coherence and allowing for easier collaborative working. However, LSPs have few real powers and even fewer resources to carry out these tasks and it is uncertain whether they will be able to bring the fragments that exist within local authorities together in a coherent manner at local level (see Geddes, 2006) let alone represent them at the city-region level.

The elaboration of Community Strategies are seen by government as having a key role in engaging neighbourhoods/communities with the LSP. Community Strategies emerged as a duty of local authorities through the 2000 Local Government Act (DETR, 2001) along with a new discretionary power to do anything they consider likely to promote or improve the economic, social or environmental well-being of their area (DETR, 2001, Part 1). The community planning process was expected to:

* allow local communities (based on geography and/or interest) to articulate their aspirations, needs and priorities;
* coordinate the actions of the council, and of the public, private, voluntary and community organisations that operate locally;
* focus and shape existing and future activity of those organisations so that they effectively meet community needs and aspirations; and
* contribute to the achievement of sustainable development both locally and more widely, with local goals and priorities relating, where appropriate, to regional, national and even global aims. (DETR, 2000b, section 10)

Within this process, government guidance indicates that, where there is an LSP, the LSP has a responsibility for developing and driving the implementation of the Community Strategy (CLG, undated). However, in practice and to date, local authorities have played the leading role in preparing Community Strategies (see Raco et al, 2006). This situation seems largely to be the result of the failure of LSPs to firmly establish their strategic coordinating position with the locality and their lack of resources. The fact that local authorities have tended to play the major role in the development of Community Strategies runs the risk of the Community Strategy being seen as a creature of local government and key partners. Indeed, one study of the preparation of a Community Strategy in an urban authority noted that:

> … rather than encouraging greater openness and pluralism in decision making processes in the town, the [Community Strategy] has in practice, reflected and reproduced the power of small elite groupings of politicians, … officers, and key 'included stakeholders'. (Raco et al, 2006, p 486)

Moreover, as indicated above, the power to promote or improve economic, social or environmental well-being is invested in the local authority rather than the LSP. This tends to reinforce the view that Community Strategies are the creatures of local government rather than of a wider constituency. This is a difficult predicament for local authorities where they have few additional resources to implement this power of well-being.

Local Area Agreements (see ODPM, 2004b) were in part a response to the perceived 'failure' of LSPs to develop a strategic focus on service delivery but also to local authority complaints about continued central control, the plethora of central funding streams and associated targets and the difficulty of 'joining up locally' to focus on the problems of a locality. The general intention was to allow for more local autonomy in addressing local problems, improving service performance and enhancing the community leadership role of local authorities, and overall to improve governance within a locality. It has even been suggested that there could be what the Local Government Association called 'small scale LAAs between the council and neighbourhoods ... as [a] model for extending community engagement' (LGA, 2005, p 12). Local Area Agreements could offer a mechanism for developing targets/indicators that link into Community Strategies and thus to the strategic goals of LSPs in the 'form of dialogue and engagement with local people to understand what "well-being" and "quality of life" mean for a specific local population' (LGA, 2005, p 13). Such activities could then give a more precise sense of what neighbourhoods want and provide a framework for public services to address those needs.

The 2006 Local Government White Paper (CLG, 2006, p 102) acknowledges that 'at present LAAs are an important, but not central part of the performance framework'. This may be seen as something of an understatement suggesting that there is still some way to go before they achieve the prominence government wants to see. Also the fact that local authorities rather than LSPs are responsible for setting up and coordinating LAAs with government creates a degree of uncertainty regarding the role of the LSP in this process. However, whether LSPs and local authorities have the capacities and will to do this remains unclear because it requires a fundamental rethink of governance arrangements vis-à-vis all public services provided within a locality.

The combination of LSPs, Community Strategies, LAAs and MAAs holds out possibilities for the restructuring of local governance systems, facilitated by GOs, but the extent to which this has actually taken place remains uncertain and the link to strategic thinking and action at the city-region and regional levels has not even begun to be addressed. It would appear that what we have are two parallel processes of governance developing. On the one hand there is a compartmentalisation of governance in the sense that one focus is largely on trying to redress ongoing problems in the relationship between centre and locality. On the other hand there is an attempt to reorganise governance within local authorities and neighbourhoods. However, in neither instance does it appear that the emerging levels of governance between the national and local levels have been taken into account.

Conclusion

In formal terms the city-region level of governance remains relatively underdeveloped in terms of its institutional capacity to effect change and in terms of how it relates, politically and democratically, to the constituent administrative units (for example the local authority and the neighbourhood) that make up a city-region. Although the Local Government White Paper offers the promise of the development of a more formal city-region administrative structure in some areas, its proposals remain vague and much of the real detail seems likely to emerge from the 2007 Comprehensive Spending Review. However, we know even less about the informal aspects of city-regional governance and its links to the neighbourhood. Thus, while it is widely recognised that new forms of multi-level (urban) governance have developed over the last 20 years, surprisingly little is known about the formal, let alone the informal, architecture of this system, even in particular localities (see Stewart, 2003, for a rare exception). Even less is known about the power dynamics and flows that shape such a system and its activities. What we can agree on is that this is an evolving and dynamic situation.

More recently, the neighbourhood, which until recently has largely existed in policy terms as a site of urban policy intervention (for example through the National Strategy for Neighbourhood Renewal) in *deprived* neighbourhoods, has begun to figure more prominently in thinking as a site of service delivery and potential democratic engagement. Yet we know little about how the neighbourhood might function within the city-region system of governance either now or in the future. What is the nature of the links between the two levels? At the moment these links largely do not exist (for instance the links between the National Strategy for Neighbourhood Renewal in a region are only weakly, if at all, linked to the Regional Economic Strategy and the Regional Spatial Strategy) and they are likely to prove difficult to construct in the complex system of multi-level governance that characterises both regions and city-regions today. One of the main problems to be confronted is how the regional level of governance (Regional Development Agencies and GOs) link to the city-region, local authorities (and LSPs) and neighbourhoods in a strategic sense. There is currently a lack of transparency, in terms of multi-level governance, relating to how collective choices will be made and who is accountable for them.

Nevertheless, this chapter suggests that LSPs, Community Strategies and LAAs (and possibly MAAs) may provide methods for building up links between the neighbourhood, the local authority and city-region levels. However, it also points out that these instruments are overwhelmingly focused on the local authority spatial unit and in themselves provide no direct link to the city-region. While MAAs may offer an alternative way of constructing links between contiguous local authorities, these are embryonic and much uncertainty surrounds how they will operate. While GOs are involved in facilitating their collective development there is no evidence that they have sought to link them in a strategic manner to issues beyond the local authority and Regional Development Agencies have shown little interest in building links to regional economic strategy. Within a city-region there will be several LSPs and Community Strategies plus LAAs (possibly through MAAs) that will need to be aggregated into an overarching strategic document and action plan for the city-region, which in turn will need to be integrated into wider strategic economic development plans for the city-region. It is not difficult to imagine that this will be a process fraught with tensions and disagreements as the constituent parties argue over the nature of an overarching and integrative strategy for the city-region. In many cases local authorities (and LSPs) on the edge of a city will simply not wish to cooperate with the adjacent city in an attempt to develop a common framework of action (on the case of Bristol see Boddy et al, 2004). In such cases a common city-region framework will remain a chimera, although of course in other city-regions the opposite will be the case.

Moreover, the neighbourhood remains an elusive notion. Most attention has been focused on deprived neighbourhoods and relatively little is known about affluent neighbourhoods, what their needs are and what their inhabitants want. Such neighbourhoods only tend to organise themselves collectively when seeking to respond, often negatively, to proposed new developments in their area. In fact it is questionable whether the residents of most neighbourhoods actually want to participate in developments at the city-region level. It is likely that the vast majority of residents will be largely uninterested. A small number of community leaders will recognise the potential importance of participating and seeking to influence the decision-making process at the city-region level, but this will only be the case if they can be persuaded that this is something worth getting involved in. Thus, in part the onus lies on actors at the city-region level to 'reach out' to these local leaders and demonstrate to them that it is worthwhile (for their neighbourhoods) expending their time, energy and resources on engaging with the city-region. Also it will be necessary to provide some resources to support the development of neighbourhood engagement at this level if it is not to run the risk of diverting scarce resources away from more immediately neighbourhood issues.

References

Ache, P. (2000) 'Cities in old industrial regions between local innovative milieu and urban governance: reflections on city region governance', *European Planning Studies*, vol 8, no 6, pp 693-709.

Atkinson, R. (1999a) 'Countering urban social exclusion: the role of community participation in urban regeneration', in G. Haughton (ed) *Community Economic Development*, London: The Stationery Office.

Atkinson, R. (1999b) 'Discourses of partnership and empowerment in contemporary British urban regeneration', *Urban Studies*, vol 36, no 1, pp 59-72.

Atkinson, R. (2001) 'The emerging "urban agenda" and the European spatial development perspective: towards an EU urban policy?', *European Planning Studies*, vol 9, no 3, pp 385-406.

Atkinson, R. (2003a) 'Addressing social exclusion through community involvement in urban regeneration', in R. Imrie and M. Raco (eds) *Urban Policy, Community, Citizenship and Rights*, Bristol: The Policy Press, pp 101-19.

Atkinson, R. and Cope, S. (1997) 'Community participation and urban regeneration in Britain', in P. Hoggett (ed) *Contested Communities*, Bristol: The Policy Press, pp 201-21.

Atkinson, R. and Moon, G. (1994) *Urban Policy in Post-war Britain: The City, the State and the Market*, London: Macmillan.

Boddy, M. (2002) 'Linking competitiveness and cohesion', in I. Begg (ed) *Urban Competitiveness: Policies for Dynamic Cities*, Bristol: The Policy Press, pp 33-53.

Boddy, M., Bassett, K., French, S., Griffith, R., Lambert, C., Leyshon, A., Smith, I., Stewart, M. and Thrift, N. (2004) 'Competitiveness and cohesion in a prosperous city-region: the case of Bristol', in M. Boddy and M. Parkinson (eds) *City Matters: Competitiveness, Cohesion and Urban Governance*, Bristol: The Policy Press, pp 51-69.

CEC (Commission of the European Communities) (1997) *Towards an Urban Agenda in the European Union*, Communication from the Commission, COM(97) 197 final, 06.05.97, Brussels: European Commission.

CEC (1998) *Sustainable Urban Development in the European Union: A Framework for Action*, Communication from the Commission, COM(1998) 605 final, 28.10.98, Brussels: European Commission.

CLG (Communities and Local Government) (2006) *Strong and Prosperous Communities: The Local Government White Paper*, Cm 6939-I, London: The Stationery Office.

CLG (undated) *Preparing Community Strategies: Government Guidance to Local Authorities*, available at www.communities.gov.uk [URL correct as of February 2007].

Cockburn, C. (1977) *The Local State: Management of Cities and People*, London: Pluto.

Core Cities Working Group (2004) *Our Cities are Back: Competitive Cities make Prosperous Regions and Sustainable Communities*, Third Report of the Core Cities Working Group, London: ODPM.

DETR (Department of the Environment, Transport and the Regions) (2000a) *Local Strategic Partnerships*, London: DETR.

DETR (2000b) *Preparing Community Strategies: Government Guidance to Local Authorities*, London: DETR.

DETR (2001) *Power to Promote or Improve Economic, Social or Environmental Well-being: Guidance to Local Authorities from the DETR*, London: DETR.

Florida, R. (2000) *Competing in the Age of Talent: Quality of Place and the New Economy*, Report prepared for the K Mellon Foundation, Heinz Endowments and Sustainable Pittsburgh, Pittsburgh, PA: Mellon Foundation.

Florida, R. (2002) *The Rise of the Creative Class*, New York: Basic Books.

Geddes, M. (2006) 'Partnership and the limits to local governance in England: institutionalist analysis and neoliberalism', *International Journal of Urban and Regional Research*, vol 30, no 1, pp 76-97.

Harding, A., Deas, I., Evans, R. and Wilks-Heeg, S. (2004) 'Reinventing cities in a restructuring region? The rhetoric and reality of renaissance in Liverpool and Manchester', in M. Boddy and M. Parkinson (eds) *City Matters: Competitiveness, Cohesion and Urban Governance*, Bristol: The Policy Press, pp 33-49.

Harris, M., Cairns, B. and Hutchinson, R. (2004) '"So many tiers, so many agendas, so many pots of money": the challenge of English regionalization for voluntary and community organizations', *Social Policy and Administration*, vol 38, no 5, pp 525-40.

Johnson, C. and Osborne, S. P. (2003) 'Local strategic partnerships, neighbourhood renewal and the limits to co-governance', *Public Money and Management*, vol 23, no 3, pp 147-54.

Kearns, A. and Parkinson, M. (2001) 'The significance of neighbourhood', *Urban Studies*, vol 38, no 12, pp 2103-10.

Kelly, R. (2006) Speech by Ruth Kelly, Secretary of State for Communities and Local Government, to the Core Cities Summit, Bristol, 26 June.

Kooiman, J. (ed) (1993) *Modern Governance*, London: Sage Publications.

Le Galès, P. (2002) *European Cities: Social Conflicts and Governance*, Oxford: Oxford University Press.

LGA (Local Government Association) (2005) *Leading Localities: Local Area Agreements*, London: LGA.

MacLeod, G. and Goodwin, M. (1999) 'Space, scale and state strategy: rethinking urban and regional governance', *Progress in Human Geography*, vol 23, no 4, pp 503-27.

Milburn, A. (2004) 'Localism: the need for a new settlement', Speech to a Demos seminar, London.

Miliband, D (2005a) 'Power to the neighbourhoods: the new challenge for urban regeneration', Speech by David Miliband, Minister for Communities and Local Government, to the British Urban Regeneration Association, 12 October.

Miliband, D. (2005b) 'Civic pride for the modern age', Speech by David Miliband, Minister for Communities and Local Government, to the Core Cities Group, 20 May.

Miliband, D. (2006) 'Empowerment and the deal for devolution', Speech by David Miliband, Minister for Communities and Local Government, to the annual conference of the New Local Government Network, 18 January.

Murie, A., Beazley, M. and Carter, D. (2003) 'The Birmingham case', in W. Salet, A. Thornley and A. Kreukels (eds) *Metropolitan Governance and Spatial Planning*, London: Spon Press, pp 57-76.

ODPM (Office of the Deputy Prime Minister) (2003) *Evaluation of Local Strategic Partnerships: Report of a Survey of all English LSPs*, London: ODPM.

ODPM (2004a) *LSP Evaluation and Action Research Programme: Case-Studies Interim Report: A Baseline of Practice: Executive Summary*, London: ODPM.

ODPM (2004b) *Local Area Agreements: A Prospectus*, London: ODPM.

ODPM (2005) *Sustainable Communities: People, Places and Prosperity*, London: ODPM.

ODPM (2006a) *State of the English Cities: Volume I*, London: ODPM.

ODPM (2006b) *State of the English Cities: Volume II*, London: ODPM.

ODPM (2006c) *A Framework for City-regions*, London: ODPM.

Pierre, J. (ed) (2000) *Debating Governance: Authority, Steering and Democracy*, Oxford: Oxford University Press.

Pratchett, L. (2004) 'Local autonomy, local democracy and the "new localism"', *Political Studies*, vol 52, no 2, pp 358-75.

Raco, M., Parker, G. and Doak, J. (2006) 'Reshaping spaces of local governance? Community strategies and the modernisation of local government in England', *Environment and Planning C: Government and Policy*, vol 24, no 4, pp 475-96.

Rhodes, R.A.W. (1995) *The New Governance: Governing without Government*, London: ESRC.

Rhodes, R.A.W. (1997) 'From marketization to diplomacy: it's the mix that matters', *Public Policy and Administration*, vol 12, no 2, pp 31-50.

Salet,W.,Thornley,A. and Kreukels,A. (eds) (2003) *Metropolitan Governance and Spatial Planning*, London: Spon Press.

SEU (Social Exclusion Unit) (1998) *Bringing Britain Together:A National Strategy for Neighbourhood Renewal*, Cm 4045, London:The Stationery Office.

SEU (2001) *A New Commitment to Neighbourhood Renewal: National Strategy Action Plan*, London: SEU.

Simmie, J. (1974) *Citizens in Conflict: The Sociology of Town Planning*, London: Hutchinson.

Stewart, M. (2003) 'Towards collaborative capacity', in M. Boddy (ed) *Urban Transformation and Urban Governance*, Bristol: The Policy Press, pp 76-89.

Stoker, G. (1998) 'Governance as theory: five propositions', *International Social Science Journal*, no 155, pp 17-28.

Taylor, M. (2003) *Public Policy in the Community*, Basingstoke: Palgrave Macmillan.

Willmott, P. (1989) *Community Initiative: Patterns and Prospects*, London: Policy Studies Institute.

FIVE

More local than local government: the relationship between local government and the neighbourhood agenda

Eileen Lepine and Helen Sullivan

Introduction

Tracing the fortunes of English local government, from the establishment of the principle of elected local self-government in the mid-19th century through to the programme of 'modernisation' that the system is undergoing in the 21st century at the behest of 'New Labour', reveals the extent to which change has been the dominant feature of its history (Wilson and Game, 1998). Post-1945 much of that change has been driven by central government reform and, while local government has been able to draw on its own institutional resources to help it adapt and absorb some of the more radical reform proposals (Sullivan, 2003; Lowndes, 2004), nonetheless, central government interventions have had important consequences for local government's structures and processes, role and purpose, and relationships with citizens. They have also played an important role (directly and indirectly) in influencing local government's perspective on and its interactions with the neighbourhood. Two vignettes serve to illustrate the point.

The attempt by the post-war Labour administration to rid society of all major ills was manifest in the development of new institutions, centrally organised and administered. While some of the local discretion and variation enjoyed by local government in the period of expansion up to the 1930s began to diminish, local government assumed significant delivery responsibilities for welfare state services. This led to the creation of local government units far larger than many European counterparts. At this time it seemed that local government did not have to pay much attention to the neighbourhood. Autonomous, self-confident, delivering the valued services of the post-war welfare state, its connection with locality was at the authority-wide level at which it embodied civic pride. Internal divisions were based on service departments, not sub-localities. Neighbourhood seemed in any case to be declining in significance in the face of prosperity and social mobility.

Contemporary narratives provide a sharp contrast. Following decades of reform under the Conservatives, coupled with the emergence of a new, more challenging governance environment, local government is depicted as a shadow of its former self. Reduced in powers, no longer confident, struggling to assert civic leadership, its capacity to engage with others is as important as its internal organisation. Its partners are important both as means of achieving improved service delivery (local government is now oriented towards commissioning and purchasing services, rather than providing them) and as collaborators in a form of 'network governance' (Stoker, 2004). In mid-2006, central government proposals, in which 'power was to be devolved firstly from central government to local government and secondly beyond the local authority to neighbourhoods and individual citizens' (ODPM, 2006a, p 4), appeared to offer another challenge to local government's sense of identity and purpose. The further development of these proposals in the recent White Paper (CLG, 2006) is discussed later in this chapter.

In the intervening period, neighbourhood – a 'chaotic concept with a tangential and shifting association to notions of community' (Kennett and Forrest, 2006, p 715) – has often had a significant place in the narratives of local governance. Decentralisation on an area basis, to a level below the local authority, often referred to as the neighbourhood, has been pursued in different forms and for various purposes – in centrally driven area management initiatives in the 1970s, in locally inspired decentralisation programmes in the 1980s and 1990s and in the apparently shared agenda for 'new localism' that has obtained a high profile in the 2000s (ODPM, 2006a).

This chapter considers the relationship between neighbourhood, decentralisation and elected local government in the context of prevailing central–local relations. It examines the variety of motivations that have underpinned local authorities' 'move to the neighbourhood' over time, highlights some of the trends in decentralisation strategies, and identifies the key 'trade-offs' that have confronted local authorities pursuing a neighbourhood agenda. The exploration of this relationship draws on interpretive approaches to policy analysis to argue that objective conditions are seldom 'so compelling and unambiguous that they set the policy agenda' (Majone, 1989, p 24); rather, 'the language of policy and planning analyses not only depicts but also constructs the issues at hand' (Fischer and Forester, 1993, p 1), making it necessary to consider how problems are constructed and framed, what claims are made and how they are made. As the earlier vignettes indicate, the chapter pays particular attention to the role of 'decentralisation' and 'neighbourhood' in policy discourses and in those 'processes of argument, acceptance and change' through which 'administrative doctrines' – ideas about what is to be done – gain ground, while competing doctrines are ignored or treated 'as heresies or outdated ideas' (Hood and Jackson, 1991, p 17).

The chapter considers whether the persistent attraction of neighbourhood in the narratives of local governance lies in its imprecision – in its ability to contain contradiction and convey much that cannot quite be spelt out. Neighbourhood can frequently be seen as a proxy for community, which itself has 'a multi-faceted appeal precisely because it draws on diverse sets of images, not all of them compatible' (Newman, 2001, p 147; see also Chapter Two's exploration of these issues). It has been suggested that decentralisation has similar properties – its 'ubiquity … a measure of its malleability' (Paddison, 1999, p 107). Community, neighbourhood and decentralisation are therefore a potent rhetorical mix, an appreciation of which is vital in any assessment of their contribution to the changing paradigms of local governance.

Size, democracy and local government

The interaction between size and democracy has long been of interest to designers of government systems seeking to explore the capacity of different institutional configurations to deliver particular purposes. Following Dahl and Tufte's (1973) classic analysis, small-scale governance is generally associated with participation and responsiveness and large-scale governance with efficiency and equity (Dahl and Tufte, 1973; Newton, 1982). Interestingly Dahl and Tufte were never completely clear as to what exactly constituted 'smaller' and 'larger', arguing, for example, that the immediacy and comprehensibility of *local* politics may make this a good level at which to cultivate 'the virtues of democratic citizenship' (1973, p 60) but also that units significantly *smaller* than the typical local government level may be required for participation (1973, pp 53-61). Other writers did not share their reticence, however, arguing instead that the concept of decentralisation was only viable when it addressed the shift of power and organisational responsibility from national to local level, but not beyond to neighbourhoods (Smith, 1985; Wolman, 1990). For these writers the neighbourhood was simply too small to develop and deploy sufficient capacity for governance tasks.

Justifications for elected local government typically include its place in a necessary diffusion of power, its role as a basis for political participation, its creation of an arena in which the art of politics is learnt, its appeals to community and locality and its strengths in identifying and responding to local demands (Leach, 1996, pp 26-9). However, over time, local government has struggled to support its claims to be 'representative, participatory, responsive, accountable...' (Goldsmith, 1992, p 394). Low voter turnout has challenged its representative claims. Remoteness, prompted by organisational size, structure and culture, has limited confidence in its ability to be responsive and accountable, while both the increasing strength of professionals and the party political dominance of councillors have led some to question its capacity to facilitate participation (Sharpe, 1979; Stoker and Young, 1993; Burns et al, 1994).

The turn to decentralisation by local government can be seen as a means of responding to the challenges it faces and claiming some of the advantages Dahl and Tufte associate with larger and smaller democracies – offering within its area that mix of units and relationships that serves the area best (in terms of service improvement and public participation) and makes effective wider connections. There is evidence for this in research that examines the purposes local authorities have associated with decentralisation schemes. Sullivan et al's (2001) review of a range of decentralisation initiatives, from the 1970s to 2000, identified four core motivations and related purposes (see also Table 5.1):

- to reconnect locally elected members with their communities and to enhance the representative role of the councillor;
- to improve the quality and value for money of local authority service provision;
- to improve the quality of democracy by finding new ways to facilitate citizen participation in local government;
- to develop coherence in policy and service coordination in a fragmented governance environment.

The predominance of one or other set of motivations and purposes at different points in time and in different local contexts will be explored in the following sections.

Table 5.1:The purposes of decentralisation

Politicians: roles and relationships	Service delivery	Community involvement	Coordination
Improving the quality of decision making	Improving access to service information and advice	Raising awareness about local government	Integrating local authority services
Improving local authority/sub-local-level relations	Improving access to service delivery	Broadening and deepening citizen involvement in local governance	Improving the linkages between all local service providers
Enhancing the role of elected members within sub-localities	Maximising the responsiveness and appropriateness of services	Increasing involvement of marginalised communities	Better reflecting neighbourhood/community identities in policy making and service planning
Developing community leadership in neighbourhoods	Improving quality of services	Increasing the capacity of all citizens as decision takers	Rationalising and enhancing partnership working
		Generating community cohesion	

Source: Adapted from Sullivan et al (2001, p 17)

Area management, participation and the rediscovery of neighbourhood poverty

In the 1960s the practical and political imperatives for decentralisation to the neighbourhood elicited responses both from central government and from local political parties and other local bodies. 'Top-down' responses saw central government departments attempting to make sense of the impact of economic restructuring (which had exacerbated poverty for many communities) and local government reorganisation (which had further increased the size of many local authorities) on localities, via the initiation of:

- area management initiatives – an attempt to apply a corporate approach to local government activities at neighbourhood level (Horn et al, 1977);
- zoning initiatives – designated areas of special interest for one or more reasons, including Urban Programme areas, Housing Action Areas, Education Priority Areas; and
- the Community Development Projects – a 'partnership' between the Home Office, local government and a local university, working within targeted communities to develop the capacity of people in localities to help themselves (Loney, 1983).

By contrast, 'bottom-up' responses were led by grassroots organisations attempting to increase citizen influence over policy makers. While some of this activity was party political, for example through the then Liberal Party, much was carried out outside the framework of formal party structures and can be classified in terms of *pressure groups* campaigning on particular issues and *neighbourhood groups* campaigning for the needs of an area, most obviously represented through the Neighbourhood Councils movement, which sought to establish urban parish councils in metropolitan areas as a means of bringing government closer to communities (Cockburn, 1977).

Webster (1982, p 167) identifies a key concept in the narrative of decentralisation – responsiveness – and examines this in the context of the 'area management' initiative. She suggests that area management was informed by a 'set of related ideas' in which responsiveness was a common strand, emerging as a consequence of the perceived failure by local government to 'respond to the needs and problems of the community … it serves' (p 168). Webster distinguishes several distinct elements to responsiveness, all of which have a contemporary ring. First, that *diversity* of need requires a local and differentiated response. In part this is an argument that it is at the very local level that particular needs are best identified and addressed, but there are also equity arguments for increased resource allocation to 'pockets of disadvantage'. Second, that the complexity of problems demands a *joined-up* approach and that decentralisation can help secure this, at the level at which problems are intense and perhaps intensified. Third, that there is a need to *reflect community definitions* of problems and priorities in whatever approach is adopted.

Counterarguments (some of which are outlined by Webster) are familiar too, reflecting the commonly recognised tensions associated with decentralisation at any level. Against differentiation may be set the need for universal standards, the risk of 'postcode lotteries' and a concern that a focus on locality may expose conflicts of interest between localities. Webster's discussion of joined-up service delivery suggests that not all problems at that time required such solutions and notes that the idea of a joined-up approach to complex and intractable issues at that time ran counter to the functional bases of organisations and the power hierarchies associated with these; partnership has since become a much more taken-for-granted approach (Sullivan and Skelcher, 2002).

The development of corporate management and of approaches to local participation, both a feature of decentralisation strategies at this time, are examined in Cockburn's work on Lambeth, in which she argues that they were means by which the system 'was being geared up to govern more intrusively and more effectively' (1977, p 12) in the face of the rediscovery of poverty and of increased working-class militancy. In Lambeth, developments in participation included the introduction of a number of neighbourhood councils, which varied in scale, organisation, interests and relationship with the local council. Most, Cockburn suggests, 'kept the council on its toes without treading on them too often' (1977, p 142), but there were exceptions: an early indication of the challenge an alternative source of legitimacy may present to established relationships between neighbourhood and local authority.

Such developments were not the property of left or right and, although central government drivers were important, there was no simple imposition of change on local government. Some authorities and institutions supportive of local government played a key part in the development of corporate management. Cockburn also suggests that support for participation in Lambeth stemmed in part from a wish to be identified as progressive – ahead of, but in line with, expected national developments (1977, p 134). Decentralisation also provided a means of responding to low electoral turnout in the borough and a decline in activity levels in the ruling Labour Party (1977, p 92).

It is now largely accepted that the late 1960s/early 1970s was the period in which the post-war consensus began to break down. For local government this meant that departmental service hierarchies and divisions were challenged by both corporate and area management. Diversity of need assumed greater significance and, as local government's capacity to respond to it was doubted, its democratic legitimacy also began to be challenged. The language of crisis was heard as local government faced problems of increasing need and declining resources. Much of that need was located in the neighbourhoods in which poverty, having been 'rediscovered', was to be addressed and to which it could be confined in the popular imagination. The view that, since the causes of disadvantage are mostly not local, local responses are not the most appropriate or effective, can be traced back at least as far as the critiques arising from the Home Office Community Development Projects. Nonetheless, spatially located disadvantage achieved significance in this period that it continues to retain as evidenced by more recent discourses. The beginnings of the discourse of partnership can also be heard in the initiatives of this time.

Politics, conflict and the rise of managerialism

Ideas about local government, decentralisation and neighbourhood were hotly debated in the intensely political atmosphere of the Conservative governments of the 1980s and 1990s. Few sought to defend a paternalism in delivery that was subject to criticism from left and right, nor the bureaucracy associated with it. Red tape and remoteness were key aspects of the way in which the 'problem' of local government was now being 'framed' (Rein and Schon, 1993). The freshly painted front door of the council home purchased under 'right to buy' policies emphasised the claims of individuality (and consumption) over universalism. In central government's narrative the costliness of local government and the superior claims of private sector and market were also important. A sense of crisis was significant in generating the motivation for change, but not in creating consensus about the appropriate response.

The 'urban left' (Stoker, 1998, p 192) experiments in decentralisation in the 1980s are often characterised as a response to crisis, offering not only an alternative to the market approaches then being pursued by the Conservatives but a response to a wider social and economic breakdown. Decentralisation was a source of hope and renewal for these local authorities, combining the narrative of service improvement through neighbourhood-based interventions with one of democratic revitalisation. Here the neighbourhood appeared as the level at which citizenship could be 'operationalised' and 'the right to contribute to the production of policies and the shaping of choices' could be exercised (Warren et al, 1992, cited in Burns et al, 1994, p 267).

Initiatives varied in their political leadership, approach and scale and the elasticity of the term 'neighbourhood' is striking. In Islington, a Labour council established 24 neighbourhood offices, through which key services were delivered, along with parallel consultative forums. In Liberal-led Tower Hamlets there was a significant devolution of responsibility for services to seven (much larger) neighbourhoods; the key committees were councillor led, although here too there were consultative forums. In Seabrook's (1984) study of decentralisation in Walsall, where local housing offices were the main feature, neighbourhood appears as a site of resistance to a perceived attack, not only on local services and local democracy but on the welfare state and working-class communities, with neighbourhood offices described as places where it was possible to rebuild working-class solidarity, express dignity and pride and revitalise democracy.

Not to be outdone, central government adopted its own narrative for decentralisation, emphasising it as a route to service improvement via the 'empowerment' of staff (as managers) and service users (as customers) and the adoption of private sector methods, such as contracts. In the decentralisation of NHS trusts, schools and social housing, there is no assumption of decentralisation to locality; instead it takes place within functional areas and is driven by market models. Nor was there any intention through such policies to support and revive local government, although some local authorities did develop their own programmes of decentralisation based on these principles. For example, Brent's programme of 'Real Devolution' (begun in 1992) recast and restructured the local authority as a business pursuing customer satisfaction and value for money. The assumed benefits of these various forays into managerial decentralisation included increased freedom for managers, reduction in bureaucratic hierarchies and speedier and more responsive services (Pollitt et al, 1998, p 1). Clearly there is a similarity here with claims made for area or neighbourhood decentralisation. Responsiveness again appeared as the Holy Grail and managerialism was on the rise as a means to provide it.

For some commentators, decentralisation within localities, for example to neighbourhoods, offers a connection not only to the individual but to the collective in which individuals appear as active and empowered citizens (Burns et al, 1994, p 51), involved in decisions about services that both demand and reflect political choices. Of course, ideal-type contrasts do not exist in their pure form and narratives too will exhibit inconsistencies. Managerialism was not absent from the 'urban left's' initiatives. The Leader of Islington Council referred to motives, which were 'highly pragmatic, concerned with the efficiency and coordination of the service that we provide' (Hodge, 1987, p 32). Harlow's programme of decentralisation combined a commitment to citizen participation with a determination to manage (via the operation of a matrix management system) the strategy/neighbourhood tension apparent in other high-profile initiatives such as Tower Hamlets (see Lowndes and Stoker, 1992). The rise of the manager evident in such schemes was a source of some (bitter) professional resistance to town hall decentralisation.

Cockburn's (1977) discussion of corporate management and participation makes connections between public sector developments and the nature of the private sector of the 1970s. Similar connections may be seen in the 1980s/1990s. A shift in the private sector away from traditional hierarchy to a decentralised or core-periphery model was highlighted by Hambleton et al (1996) in support of claims for decentralisation as an increasingly mainstream development within and beyond local government. Newman (2001, p 31) argues, however, that rather than 'complete closure around a new paradigm' there was "an 'unstable settlement" between bureau-professional power and new managerialism'.

The conditions for the emergence of the 'collaborative discourse' (Clarence and Painter, 1998) were also laid in this period. The local authority was certainly no longer alone, nor autonomous, in its locality or sub-localities. Many changes had been made at the expense of elected local government, which faced a 'hollowing out' as its powers were moved up, down or away (Pollitt et al, 1998). These changes can be clearly identified in the shifting emphases of local authority decentralisation schemes over the 1980s and 1990s (see Table 5.2).

For some, local government's 'continued existence is dependent on the contribution it can make to good governance' (Widdecombe Report, 1986, cited in King and Stoker, 1996, p 214) – making explicit that local councils do not 'spring from some ancient right of grass roots self government ... but are ... subject to central government' (Cockburn, 1977, p 7). Among commentators there was a consensus that local government's future role was linked to its capacity as 'an enabling authority', although again there were different interpretations of what this might mean (Osborne and Gaebler, 1992, Stewart and Stoker, 1995). The battle over the enabling discourse would become a key site of central–local government engagement in the late 1990s and decentralisation would re-emerge as a weapon that both would deploy.

New Labour and the neighbourhood – a return to (new) localism?

Since 1997, neighbourhood has appeared in the context of the present government's attempts to construct 'a new social settlement around the *modernisation* of the welfare state', 'based on a modernised image of civil society' (Newman, 2001, p 144). Modernisation is itself a key

Table 5.2: Changing emphasis of decentralisation

1980s	Key features	1990s
One-stop shops – service delivery and access a prime feature	Localisation	Access remains important but emphasis on influencing purchasing or commissioning
Generic working and flexible staff relationships encouraged within the local authority	Flexibility	Development of new skills in working across boundaries with other organisations
Decision-making power and budget responsibilities to sub-local level. Few local authorities devolved budgets	Devolved management	Coordination of activities locally, influencing policy with locality perspective. Getting the strategic/local relationship right. Certain budgets devolved following legislation eg housing, social services
New organisational values to enhance user empowerment and democracy through improved relationships between staff and staff and users	Organisational culture change	New organisational values to enhance user empowerment and democracy through new roles and relationships for staff and citizens and between the local authority and other organisations
Development of area committees made up of elected representatives. Some with decision-making power, many advisory	Democratisation	Area committees supplemented with focus on participative structures and processes involving citizens and other partners in deliberation. Setting up of citizen-led bodies eg Neighbourhood Forums

Source: Sullivan et al (2001, p 19)

part of the project – localism as well as Labour must be new. An aspect of that modernity is the claim of a pragmatic focus on what works – evidence based and non-ideological – but Hood and Jackson (1991, p 17) remind us to be wary of appeals to evidence, suggesting that rises and falls in the favour in which administrative doctrines are held have little to do with hard data.

In the discourses of New Labour, disparities between places are significant (Hall, 2003). The focus of the National Strategy for Neighbourhood Renewal was on narrowing the gap between deprived *neighbourhoods* and the rest of the country. Its appeal to neighbourhood and community was direct; it looked to neighbourhood as the source of local intelligence, community motivation and momentum for renewal (SEU, 1998). Its initiatives have been described as focused on 'collective action from communities in particular places and for highly instrumental ends', forming part of a 'spatialisation of national policy domains that have traditionally been differentiated functionally rather than territorially' (Amin, 2005, p 615).

Local government too must be modernised and the Local Government Modernisation Agenda was intended to renew public confidence in local democratic institutions and enhance the capacity of local government both to provide community leadership and to respond to diversity within a framework of national standards (Burgess et al, 2001). However, in spite of this agenda and the stated interest in mainstream change in the National Strategy for Neighbourhood Renewal, various National Strategy for Neighbourhood Renewal initiatives have tended to bypass local government rather than awarding it a clear leadership role (Sullivan, 2002). At the same time, research published by the Local Government Association (LGA, 2004) suggests that more than 50% of councils have area consultative forums of some kind and just over 25% have area-based decision-making bodies, indicating that decentralisation still has some purchase on local authorities, perhaps stimulated by changes in political management arrangements in which an 'executive/non-executive' split has left many councillors with the need to develop their ward role.

Partnership is now a dominant strand in the narrative and here too central government's uncertainty about local government has often translated into policies that treat local government as a 'service providing agency like any other' (Sullivan, 2001, p 33). However, in its third term, 'New Labour' has introduced policies (for example Local Area Agreements) that delineate more clearly a leadership role for local government with partners, a shift in emphasis given additional support by the contents of the 2006 White Paper *Strong and Prosperous Communities* (CLG, 2006).

Neighbourhoods are sometimes a focus for efforts at collaboration but neighbourhood is certainly not the only or even the main level at which partnership is pursued. Nor should choice of a neighbourhood basis for a joined-up approach be assumed to imply a community-focused, participative approach (Sterling, 2005).'New Labour's' neighbourhood management initiatives have been seen as essentially managerial, with an emphasis on service coordination, which tends to narrow citizen involvement to a consumer role (Sullivan, 2001). Here 'neighbourhood' seems to be stripped, in practice, of some of the rhetorical meaning it often carries. The forms of engagement now to be found at work in the Neighbourhood Management Pathfinders are discussed in some detail in Chapter Six.

There are those now who see, in the 'New Localism' agenda, signs of a 'rapidly growing acceptance that the centre needs local government as a partner in achieving ... [its] ... aims' of service improvement and citizen empowerment (Randle, 2005, p 1). In order to justify their claims to legitimacy, local authorities must turn again to decentralisation. However, suspicion and antagonism can be seen to have characterised New Labour's view of 'local municipalism' (Hastings, 2003, p 97) and lessons from the urban left are particularly problematic – these after all were the 'loony lefties' of tabloid tales in the 1980s. Any return to decentralisation must therefore be constructed in 'complete or tactical ignorance' of the past life of this approach (Hood and Jackson, 1991, p 6); hence, 'new' localism.

Randle's (2005) work on decentralisation initiatives appears keen to make distinctions between 'radical' experiments, characterised as belonging to a past era, and current forms of decentralisation, described as: less radical; placing a stronger emphasis on the role of the centre; more cautious in relation to speed and scale; and no longer identified with the left (nor instead with the right). A number of 'consistent and explicit' motivations for decentralisation referred to by Randle (2005, p 9) are familiar (see Table 5.1) and suggest a persistence in the narrative of local government of issues of bureaucracy, departmentalism and failures in legitimacy. These have motivated decentralisation in the past and form the image of local government that underpins New Labour's reform agenda (Stoker, 2004, pp 54-8). Randle also points to a number of less explicit motivations including political positioning in relation to expected developments in government policy, echoing Cockburn's assessment of Lambeth in the 1970s.

Managerialism remains significant in the discourses of change, as does consumerism, and both have appeared in proposals for 'double devolution' (devolution from central to local government and beyond to communities). The many contributions to this (2005-06) debate made reference to a spectrum of individual choices and collective participation, echoing Newman's (2001, p 49) characterisation of the 'sceptical citizen consumer' as 'a central reference point in Labour's discourse of modernisation'. Action was said to be necessary partly because some things cannot be delivered without the exercise of *personal* responsibility, but also because democratic legitimacy and civic engagement demand more than the 72 minutes a lifetime said to be spent voting (ODPM, 2006a, p 11).

For central government, concern with performance remains paramount and, if it now believes it needs local government, it is less clear that it entirely trusts it to deliver. Proposals for change therefore are about rebalancing the performance framework, ensuring that central government retains the 'right to secure minimum standards – particularly for the protection of the most vulnerable ... and driving improvement in priority areas', but making the 'public's views on service quality the core test of local performance' (CLG, 2006, p 114).

This is intended to enable local authorities to respond better to bottom-up pressures for service improvement. The 2006 White Paper contains a number of proposals to help effect this change, including proposed requirements to reform the Best Value regime so that local citizens and communities are informed, consulted, involved and have services devolved to their control where appropriate; the introduction of a 'Community Call for Action' to be used by local councillors to raise key issues of local importance; encouraging the devolution of small budgets to ward or neighbourhood level; supporting community management of local assets; extending neighbourhood and tenant management schemes; and developing 'local charters' within which service standards and priorities are agreed between local people and service providers.

The 2006 White Paper, like the consultation papers that preceded it, offers no single model for devolution from central to local government and then to neighbourhoods and citizens. Nor does it directly address the question of whether these proposals are, at heart, concerned with particular, disadvantaged, neighbourhoods or whether we are all to spend more than 72 minutes engaged in democracy.

Critiques of the 'double devolution' approach connect with familiar arguments about the trade-offs between the smaller and larger democracy. Jones and Stewart (2006), for example, have argued that neighbourhood is not the appropriate level for some functions because 'an overemphasis on neighbourhoods might overlook more relevant communities' and that neighbourhood is not necessarily the 'natural unit for expressing a sense of community'. They also point out that the area committees currently becoming common in local governance are generally not at the 'neighbourhood' level – although, as they concede, it is seldom clear in any of these narratives quite what a neighbourhood is.

Narratives and choices – what next for local government and the neighbourhood?

The elements of responsiveness identified by Webster in 1982 remain relevant today to narratives of governance and neighbourhood, which identify neighbourhoods as sites for meeting diverse needs, for coherent and effective service delivery and for the renewal of community, citizenship and democracy. While direct participation at the neighbourhood level may represent a challenge to traditional forms of representative democracy, local government's claims of civic leadership appear to be strengthened if local authorities can claim an ability to connect to the sub-locality and to manage the tensions that arise there. However, much weight continues to be attached by central government to matters of performance and delivery, which have resulted in constraints on local discretion. It is certainly not yet clear that the paradox to which Newman (2001, p 81) draws attention – that 'the very systems of governance required to address complex and interlocking problems tend to reduce the capacity of government to control the delivery of its political programme' – can be resolved through decentralisation in the form proposed in the 2006 White Paper.

Again, the persistent question of the trade-offs involved in decentralisation is significant. Dahl and Tufte (1973, p 138) conclude that '[n]o single type or size of unit is optimal for achieving [the] twin goals of citizen effectiveness and system capacity to respond'. What is needed, therefore, is consideration of 'the optimal number of units, their characteristics, similarities and differences, the nature of a good political life in each type of unit, and the proper relationships among them' (1973, p 142). Since there is no one way to divide up power, or decide which services are provided at which level, decentralisation remains ultimately a political not a technical question and '[d]ifferent interests will perceive different structures of decentralised government as being to their advantage materially and therefore politically' (Smith, 1985, p 206).

Perhaps one important lesson from these repetitive narratives is simply that these are not matters to be resolved once and for all. Continued argument and persuasion are inevitable and also quite proper elements in the policy process, matters not of spin but of contest between different ways of framing our understanding of 'problems' and 'solutions'. Nor is persuasion relevant only between obviously competing claims. '[N]ew arguments are constantly needed to give ... different policy components the greatest possible internal coherence and the closest fit to an ever-changing environment' (Majone, 1989, p 32).

> Governments need narratives – stories – to explain simply what they are for ... and giving people more control, more ownership, more power over their lives is a clear story to tell ... it fits into our overall approach, it can be demonstrated with practical policies (such as neighbourhood governance), it helps answer the critics of government and politics ... and it helps us run public services more efficiently. (Blears, 2004)

When the narrative takes this turn, step by step, through self-help, the new model citizens of neighbourhood governance emerge from the worst-off neighbourhoods. It is far from clear, however, that this model of engaged democracy is one the better off are seriously meant to emulate. In any case, some caution is indicated with regard to the empowerment intended, given the tendency for neighbourhood to appear as object rather than subject in these discourses in which directly expressed neighbourhood motivations are seldom heard.

One can see, in past initiatives and current proposals, attempts to create the circumstances in which various explicitly stated gains might be made and neighbourhood might gain its own place in the complex polity discussed by Dahl and Tufte (1973). At times, however, it appears that neighbourhood and decentralisation are called on in order to justify positions, or win hearts and minds, in part through connection with what has been described, in the policies of New Labour, for example, as a 'confused but effective babble of community' (Amin, 2005, p 620).

A number of 'keys to persuasion', which make it more likely that an administrative doctrine will become dominant, have been seen at work here. Claims of *symmetry* have been made, between various public sector developments and a wider context of change. Appeals to crisis, and 'newism', have also been identified, assisting in a necessary '*suspension of disbelief*', which avoids arguments that 'the same doctrines have been tried before, shown to be unsatisfactory in particular cases, and abandoned' (Hood and Jackson, 1991, p 194). Ideas about responsiveness, democracy, neighbourhood and community weave in and out of the narrative. These ideas are often used with the kind of imprecision that helps make *ambiguity* another effective persuasive mechanism.

One view of the current discourse is that there is now, at various levels, a particular focus on the significance of diversity and recognition of the limitations of command and control as a response. The authors of *All Our Futures* (ODPM, 2006b) argue that 'a distinguishing feature of society in 2015 will be difference and variation' and central government's capacity to respond will depend on a significant shift in *local* government and governance (2006b, p 4). Perhaps then this is one of those points when 'a new style of management is looked for ... [because] existing means of control are under pressure' (Cockburn, 1977, p 7). However, in relation to vexed issues of diversity and cohesion, talk of the neighbourhood appears again to be serving partly rhetorical purposes – asked to do 'all the ideological work of expressing cosy inclusivity, while also carrying ... unspoken connotations of exclusion' (Fraser, 1996, p 100 – see also Chapter Eight).

If there are signs of consensus here in how problems are now being framed, it is much less clear that an agreed model of local government's future and its relationship with the neighbourhood is emerging. Of course, neighbourhood can hold a place in both the rhetoric and reality of developments in governance. However, there are dangers in the use of terms like neighbourhood and decentralisation as primarily rhetorical devices or 'keys to persuasion'. The persistence of some key issues and tensions in relation to decentralisation, to which this analysis has drawn attention, suggests that learning from other times and other places is likely to be of value. Amnesia and newism *may* create a (more or less willing) suspension of disbelief, but to the extent that they are effective, they are bound to limit such learning from past initiatives. Moreover, if decentralisation and neighbourhood make their appearance mainly to help secure acceptance, through an imprecision and ambiguity in the terms, any realistic consideration of the part each might play in the design and performance of good governance will be correspondingly limited.

References

Amin, A. (2005) 'Local community on trial', *Economy and Society*, vol 34, no 4, pp 612-33.

Blears, H. (2004) 'Neighbourhood governance and management: challenge or opportunity for local government', Speech to the New Local Government Network, 14 December.

Burgess, P., Hall, S., Mawsom, J. and Pearce, G. (2001) *Devolved Approaches to Local Governance: Policy and Practice in Neighbourhood Management*, York: Joseph Rowntree Foundation.

Burns, D., Hambleton, R. and Hoggett, P. (1994) *The Politics of Decentralisation: Revitalising Local Democracy*, Basingstoke and London: Macmillan.

Clarence, E. and Painter, C. (1998) 'Public services under New Labour: collaborative discourses and local networking', *Public Policy and Administration*, vol 13, no 3, pp 8-22.

CLG (Communities and Local Government) (2006) *Strong and Prosperous Communities: The Local Government White Paper*, Cm 6939-I, London: The Stationery Office.

Cockburn, C. (1977) *The Local State: Management of Cities and People*, London: Pluto Press.

Dahl, R. A. and Tufte, E. R. (1973) *Size and Democracy*, Stanford, CA: Stanford University Press.

Fischer, F. and Forester, J. (eds) (1993) *The Argumentative Turn in Policy Analysis and Planning*, London: UCL Press Limited.

Fraser, E. (1996) 'The value of locality', in D. King and G. Stoker (eds) *Rethinking Local Democracy*, Basingstoke and London: Macmillan, pp 89-110.

Goldsmith, M. (1992) 'Local government', *Urban Studies*, vol 29, no 3/4, pp 393-410.

Hall, S. (2003) 'The "Third Way" revisited: "New" Labour, spatial policy and the National Strategy for Neighbourhood Renewal', *Planning, Practice and Research*, vol 18, no 4, pp 265-77.

Hambleton, R., Hoggett, P. and Razzaque, R. (1996) *Freedom within Boundaries: Developing Effective Approaches to Decentralisation*, Luton: Local Government Management Board.

Hastings, A. (2003) 'Strategic, multi-level, urban regeneration: an outward looking approach at last?', in R. Imrie and M. Raco (eds) *Urban Renaissance: New Labour, Community and Urban Policy*, Bristol: The Policy Press, pp 85-100.

Hodge, M. (1987) 'Central/local conflicts: the view from Islington', in P. Hoggett and R. Hambleton (eds) *Decentralisation and Democracy: Localising Public Services*, Occasional Paper 28, Bristol: School for Advanced Urban Studies, pp 29-36.

Hood, C. and Jackson, M. (1991) *Administrative Argument*, Aldershot: Dartmouth.

Horn, C. J., Mason, T., Spencer, K. M., Vielba, C. A. and Webster, B. A. (1977) *Area Management Objectives and Structures*, Area Management Monitoring Project, 1st Interim Report, Birmingham: INLOGOV.

Jones, G. and Stewart, J. (2006) 'Seeds of change', *Public Finance*, 12 May, www.publicfinance.co.uk/features_details.cfm?News_id=27547 [URL correct as of February 2007].

Kennett, P. and Forrest, R. (2006) 'The neighbourhood in a European context', *Urban Studies*, vol 43, no 4, pp 713-18.

King, D. and Stoker, G. (eds) (1996) *Rethinking Local Democracy*, Basingstoke and London: Macmillan.

Leach, S. (1996) 'The dimensions of analysis: governance, markets and community', in S. Leach, H. Davis and associates (1996) *Enabling or Disabling Local Government*, Buckingham: Open University Press, pp 25-40.

LGA (Local Government Association) (2004) *Making Decisions Locally: A Survey of Local Authorities on Area Committees and Area Forums*, LGA Research Report 15/04, London: LGA.

Loney, M. (1983) *Community against Government: The British Community Development Project 1968-78*, London: Heineman.

Lowndes, V. (2004) 'Reformers or recidivists? Has local government really changed?', in G. Stoker and D. Wilson (eds) *British Local Government into the 21st Century*, Basingstoke: Palgrave, pp 230-46.

Lowndes, V. and Stoker, G. (1992) 'An evaluation of neighbourhood decentralisation: part two', *Policy & Politics*, vol 20, no 2, pp 143-52; (see also part one: *Policy & Politics*, vol 20, no 1, pp 47-61).

Majone, G. (1989) *Evidence, Argument and Persuasion in the Policy Process*, New Haven, CT and London: Yale University Press.

Newman, J. (2001) *Modernising Governance, New Labour, Policy and Society*, London: Sage Publications.

Newton, K. (1982) 'Is small really so beautiful? Is big really so ugly? Size, effectiveness, and democracy in local government', *Political Studies*, vol 30, no 2, pp 203-20.

ODPM (Office of the Deputy Prime Minister) (2006a) *Empowerment and the Deal for Devolution*, Speech by David Miliband, Issued as part of a dialogue on the future of local government, London: ODPM.

ODPM (2006b) *All Our Futures: The Challenges for Local Governance in 2015*, Tavistock Institute, SOLON Consultants, Local Government Information Unit, London: ODPM.

Osborne, D. and Gaebler, E. (1992) *Reinventing Government*, Reading, MA: Addison-Wesley.

Paddison, R. (1999) 'Decoding decentralisation: the marketing of urban local power?', *Urban Studies*, vol 36, no 1, pp 107-19.

Pollitt, C., Birchall, J. and Putman, K. (1998) *Decentralising Public Service Management*, Basingstoke and London: Macmillan.

Randle, A. (2005) *Councils Embracing Localism: Lessons in Decentralisation from Birmingham, Wakefield and West Sussex*, Summary version available at www.nlgn.org.uk/nlgn.php, London: New Local Government Network [URL correct as of February 2007].

Rein, M. and Schon, D. (1993) 'Reframing policy discourse', in F. Fischer and J. Forester (eds) *The Argumentative Turn in Policy Analysis and Planning*, London: UCL Press Limited, pp 145-66.

Seabrook, J. (1984) *The Idea of Neighbourhood: What Local Politics Should be About*, London: Pluto Press.

SEU (Social Exclusion Unit) (1998) *Bringing Britain Together: A National Strategy for Neighbourhood Renewal*, Cm 4045, London: The Stationery Office.

Sharpe, L. J. (ed) (1979) *Decentralist Trends in Western Democracy*, London: Sage Publications.

Smith, B. (1985) *Decentralisation: The Territorial Dimension of the State*, London: George Allen and Unwin.

Sterling, R. (2005) 'Promoting democratic governance through partnerships?', in J. Newman (ed) *Remaking Governance: Peoples, Politics and the Public Sphere*, Bristol: The Policy Press, pp 139-57.

Stewart, J. and Stoker, G. (1995) 'Fifteen years of local government restructuring 1979-1994: an evaluation', in J. Stewart and G. Stoker (eds) *Local Government in the 1990s*, Basingstoke: Macmillan, pp 191-209.

Stoker, G. (1998) *The Politics of Local Government*, London: Macmillan.

Stoker, G. (2004) *Transforming Local Governance: From Thatcherism to New Labour*, Basingstoke: Palgrave Macmillan.

Stoker, G. and Young, K. (1993) *Cities in the 1990s*, London: Macmillan.

Sullivan, H. (2001) 'Maximising the contribution of neighbourhoods: the role of community governance', *Public Policy and Administration*, vol 6, no 2, pp 29-48.

Sullivan, H. (2002) 'Modernisation, neighbourhood management and social inclusion', *Public Management Review*, vol 4, no 4, pp 505-28.

Sullivan, H. (2003) 'Local government reform in Great Britain', in N. Kersting and A. Vetter (eds) *Reforming Local Government in Europe: Closing the Gap between Democracy and Efficiency?*, Opladen: Leske and Budrich, pp 39-64.

Sullivan, H. and Skelcher, C. (2002) *Working across Boundaries: Collaboration in Public Services*, Basingstoke: Palgrave.

Sullivan, H., Root, A., Moran, D. and Smith, M. (2001) *Area Committees and Neighbourhood Management: Increasing Democratic Participation and Social Inclusion*, London: Local Government Information Unit.

Warren, R., Rosentraub, M. S. and Welschler, L. F. (1992) 'Building urban governance: an agenda for the 1990s', *Urban Affairs Quarterly*, vol 14, no 3/4, pp 399-422.

Webster, B.A. (1982) 'Area management and responsive policy making', in S. Leach and J. Stewart (eds) *Approaches in Public Policy*, London: Allen and Unwin, pp 167-98.

Widdecombe Report (1986) *The Conduct of Local Authority Business*, Cm 9798, London: HMSO.

Wilson, D. and Game, C. (1998) *Local Government in the UK* (2nd edition), Basingstoke: Macmillan.

Wolman, H. (1990) 'Decentralisation: what it is and why we should care', in R. J. Bennett (ed) *Decentralisation, Local Governments and Markets*, Oxford: Clarendon Press, pp 29-43.

SIX

Neighbourhoods, democracy and citizenship

Joanna Howard and David Sweeting

The focus of this chapter is an exploration of the nature of democracy in neighbourhoods in England in the context of the government's neighbourhoods agenda. The emphasis on neighbourhood governance in Labour's third term promises to reconfigure local democracy and the neighbourhood level is presented as having the potential for widespread citizen participation and engagement. Nevertheless, aside from a vague and often repeated assertion that 'neighbourhood arrangements must be consistent with local representative democracy' (ODPM/HO, 2005, p 16), government prescription on the nature of democracy in neighbourhoods is ambiguous.

The chapter is divided into three sections. First, the following (not mutually exclusive) forms of democracy are presented: representative, participatory and market democracy. For each form of democracy, theoretical underpinnings and hallmarks are discussed and the conceptualisation of the identity and role of the citizen is sketched briefly. It will be argued that each form of democracy upholds a different relationship of the individual with the state (voter citizen, active citizen, consumer citizen) and that these relationships suggest different bundles of rights and responsibilities and differing degrees of agency. Second, New Labour government policy documents on neighbourhoods are considered and the chapter identifies the forms of democracy and citizenship that emerge or are implied in the discourse. A third section discusses research carried out into the Neighbourhood Management Pathfinders (NMPs) and the New Deal for Communities (NDCs) to explore how the particular form(s) of democracy and citizenship emphasised in these programmes are played out in practice in neighbourhood governance spaces. In particular, this draws on research carried out by the authors in consortium with other research institutes, published in the NMP 2004 and 2006 reports and the NDC interim report (SQW, 2004, 2006; CRESR, 2005). The chapter ends by drawing some observations and conclusions on the changing emphases between participatory, representative and market forms of democracy in the UK.

Forms of local democracy and citizenship

The chapter draws inspiration from several academic contributions that have posited variations of forms or models of local governance and democracy. For example, Denters (2002) offered the 'representative democratic model', the 'individualist model' and the 'direct-democratic model'. Miller et al (2000) put forward the 'localist', the 'individual', the 'centralist' and the 'mobilisation' models. Naschold (1996) talked about differences between representative, industrial, user and direct democracy, while Haus and Sweeting (2006) used models of representative, participatory, user and network democracy.

This chapter focuses on the distinctions between three forms of democracy: representative, participatory and market democracy. Its primary interest is in the way that local citizens and institutions interact and the forms of democracy and citizenship that are apparent in neighbourhoods. These different forms of democracy are likely to co-exist at a neighbourhood level and they are not exclusive to any organisational type, nor are they mutually exclusive in an empirical sense. However, there are differences at a conceptual level that are significant. The chapter therefore concentrates on differences that relate to the values that underpin the forms of democracy, their prime modes of participation and the key characteristics of citizenship that flow from each form. The main characteristics are shown in Table 6.1.

The different forms of democracy in neighbourhoods are related to the exercise of citizenship. Marshall's (1965) classic construction of citizenship saw citizens as having legal, political and social rights. Nevertheless, within the confines of the representative democratic system, the active elements within this approach were difficult to realise and citizenship was perceived as largely passive (Marinetto, 2003, p 106). In the 1980s and early 1990s, Conservative governments emphasised 'active citizenship' as a way of increasing individual responsibility and discouraging reliance on the welfare state (NCVO, 2005, p 9). This approach reaffirmed the liberal–individualist perspective of citizenship, where individual rather than collective interests took precedence and citizens were conceptualised both as private individuals and increasingly as consumers of services. The Citizen's Charter also placed emphasis on the individual citizen rather than the collective (NCVO, 2005, p 9). Under New Labour, active citizenship has developed a different emphasis, drawing more on communitarian theories of democracy.

Table 6.1: Main characteristics of forms of democracy

	Values/assumptions	Forms of participation	Citizenship
Representative	Electoral accountability, competing interests	Elections, political parties	Voter
Participatory	Deliberation, interaction, consensus	Deliberative fora: neighbourhood forums, tenants' and residents' associations, and participatory spaces in neighbourhood regeneration initiatives, eg project boards, steering groups, theme groups	Active citizen
Market	Consumer sovereignty, responsiveness	Choice between providers, focus groups, surveys	Consumer

Marinetto (2003, p 117) describes how urban policy pursued since 1997 has 'played an integral part in the burgeoning of active citizenship, using policy intervention in such areas as urban regeneration and local government to intervene deliberately in supporting active citizenry'.

Representative democracy is the predominant form of democracy apparent in national and local governments in the modern era. In a representative democratic system there is an assumption that often citizen preferences will conflict and that there will be competing (perhaps irreconcilable) interests between different groups. These competing preferences and different interests are most obviously reflected in the party system, with different interests represented by different parties. Voting in elections is the prime method of citizen participation, with representatives chosen according to the number of votes cast. Representatives can have different degrees of freedom from the views of their constituents and, to a greater or lesser extent, can be considered as 'trustees' or 'delegates' (Judge, 1999).

This 'aggregative' (Cohen and Sabel, 1997) way of organising citizen participation is a way of ensuring that decision making continues in the face of competing citizen interests. Provided that the procedures for aggregating preferences are seen as broadly fair, citizens have sound reasons for accepting decisions, even if they do not agree with them. Decision makers are held to account through the representative process. Should citizens be unhappy with the performance of decision makers, they can remove them in a subsequent election. Although voting in elections is the basic act of participation for most citizens, there is 'supplementary value' (Denters, 2002, p 2) in other forms of citizen participation. However, the primacy of the representative process is unchallenged, with elected representatives the ultimate decision makers. The view of citizen therefore is that of voter, with the act of voting in elections as a way of expressing preferences the key political act.

There are many criticisms of this model of democracy. Elections can be a poor means of gauging citizen preferences (Riker, 1982). Voting alone is not enough to reflect the true nature of responsibility placed on citizens in a democracy (Barber, 1984). Low levels of turnout in elections can undermine the legitimacy of decision makers and the decisions they make. The rise of a new political culture (Clark, 1998), entailing a blurring of the old left/right continuum and questioning the traditional pillars of representative democracy, casts doubt on the relevance of political parties in the modern era.

In part as a response to the failings of the representative process, but also a rejection of the fundamental tenets that underpin it, many theorists have posited other forms of democracy as either complementary to or replacements for the representative process. These various schools of thought are grouped here under the label *participatory democracy*. Calls for participatory democracy became popular in the 1960s and 1970s (for example, Arnstein, 1969; Pateman, 1970) and have re-emerged more recently, as democracy is said to have taken a 'deliberative turn' (Goodin and Niemeyer, 2003; Parkinson, 2003). Deliberation is a key feature of participatory democracy. Deliberative decision making requires that decisions proceed 'on the basis of free public reasoning among equals; interests unsupported by considerations that convince others carry no weight' (Cohen and Sabel, 1997, p 320). 'Consensus seeking' between participants is a feature of deliberative decision making (Klausen et al, 2006, p 193). In the context of local democracy, deliberation has been defined as 'the process by which views are tested and arguments are put forward and countered in discussion. It involves discourse about an issue and reflection on what is said' (Stewart, 1996, p 32). It has been argued that democracy involving more deliberation could enhance the decision-making process, especially locally (Fishkin, 1991). Deliberation is interactive and involves hearing and listening to others, as well as putting forward one's own point of view.

There is a variety of techniques for citizen participation in participatory democracy and part of the institutional design of participatory democracy should be related to allowing deliberation to flourish. Examples range from public meetings and focus groups to more formally constituted decision-making arenas, such as those described by Burns (2000) and used by the 'new urban left' in the 1980s in the UK. Active citizenship is a key component of the participatory model and extends into both decision making about and production of public goods and services. There is emphasis on 'doing things *with* people rather than *for* them' (Miller et al, 2000, p 31; emphasis in original). Active citizenship and community involvement are key planks in the government's approach to urban regeneration with the community involved, often at neighbourhood level, as part of their commitments and obligations as citizens (Marinetto, 2003).

Critics of the participatory model point to the time demands placed on individual citizens (Denters, 2002). Criticisms also relate to the representativeness of participatory fora and to the problems associated with organising participation on a large scale (Haus and Sweeting, 2006). This model is also said to favour 'vocal minorities' at the expense of the 'silent majority' (Miller et al, 2000, p 30).

The third form of democracy is the *market* model (Miller et al, 2000, p 30; Denters, 2002, pp 3-5). Whereas representative and participatory models are geared towards making collective decisions, market democracy is geared to the individual making decisions. As Miller et al (2000, p 30) point out:

> The emphasis is not on facilitating collective choice by the local community but rather on ensuring that the system of local governance is designed in a way that ensures that individual consumers obtain the right bundle of services to meet their personal needs.

This perspective is as critical of representative democracy as the participatory view (Haus and Sweeting, 2006, p 275). Its point of departure is that the market and consumer sovereignty are the most appropriate ways to reveal citizen preferences. This type of democracy places emphasis on values traditionally associated with the private sector, such as customer care, consumer responsiveness, sensitivity to demand and competition within the public sector. Citizens make choices between different service providers in quasi-markets giving 'exit' options, with popular providers rewarded by attracting most consumers. For example, parents can choose between different schools, with those schools attracting most pupils rewarded with higher budgets. Responsiveness to consumer preferences will also be ensured by providers using private sector-style techniques to gauge the demands of their consumers, such as surveys and customer suggestion schemes – giving consumers 'voice'. Consumers also make use of information about the merits or otherwise of different service providers – for example by using league tables for schools or hospitals.

The market model is backed by a system of consumer rights and citizenship is based on a conception of the individual as consumer. Citizens' charters can help to lay down what consumers can expect, how they can complain and to whom they might appeal (Miller et al, 2000, p 30). This system allows consumer citizens to defend their interests against suppliers of goods and services.

Critics of this form of democracy argue that the consumer power demanded by the model is difficult to secure in practice, as exit options might be impractical or non-existent depending on location of residence and providers may be unwilling to heed to the voice of consumers (Denters, 2002, p 5). Moreover, it is unlikely that some issues will be addressed by market democracy. For example, addressing the root causes of unemployment is likely to require multi-agency, long-term action that will not be triggered by market democracy (Haus and Sweeting, 2006, p 277).

UK policy on neighbourhoods, and the forms of democracy and citizenship implied

As discussed in Chapter One, there are a number of key New Labour policy drivers relating to neighbourhoods that both shape the spaces in which democracy takes place and reinterpret the role of citizens within them. This section considers these policy drivers, the new democratic spaces that their discourse suggests and the role of citizens within them. The relevant policy drivers are the National Strategy for Neighbourhood Renewal (NSNR), the Local Government Modernisation Agenda (LGMA) and the Home Office's 'Civil Renewal' programme (now transferred to the new Department for Communities and Local Government).

For New Labour, neighbourhoods are the site at which to tackle deprivation and to reconnect citizens with government. Hence, policy discourse emphasises engaging residents of deprived neighbourhoods as key players in the multiple and overlapping tasks of tackling social exclusion, reforming local services and promoting democratic renewal. This multifaceted conceptualisation of citizenship has evolved from the 1970s' community development focus and the 1980s' citizen as consumer emphasis to a focus on democratic renewal – reconnecting all levels of government with the people and promoting 'active citizenship' for civil and community renewal (Barnes et al, 2004). In its third term, the New Labour government created a new Minister and then Department for Communities and Local Government (known as Communities and Local Government), reaffirming its commitment to community engagement in order to improve public services at neighbourhood level and to bridge the gap between citizens and democracy (ODPM, 2006).

The first policy driver – the *A New Commitment to Neighbourhood Renewal: National Strategy Action Plan* (SEU, 2001) – was developed by the government's Social Exclusion Unit to address the economic, political and social exclusion experienced in deprived neighbourhoods. It identified the neighbourhood level as being the place where the interplay between social exclusion and political participation was most acutely experienced (see also SEU, 1998; Sullivan, 2002; Sullivan and Howard, 2005). What made this strategy different from its predecessors was its emphasis on partnership and joining up services, and its focus on residents and 'communities' as key actors in tackling the persistent problems of disadvantaged neighbourhoods (Taylor, 2007). The Local Strategic Partnership (LSP) was assigned a key role in joining up services locally (see Chapter Four), with representation on its board and theme groups from neighbourhoods themselves through the voluntary and community sector.

These LSPs and the neighbourhood partnerships that have sprung up through the various programmes funded as part of neighbourhood renewal are the new democratic spaces of this policy driver. Within them, the discourse identifies citizens geographically as 'residents' and 'communities' of the target deprived areas, who are offered new mechanisms for empowerment and a powerful voice. Citizens are broadly conceptualised, in part as potentially active citizens to be empowered through participating in the new democratic spaces, in part as service users to be involved and consulted in order to improve the information available to service providers, and in part as service providers. The role of citizens in individual programmes within the strategy is more nuanced, and this will be discussed later in the section.

A second broad policy driver that influences the relationship between the citizen and the state at the neighbourhood level is the LGMA.

The 1999 White Paper *Modernising Government* (Cabinet Office, 1997) provides a backdrop of market democracy to the modernisation agenda, with citizens as individual users or consumers of services. The LGMA builds on this with a bundle of policies primarily concerned with improving the efficiency and transparency of local government processes through top-down changes to local government's political management arrangements. In addition to improving access and information to individual citizens, the LGMA encourages local authorities to involve citizens and service users in policy formulation through a range of deliberative mechanisms such as citizens' panels, citizens' juries, user forms and area-based forums (Newman et al, 2004), as well as innovations in electoral procedures to increase voter participation. This focus conceptualises citizen participation as a way of enhancing and reinvigorating representative democratic institutions and decision making.

The democratic spaces suggested by this policy driver are either extensions of local government structures into the community, as is the case with area committees, or participatory democratic spaces for planning, debating and monitoring local needs and services. The former conceptualises citizens as voters who engage with government via their 'modernised' local councillor, while the latter engages with residents as active citizens who engage directly with government via mechanisms for participatory governance. More recently, the 2006 Local Government White Paper emphasises the role of citizen as consumer, stating that 'the simplest and most direct way to increase people's control [over public services] is to give them more choice' (CLG, 2006, p 27).

The third major policy driver concerned with democracy and neighbourhoods is what the Home Office under David Blunkett termed 'civil renewal', which draws on neighbourhoods both as communities of place and as the potential site of engagement for active citizens in participative democracy. Its core components are: active citizenship, which gives more opportunities to citizens to define and address key problems; stronger communities and community development, generating grassroots organisations that can respond themselves to key local concerns; and finally, more involvement of citizens in the decision-making processes of public agencies (Sullivan and Howard, 2005).

In late 2004, the first policy papers towards a new local government strategy began to emerge, heralding the growing support at that time for 'double devolution'. *The Future of Local Government: Developing a 10-year Vision* (ODPM, 2004, p 14) argued that:

> ... the health of representative and participative democracy
> are interrelated. Alongside local elections, as well as voter
> turnouts, there need to be more and better opportunities to
> participate and exert influence on local issues and decisions.
> Devolution should not stop at the town hall.

While the terminology of 'double devolution' is no longer in vogue,
the most recent White Paper (CLG, 2006), which is the culmination of
the process begun in 2004, puts flesh on these bones, detailing a range
of ways in which citizens, usually through their ward councillor, can
hold public service providers to account, promoting the extension of
neighbourhood management and encouraging the development of a
range of forms of neighbourhood governance.

Sullivan (2002, p 513) argues that New Labour policy drivers
for neighbourhoods cover four dimensions of integration, which
together combine to generate social inclusion, which she defines as
the integration of civic, economic, social and interpersonal systems.
Adapting Sullivan's interpretation to include the models of democracy
discussed in this chapter, it is possible to argue that:

- The LGMA promotes decentralised decision making to enhance
  representative democracy and facilitate wider citizen participation
  (civic integration; representative democracy, citizen as voter, and
  elements of active citizen). The modes of participation include
  traditional and electronic ballot, area committee, area forum and
  parish council.
- Aspects of the NSNR promote local access and resources to
  improve education, training and employment opportunities
  (economic integration; market democracy, citizen as user/consumer
  of services). The modes of participation include individual service
  user groups and project steering groups.
- The LGMA and NSNR promote service coordination to raise
  service standards, enhance coherence of service provision and
  improve service responsiveness to user needs (social integration;
  market democracy, citizen as user/consumer of services).
- Civil renewal and the NSNR promote capacity building to help
  sustain and enhance community networks and social capital
  (interpersonal integration; participatory democracy, active
  citizen).

There are several government strategies to engage citizens at work
here, which combine a variety of modes of neighbourhood governance

(Lowndes and Sullivan, forthcoming, 2008). So there is a contract in neighbourhood renewal between service users and providers as partners both in identifying neighbourhood needs and planning better responses to meet these. The focus on exclusion and deprived neighbourhoods gives an implicit meaning to citizenship, in that the people to be targeted by these initiatives are consumers/users who are unable to access adequate public services. Policy interventions therefore focus on social and economic inclusion and citizenship. At the same time, there is also a strong focus on re-engaging citizens of disaffected areas with democracy, which requires participatory mechanisms for deliberation rather than for user/client consultation.

The two key programmes of the NSNR that were developed to target individual areas of multiple deprivation are the NDCs and the NMPs (see Chapter One). Both were introduced as a new approach to tackling deprivation and exclusion through creating neighbourhood-based infrastructure (a manager, small staff and office) and with funds for capacity building with community groups. Neighbourhood Management Pathfinders, however, have only a small budget for leverage with other service providers and are expected to facilitate a more coordinated approach in local service delivery, increase user influence over service delivery and influence mainstream providers to improve the quality of their services by adopting and mainstreaming practices piloted by the Pathfinder (see Chapter Nine). The NDCs on the other hand have large budgets relative to other regeneration funding (£2 billion distributed to 39 NDCs) to work across the areas of health, education, housing and physical environment, worklessness and crime. These resources are intended to impact on local services to increase their effectiveness and responsiveness and on community capacity to enable citizens living in deprived areas to 'do more for themselves', as well as to provide better information to service providers.

The NMP and NDC policy documents that were developed within the NSNR in New Labour's first administration speak in terms of power: 'NDCs will represent a major shift of power and responsibility down to the neighbourhood level' (SEU, 1998, p 6), and neighbourhood management is described as a 'radical way of devolving power to neighbourhoods' (SEU, 2001, p 51). This rhetoric has been further reinforced by the introduction of the notion of further devolution of some powers to neighbourhoods and citizens (CLG, 2006).

The NMPs and NDCs have also been linked with emerging policies for reshaping public services. Neighbourhood management has been identified as an important vehicle for engagement in and delivery of Local Area Agreements (LAAs) and given a high profile in the 2006

Local Government White Paper *Strong and Prosperous Communities* (CLG, 2006).

The following section looks at how citizens engage in practice in these programmes.

Democracy in neighbourhoods: Neighbourhood Management Pathfinders and New Deal for Communities

There are a variety of arenas for democratic engagement within the NMP and NDC programmes. These include the board, theme or sub-groups, working groups, project steering groups, forums and groups organised around particular needs or demographics, for example, traders, black and minority ethnic communities, those over fifty and so on. The board is the key arena and the composition of NMP and NDC boards is very similar. The average size of boards in both cases is 22 (CRESR, 2005; SQW, 2006, p 47). Typically boards consist of local residents, community and voluntary sector representatives, representatives of local service providers (for example, the local authority, police, housing, health, Job Centre Plus), local councillors and occasionally local businesses.

For NDCs, residents constitute a majority on 24 of the 39 NDC boards. About 40% of board members are female and 20% from black and minority ethnic communities. Agency representation averages 44%, although with considerable variation. For NMPs, agency representation is slightly lower (31% for Round 1 and 33% for Round 2) (SQW, 2006, p 48). Black and minority ethnic group representation is a feature of NMPs, where there is a significant black and minority ethnic population (SQW, 2006, p 50), although only 10% of all Round 1 NMP board members are from such communities (SQW, 2004, p 7) (figures for Round 2 are not available). Overall, 31% of Round 1 NMP board members and 37% of Round 2 NMP board members are residents (SQW, 2006, p 48).

Representative democracy

In 34 out of 39 NDC areas, resident board members are elected by the local community. Research into NDC elections has found that the average turnout in 2002 was around 23.7%. This figure is a little below the average for local government elections, although the turnout for some NDC areas is higher than that for their local government elections, given that NDC areas tend to have low voter turnout rates in local authority elections (Rallings et al, 2004). Most NDC partnerships are now holding elections every year or two years, some opting to put only half the resident board members up for election each year to avoid high turnover (CRESR, 2005). Fewer NMPs use elections. At the time of the 2003/04 annual review, five of the 20 Round 1 NMPs had elected resident representatives (SQW, 2004, p 8). Only one of the 15 Round 2 NMP boards had elected residents (personal communication within research consortium). Turnouts for the elections vary, but for three areas are reported as 25%, exceeding the turnout in some local authority elections (SQW, 2004, p 11).

The interim evaluation of NDCs (CRESR, 2005) observes that board elections differ from local council elections in some interesting ways. For example, as boards are often keen to appear to be operating away from the party political elements of local politics, residents do not stand on party lines. Some areas have employed a single transferable voting system. Also, in some NDC areas, voting has been extended to residents from 15 years old and to other groups not normally entitled to vote in elections, such as refugees and asylum seekers (CRESR, 2005, p 24). Therefore it could be argued that NDC elections are more inclusive than traditional electoral processes for local government.

Where residents are elected from the local population onto NDC or NMP boards, a form of representative democracy is in practice at neighbourhood level, since some local residents are elected to represent others who participate as voters. It would, however, be simplistic to suggest that these NDCs and NMPs operate a typical or fully functioning system of representative democracy. In some cases, resident board members may feel unclear as to who they represent: 'I say my piece, but I don't know that I'm right or truly representative. I don't speak to that many residents' (Round 1 NMP resident board member, interview with author, October 2006).

In any case, as indicated earlier, many NMP boards do not elect resident representatives. Moreover, the resident board representatives are not the only decision makers for either NDCs or NMPs; whether elected or not, they also sit alongside a number of other board members (most of whom also have voting rights on the board; SQW, 2004, p 8). It would therefore be difficult, if not impossible, for the citizens in NMP and NDC areas to hold all board members to account through elections and voting.

Most NDC and NMP boards do, however, include local councillors, who generally do represent a political party and through them there is clearly a link to the representative processes of the local authority. Councillors tend either to be the ward councillor for the area of the

NMP, or NDC, or an executive member of the local authority (or both). However, their identity as party representative is often concealed under their role as representative of a ward. Further, the participation of councillors on NDC and NMP boards is variable; some partnerships have enjoyed the consistent support and attendance of a number of local councillors, while others have struggled to get any councillors to attend board meetings. Therefore, while there are elements of representative democracy apparent in NMPs with the election of resident representatives and the involvement of local councillors, none can be described as a fully functioning representative democracy.

Participatory democracy

There are many elements of participatory democracy present in NDCs and NMPs. The boards are deliberative fora, with in some cases considerable effort put into making discussions between residents and service providers meaningful. For example, some neighbourhood managers brief resident representatives before formal meetings. Resident board members are also involved in the recruitment of programme staff. Generally in NDC and NMP boards there appears to be a will to move business forward on the basis of consensus, a key trait of the participatory perspective, although in some cases this is not possible and hence there are mechanisms for issues to be voted on at board level. In their early years, a number of NDC boards experienced problems related to intra-community strife and tense relationships between agency and resident representatives (CRESR, 2005). In most cases partnerships have moved on and tensions have eased, but this demonstrates the potential difficulties and the processes involved in bringing residents and service providers together in communities experiencing multiple forms of deprivation and exclusion and trying to reach some form of common position.

Most NDC and NMP boards also operate some system of sub-groups (forums, residents' panels, project steering groups and so on) related to the themes of the organisation or some other issue (young people, long-term unemployed, long-term illness) and these are deliberative in nature as well. Other examples of participative mechanisms include capacity-building interventions and project design and delivery sub-groups, which are responsible for developing thematic strategies and commissioning projects.

Outside the members of NDC and NMP boards (and sub-groups), there are also considerable efforts made to get 'ordinary' members of the public to participate. In some cases members of the public are invited to attend board meetings and may be allowed to ask questions and to join the debate. There are also attempts to involve citizens in the production of services, broadly speaking, in that some NMPs have involved citizens in neighbourhood clean-up exercises or the monitoring of cleanliness in their own street and made moves towards the community management of local amenities. So there are elements of 'active citizenship' characteristic of the participatory perspective.

While NDCs and NMPs are not able to involve great numbers, the variety and scope of activities that they promote provide many opportunities for engagement. What is perhaps in question is the extent to which this participation is focused on empowerment, through building the capacity of residents in the deprived neighbourhood to engage actively with policy makers around decisions that affect them. Often the active citizens who end up on NDC and NMP boards and sub-groups are individuals who are already experienced in how to 'deliberate' and reach consensus alongside service providers and local councillors. Some learn as part of the process, having started out with a more confrontational approach or a focus on particular issues that they are passionate about. Clearly, a process is required that involves learning on the part of the participating citizen and also on the part of service providers who are not accustomed to discussing their actions and strategies with clients.

Market democracy

Neighbourhood management focuses on greater efficiency and effectiveness in service delivery through the joining up of services, greater responsiveness and innovation in forms of provision to improve access and targeting. 'Customer-focus, innovation and risk-taking' are necessary skills of NMPs (Lowndes and Sullivan, forthcoming, 2008, p 16). Lowndes and Sullivan therefore link neighbourhood management to market democracy 'in which accountability rests upon the principle that citizens are also consumers (who pay for services through taxation) who may choose to take their "business" elsewhere' (Lowndes and Sullivan, forthcoming, 2008, p 16).

This is evidenced in NMPs in the overall focus of the programme. The 2006 Annual Review stated that 'working with mainstream service providers to improve the quality and responsiveness of public services to local needs is the objective that lies at the heart of the Neighbourhood Management Pathfinder Programme' (SQW, 2006, p 23). This approach is apparent in both NDCs and NMPs as, in their project steering groups and theme groups, citizens interact with state actors on issues of service provision. Public sector service providers are involved in their capacity (unsurprisingly) as providers of services and local residents as service users and recipients of services, or their representatives. While there are some differences between partnerships, typically public sector board members include Primary Care Trusts, the local authority (especially environment and housing departments), housing associations, Jobcentre Plus and the police, as well as non-statutory service providers such as voluntary, business and faith organisations. The onus is on service provider representatives to improve 'their' service to local residents, and on working with other service providers to improve services. A key output that has come out of this kind of inter-agency work with representatives of different service users in NMPs has been the negotiation of Service Level Agreements for neighbourhoods (SQW, 2006, pp 62-3).

However, it would be crude to say that citizen participation as service users is simply an example of market democracy. There is a considerable blurring between what is understood to be participatory democracy – deliberative processes, which bring about the empowerment of citizens and their active participation in the public sphere – and market democracy, which provides feedback mechanisms between service providers and users to improve the service and its accessibility. A mental health service user, for example, or a social housing tenant may join a forum or project board set up by their local NDC or NMP. But through participating in this space, they both bring their concerns as service users and exercise the rights and duties of an active citizen.

It is true to say that often the involvement of local people is instrumentally geared to services and service improvement. The 2006 NMP evaluation reports on one area where 'the test which community involvement has to pass if it is to be sustained and enhanced is that it must make a difference to local service delivery and the lives of local people' (SQW, 2006, p 64). The NMPs juggle with bringing together service providers in their theme groups, in order to join up services and get providers working together better, and ensuring the meaningful and sustained involvement of citizens in this process. This can also be a balancing act faced by NDCs. Both NDCs and NMPs are partnerships, which are about 'working together', above all things (Gaventa, 2004). They promote or necessarily seek 'the acceptable face of community involvement' with a practical imperative to get service providers, councillors and residents to talk and work together constructively and deliver – illustrating 'the culture of delivery about partnerships' (Taylor, 2003, p 133). If in the end those who find the process most useful are service providers and the rest drop out, then, from some perspectives, this may be of some, but not great concern, because in the end the partnership needs to demonstrate that it is having an impact on service delivery.

Conclusions

In sum, NDCs and NMPs exhibit aspects of all three forms of democracy discussed here. Those that elect residents have a form of representative democracy in place, alongside other forms. All provide a variety of forums or spaces for the deliberative engagement of residents from the neighbourhood with local service providers and councillors. All also promote service user access to and influence over service providers, either individually through funded projects to improve their access to particular services or collectively through participation on project steering groups, monitoring of services and so on. There is a mixture of both individualist market democracy and a deliberative and collective engagement that is more resonant of participatory democracy. Often, what is nominally market democracy can be seen as a form of participative democracy that enables residents in their neighbourhoods to engage with service providers and their local councillors. This engagement connects citizens as both consumers and active democratic agents with the state and other actors in local governance.

Ultimately, the issue may not be so much whether NDCs or NMPs promote one kind of democracy more than another. It is rather about coherence and compatibility between the different conceptualisations of democracy and citizenship and the resulting strategies developed to pursue them, as well as the broader fit with local governance. There has been a retreat from a head-on conversion to participatory democracy, but a creeping move can be seen within more marketised approaches towards deliberation, empowerment and collective action. While Crow (2005) observes that many so-called mechanisms of participative democracy actually involve local people as consumers, not as citizens, the present authors argue that many consumer-focused interventions can actually encourage participation as active citizen as well as consumer.

At the beginning of the chapter, reference was made to the oft-repeated assertion that 'neighbourhood arrangements must be consistent with local representative democracy' (ODPM/HO, 2005, p 16). The extent to which this is the case remains an issue subject to considerable debate. If local representative democracy is defined as the formal representative system with elections and local councillors, the word 'consistent' leaves much room for interpretation. For example, does 'consistent' mean that neighbourhood board and local council can peacefully co-exist or that policies that are pursued by neighbourhoods must be in harmony with those at local authority level? The difference is crucial. From the evidence presented earlier, it would appear that the former, less ambitious interpretation is possible (albeit not always apparent) but there is considerable ambiguity over the role of local councillor. Local councillors can (and do) take part in neighbourhood democracy should they so wish, but they tend to have a limited role and they often come to the arena as residents rather than as elected representatives (Sullivan, 2001). The publication of the 2006 Local Government White Paper does not change this view of council and neighbourhood existing in parallel. The White Paper attempts to re-emphasise the role of local councillor, calling them 'the bedrock of local democracy' (CLG, 2006, p 52), and suggests local councillors be given small budgets, play key roles in 'Community Calls for Action', and in many different ways 'champion the interests of their communities' (CLG, 2006, p 52). Although there are proposals in the White Paper to encourage more areas to take up neighbourhood management, there is scant mention of the role of councillor in these arrangements (CLG, 2006, pp 38-9). In any case, residents elected by the local population (as with NDCs and NMPs) can claim as much legitimacy as local councillors. In that sense, councillor non-participation is not a barrier to neighbourhood democracy.

For the latter interpretation – of neighbourhood and authority policies being in harmony – there are greater barriers to overcome. Partly at issue is the extent and efficiency of linkages between local government, Local Strategic Partnership and neighbourhood governance structures, referred to in Chapter Four of this book. Related are the differences between LGMA priorities (strengthening representative democracy through engaging and activating citizens) and NSNR priorities (closing the gap between the most deprived neighbourhoods and the rest through local partnership working), which give local authorities and neighbourhood partnerships different roles at the local level.

References

Arnstein, S. (1969) 'A ladder of citizen participation', *Journal of the American Institute of Planners*, vol 35, no 4, pp 216-24.

Barber, B. (1984) *Strong Democracy: Participatory Politics for a New Age*, Berkeley, CA: University of California Press.

Barnes, M., Newman, J. and Sullivan, H. (2004) 'Power, participation and political renewal: theoretical perspectives on public participation under New Labour in Britain', *Social Politics*, vol 11, no 2, pp 267-79.

Burns, D. (2000) 'Can local democracy survive governance?', *Urban Studies*, vol 37, no 5-6, pp 963-74.

Cabinet Office (1999) *Modernising Government.*, Cm 4310, London: The Stationery Office.

Clark, T. (1998) *The New Political Culture*, Oxford: Westview Press.

CLG (Communities and Local Government) (2006) *Strong and Prosperous Communities: The Local Government White Paper*, Cm 6939-I, London: The Stationery Office.

Cohen, J. and Sabel, C. (1997) 'Directly-deliberative polyarchy', *European Law Journal*, vol 3, no 4, pp 313-42.

CRESR (Centre for Regional, Economic and Social Research) (2005) *New Deal for Communities 2001-2005: An Interim Evaluation*, Research Report 17, London: ODPM.

Crow, A. (2005) *The Community Activist Challenging Councillor's Views on 'Acceptable' Levels of Participation*, Birmingham: INLOGOV, University of Birmingham.

Denters, B. (2002) 'Citizen participation and local governance', Paper presented at the conference 'Europa I món local', Autonomous University, Barcelona, 24-25 January.

Fishkin, J. (1991) *Democracy and Deliberation*, New Haven, CT: Yale University Press.

Gaventa, J. (2004) *Representation, Community Leadership and Participation: Citizen Involvement in Neighbourhood Renewal and Local Governance*, London: ODPM.

Goodin, R. and Niemeyer, S. (2003) 'When does deliberation begin? Internal reflection versus public discussion in deliberative democracy', *Political Studies*, vol 51, no 4, pp 627-49.

Haus, M. and Sweeting, D. (2006) 'Local democracy and political leadership: drawing a map', *Political Studies*, vol 54, no 2, pp 267-88.

Judge, D. (1999) *Representation: Theory and Practice in Britain*, London: Routledge.

Klausen, J. E., Sweeting, D. and Howard, J. (2006) 'Community involvement and legitimation', in H. Heinelt, D. Sweeting and P. Getimis (eds) (2006) *Legitimacy and Urban Governance: A Cross-national Comparative Study*, London: Routledge, pp 191-208.

Lowndes, V. and Sullivan, H. (forthcoming, 2008) 'How low can you go? Rationales and challenges for neighbourhood governance', *Public Administration*.

Marinetto, M. (2003) 'Who wants to be an active citizen? The politics and practice of community involvement', *Sociology*, vol 37, no 1, pp 103-20.

Marshall, T. H. (1965) *Class, Citizenship, and Social Development*, New York: Anchor.

Miller, W., Dickson, M. and Stoker, G. (2000) *Models of Local Governance: Public Opinion and Political Theory in Britain*, Basingstoke: Palgrave.

Naschold, F. (1996) 'Partizipative demokratie: Erfahrungen mit der Modernisierung Kommunaler Verwaltungen', in W. Weidenfeld (ed) *Demokratie am Wendepunkt. Die demokratische Frage als Projekt des 21.Jahrhunderts*, Berlin: Siedler, pp 294-307.

NCVO (National Council for Voluntary Organisations) (2005) *Civil Renewal and Active Citizenship: A Guide to the Debate*, London: NCVO.

Newman, J., Barnes, M. and Sullivan, H. (2004) 'Public participation and collaborative governance', *Journal of Social Policy*, vol 33, no 2, pp 203-24.

ODPM (Office of the Deputy Prime Minister) (2004) *The Future of Local Government: Developing a 10-year Vision*, London: ODPM.

ODPM (2006) *Empowerment and the Deal for Devolution*, Speech by David Miliband, Issued as part of a dialogue on the future of local government, London: ODPM.

ODPM/HO (Office of the Deputy Prime Minister/Home Office) (2005) *Citizen Engagement and Public Services: Why Neighbourhoods Matter*, London: ODPM.

Parkinson, J. (2003) 'Legitimacy problems in deliberative democracy', *Political Studies*, vol 51, no 1, pp 180-96.

Pateman, C. (1970) *Participation and Democratic Theory*, Cambridge: Cambridge University Press.

Rallings, C., Thrasher, M., Cheal, B. and Borisyuk, G. (2004) 'The New Deal for Communities: assessing procedures and voter turnout at partnership board elections', *Environment and Planning C: Government and Policy*, vol 22, no 4, pp 569-82.

Riker, W. H. (1982) *Liberalism against Populism: A Confrontation between the Theory of Democracy and the Theory of Social Choice*, San Francisco, CA: Freeman.

SEU (Social Exclusion Unit) (1998) *Bringing Britain Together: A National Strategy for Neighbourhood Renewal*, Cm4045, London: The Stationery Office.

SEU (2001) *A New Commitment to Neighbourhood Renewal: National Strategy Action Plan*, London: The Stationery Office.

SQW (2004) *Neighbourhood Management Pathfinder Programme National Evaluation*, London: ODPM/NRU.

SQW (2006) *Neighbourhood Management: At the Turning Point?*, Research Report 23, London: ODPM/NRU.

Stewart, J. (1996) 'Innovation in democratic practice in local government', *Policy & Politics*, vol 24, no 1, pp 29-41.

Sullivan, H. (2001) 'Modernisation, democratisation and community governance', *Local Government Studies*, vol 27, no 3, pp 1-24.

Sullivan, H. (2002) 'Modernisation, neighbourhood management and social inclusion', *Public Management Review*, vol 4, no 4, pp 505-28.

Sullivan, H. and Howard, J. (2005) *Below the Local Strategic Partnerships*, Issues Paper, National Evaluation of Local Strategic Partnerships, London: ODPM.

Taylor, M. (2003) *Public Policy in the Community*, London: Palgrave.

Taylor, M. (2007) 'Community participation in the real world: opportunities and pitfalls in new governance spaces', *Urban Studies*, vol 44, no 2, pp 291-317.

SEVEN

Community leadership cycles and neighbourhood governance

Derrick Purdue

Introduction

Successive government documents have highlighted the role of the local authority in providing community leadership (HM Treasury, 2002; Home Office, 2004; CLG, 2006). This is particularly important in the context of the move to governance, which depends on collaboration between sectors, on the establishment of institutional arrangements for partnership and on the engagement of all sectors including local communities. Indeed, theories of collaboration emphasise the importance of new approaches to leadership that can articulate and resolve the tensions between sectors (Stewart, 2003). But equally significant at the neighbourhood level is the quality of leadership from within the local community itself. Few members of the 'community' will come and sit at the partnership table but these leaders from within the community will play a pivotal role in linking citizens into governance both at the neighbourhood level and potentially beyond. Theirs can be an uncomfortable role, squeezed between incorporation into the structures of the state on the one hand and representation of the interests of their neighbours on the other.

This chapter explores the concept and experience of community leadership as it applies to local residents who take up leading roles in neighbourhood governance. It draws on research carried out by the author and colleagues on community leaders in area regeneration (Purdue et al, 2000; Purdue, 2005), to explore issues of leadership succession – how community leaders emerge yet later fade away to be replaced by new faces, which in their turn come and go through leadership cycles – using Hirschman's (1970) concepts of exit, voice and loyalty, as developed by Lowery et al (1992). The chapter concludes by applying Gamson's (1975) schema for evaluating the impact of community action to the question of how effective community leaders have actually been in gaining access to and influencing 'leadership coalitions' (Miller, 1999) in their neighbourhood.

Concepts of leadership and succession

One of the aims of regeneration partnerships at the city and neighbourhood level has been to expand participation in local governance to include civil society, by including partners from the voluntary and community sectors (Miller, 1999). The inclusion of leaders (or representatives) from the local community is supposed to embed the actions of the regeneration partnership within its neighbourhood as well as building a bridge between local residents in poor neighbourhoods and local political and business leaders and thereby strengthening the legitimacy of neighbourhood governance. Hence, partnerships provide a model of participative democracy to supplement the waning legitimacy of representative local democracy. However, leaders of different sectors sitting round a table remains a corporatist form of participation, rather than broader civic participation.

In seeking to explain this phenomenon, it is necessary to refer to the literature on leadership structures in urban politics and local governance, which developed within the community power debate of the 1950s and the later 'new community power debate'. Central to these debates was whether power was concentrated in ruling urban 'elites' (Hunter, 1953; Miller, 1958; Bachrach and Baratz, 1962) and later 'growth machines' (Logan and Molotch, 1987) or dispersed between a plurality of competing social groups in a city (Dahl, 1957). The popular concept of 'urban regimes' (Stone, 1989) represents a compromise between the elite and pluralist positions, where city leaders form a regime consisting of an alliance between the business elite and a political elite around an elected mayor, with a clear social base (usually in fractions of the middle class). Terms such as 'elite' or 'urban regime' were intended to refer to stable ruling groups within North American cities. The transfer to the context of regeneration partnerships in British neighbourhoods requires a change of terminology. The fragility and relative impermanence of the relations between the individual leaders from the statutory, private, community and voluntary sectors who work together in time-limited partnerships in the neighbourhood context suggests that the term 'leadership coalition', used by Miller (1999) in a study of the role of the voluntary sector in Bristol, is a more accurate description. 'Coalition' is a term often used to indicate organisations coming together for shorter periods of time around specific interests (Diani et al, 2007).

This chapter analyses the changing role played by community leaders in neighbourhood leadership coalitions by introducing a model of community change driven by the options of loyalty to the existing status quo, exiting from the community or using one's voice to change it and uses the research findings to develop a community leadership cycle. This cycle consists of five phases through the life of a partnership – emergence, consolidation, embedding, challenge and progression. The form this cycle takes and the consolidation of neighbourhood leadership coalitions vary according to the history of each neighbourhood. In neighbourhoods with little history of funding, there is usually a full five-phase cycle, whereas in neighbourhoods where community leaders are established and used to accessing funding, the cycle stabilises much more quickly.

Both communities and partnerships are engaged in processes of change, which require innovation on the part of leaders. Not only must existing leaders change their ideas, practices and networks to keep up, but also new leaders must be admitted to bring innovation with them. Hirschman's (1970) model of exit, voice and loyalty is a useful way of looking at how community leaders relate to leadership coalitions over time and how leadership succession operates. Hirschman argued that 'exit' and 'voice' are key mechanisms for the recuperation of failing organisations. This model has been adapted to empowerment strategies for local residents wishing to change their conditions of life in a neighbourhood (Lowery et al, 1992; Stewart and Taylor, 1995). Here the model is applied more specifically to partnerships as interorganisational forms of governance.

Raising one's voice is a metaphor for engaging in political debate and protest action. The 'voice' option is therefore an approach to change, seeking inclusion in the solution of local problems. An advantage of voice is that it is directed to the future and is a precise way of indicating the change you want, but it has a downside in that it takes a large investment of time and energy.

The 'exit' option on the other hand is modelled on consumer choice (and voter behaviour). A consumer applies pressure on a company to change by buying from a competitor instead. Similarly, voters may switch parties if they are unhappy with the leadership and its policies. Exit is best adapted to voluntary forms of association where viable alternatives exist (Hirschman, 1970). However, exit is a response to the past and so is a fairly blunt instrument in shaping future alternatives as it leaves the generation of solutions to others.

'Loyalty' is a third option, which may encourage the status quo, but it also increases the barriers to exit and therefore encourages the use of voice within an organisation or partnership, especially among the most quality conscious residents, who would otherwise be the first to exit (Hirschman, 1970). Loyalty to the neighbourhood (or particular groups within it) is clearly a characteristic of those who occupy community leadership roles within regeneration partnerships, but loyalty to the partnership itself will also come to play a role.

'Alienation', although hardly an empowerment strategy, is a significant option in community responses to regeneration. Indeed, regeneration partnerships typically exist against a background of alienation from government initiatives and local politics. One respondent in the study on which this chapter is based commented: 'The worst problem is apathy of people on the estate. We expected everybody else to be as enthusiastic as us about it.' As another respondent put it, getting the community to participate is 'like pulling teeth'.

Following a brief introduction to the research, these concepts of loyalty, voice and exit are applied to the successive phases of a partnership and the involvement of local community leaders in the partnership.

Methodology: identifying community leaders

The argument put forward in this chapter is based on a study funded by the Joseph Rowntree Foundation. The fieldwork for the study involved nine case studies of Single Regeneration Budget (SRB) schemes in England and their equivalents in Scotland and Wales. The nine case study areas were chosen, in the light of advice from the Joseph Rowntree Foundation, to reflect a range of characteristics. Common to all areas was the existence of a regeneration initiative. In the English cases this was a regeneration scheme supported by the government's SRB Challenge Fund. In Scotland and Wales similar area regeneration initiatives were chosen. Table 7.1 illustrates the location of the areas covered by the study.

The case studies were chosen with a regional spread across five English regions plus one case study from Scotland and one from Wales. Cases were included from major conurbation areas (London and Glasgow), from major freestanding provincial cities (Bristol, Liverpool and Sheffield) and from a number of smaller less well-researched towns (Banbury, Chester, Pontypool and Weston-Super-Mare).

In order to identify community leaders, a combination of positional and reputational approaches was adopted (Bonjean and Olsen, 1964). First those who held positions on local partnerships were interviewed, followed by others who had a local reputation for community activism.

Table 7.1:The case study localities

Locality	Authority (status)	Region	Partnership
1) Banbury	Cherwell (district)	South East	Grimsbury Regeneration Partnership
2) Bristol	Bristol (unitary)	South West	Inner City Lifeline
3) Chester	Chester (district)	North West	Regeneration in West Chester
4) Glasgow	Glasgow (unitary)	Scotland	North Glasgow Partnership
5) Pontypool	Torfaen (unitary)	Wales	United Estates Project
6) Sefton	Sefton (metropolitan district)	North West (Merseyside)	Netherton Partnership
7) Sheffield	Sheffield (metropolitan district)	Yorkshire and Humberside	Sheffield's Growing Together
8) Tower Hamlets	Tower Hamlets (London borough)	London	Cityside Regeneration Partnership
9) Weston-Super-Mare	North Somerset (unitary)	South West	Weston-Super-Mare Regeneration Partnership

Eighty-eight interviews with community leaders were carried out by three researchers on the project team. The interviewees included 42 women (48% of the sample) and 22 from black and minority ethnic backgrounds (25% of the sample). Some of these interviewees later came together in eight focus groups.

Seven of the nine case study neighbourhoods were peripheral estates; two were inner-city neighbourhoods. Leaders in the inner cities came from the voluntary sector and were usually paid workers. On the peripheral estates most leaders came from tenants' and residents' associations, with some from churches or small voluntary projects. In one case study, local councillors controlled most of the community organisations and played a leadership role in the partnership.

The community leadership cycle

The SRB research identified a community leadership cycle as an explanatory model of the dynamics of leadership coalitions in neighbourhood-level partnerships. This cycle consists of five phases – emergence, consolidation, embedding, challenge and progression. Two of the phases (emergence and embedding) are top-down attempts by the neighbourhood regeneration partnership to build a leadership coalition, in the other three phases of this model (consolidation, challenge and progression), community leaders respond successively with the loyalty, voice and exit options as empowerment strategies. While any empirical case will obviously be more complicated than can be represented in this analytical model, within this process of emergence, consolidation and change, there is an identifiable process of leadership succession, through which community leaders enter and exit from partnerships. The community leadership cycle is summarised in Table 7.2 and Figure 7.1.

Emergence

The research suggests that a new leadership coalition emerges in a neighbourhood when a partnership is set up and starts to recruit a first generation of local activists onto the partnership. In the case study areas, such leaders were recruited from tenants' or residents' associations in peripheral estates and voluntary sector organisations in the inner cities. Recruitment was usually done on an ad-hoc basis through existing contacts. The invitation of community leaders or representatives into partnerships represents an opening up of a new governance space to the voices of civil society within the neighbourhood. However, ambiguous messages abound. Public agencies such as the local authority are often seen as the root cause of neighbourhood decline by communities, while a legacy of marginalisation in previous initiatives hangs over emergent leaders, who may feel that public agencies only want their signatures to validate already formulated partnership bids. Indeed, some community leaders in the study were shown the bid only just in time to sign before it was submitted, yet few felt able to resist the promise of exercising their voice in relation to new resources.

Consolidation through loyalty

This initial phase is followed by a consolidation phase during which community leaders respond to their sudden presence among a neighbourhood leadership coalition by attempting to develop a fuller

Table 7.2: The community leadership cycle and succession

Phase of community leadership cycle		Type of community leaders	Empowerment strategy employed by community leaders	Processes associated with community leadership phase
Emergence		Ad-hoc first generation		Bidding, recruiting community leaders
Consolidation		Ad-hoc first generation	Loyalty	Establishing trust between partners
Embedding	SUCCESSION PHASE	Embedded first generation and new second-tier leaders		Capacity building (deepening), wider recruitment (broadening)
Challenge		Embedded first generation versus new second generation	Voice	Representation crises
Progression		First and/or second generation	Exit or voice/ exit	Burnout, move on

Source: Adapted from Purdue (2005)

membership of the partnership. A community representative on one SRB partnership found it very scary at first. It meant meeting people she had never come into contact with before – millionaires, chiefs of police, chief executives. Her first response was to be argumentative, but as the meetings became more familiar, she came to see them as a useful network.

Community leaders are expected to develop a sense of loyalty to the partnership during this phase. They must demonstrate that they are able

Figure 7.1: The community leadership cycle

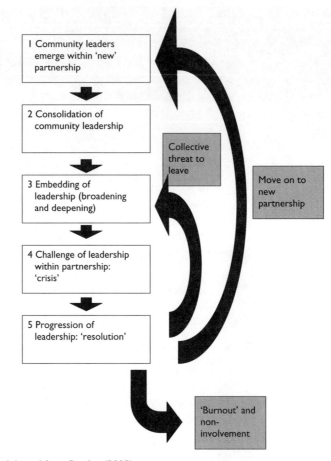

Source: Adapted from Purdue (2005)

to perform committee tasks and are often assigned mobilisation tasks to develop support for the partnership in the local community. Thus, in one case, a community partner was allowed to take the chair of the partnership but given 10 days to cut 10% off the budget and negotiate with all the projects to accept it. The success of the community team in carrying out this task proved their loyalty to the partnership and their standing in the wider community. This period of consolidation can become a comfortable state for all involved as community partners become known and accepted and neither side wishes to see any change. Once a partnership has been established, a compact of mutual loyalty is built between statutory partners (who desire a settled pattern of business) and existing community leaders (who have a new status through the partnership).

Embedding the leadership coalition through capacity building

It is generally within the interest of the neighbourhood partnership to expand the potential of residents who can demonstrate community leadership not only through developing the skills of those who have already embraced a community leadership role (deepening) but also through training new community leaders (broadening). Broadening brings in new voices and helps to ensure that the diversity of the neighbourhood is reflected; deepening is needed to help set out a strategic vision for the neighbourhood and overcome competition between rival leaders and community representatives.

Many partnerships employ capacity builders to train and develop community leaders, promoting and supporting leadership by lay members of the community. They seek to encourage the emergence of new leaders and new leadership structures, integrating leaders with conflicting aspirations into shared networks and projects. Community capacity building may take a wider more developmental form, bubbling up from the grassroots or a narrower more strategic form aimed at fitting the local community into new partnership structures (Banks and Shenton, 2001). Either way the aim is to broaden and embed the leadership coalition within the local community, through developing a 'second generation' of leadership.

This 'second generation' of community leaders may remain as a second tier of leadership with narrower, more immediate concerns, connected to specific projects and groups. However, the study suggested that the relationship between the two generations of leaders can frequently be problematic. In some cases the new leaders felt inhibited by, or unconnected to, those who had hitherto officially represented them, while in other cases they felt open hostility to the established community leaders, whom they saw as unrepresentative or obstructive gatekeepers (see Harrison et al, 1995). In the view of one new activist, members of her local residents' association were 'like Masons' with their 'little secret meetings'. Some of the 'new' leaders had, in fact, initiated and/or been running projects in the field for a number of years but had kept their distance from the partnerships. As they were drawn into engagement through the capacity-building process, they encountered the established leaders less as a representative organ than as an entrenched power structure.

In other areas, the existing community leaders restricted the scope of capacity building, preventing potential succession conflicts from emerging. In one inner-city case study, on the initiative of the established community leaders, a capacity-building project designed from outside the neighbourhood was deemed inappropriate, closed down and replaced with research into local views of the neighbourhood. While a second layer of leaders existed outside the partnership, they were very busy voluntary sector project managers rather than grassroots community members and were too engaged in their own work to get involved in partnerships. In another area, capacity building was tightly constrained by councillors who had control of all the local community organisations and regeneration activities. Either way, these gatekeepers prevented direct access to the local residents they purported to represent.

Despite these negative examples, the evidence is that capacity building can expand the available core of community leadership and can add new community voices to the partnerships. The empowerment of new leaders can increase the power and effectiveness of the community sector as a whole, giving support to those leaders who actually sit on the partnership and increasing their power within a local leadership coalition. However, encouraging new leaders and developing new structures can challenge the power and legitimacy of the established leaders.

Challenging established leaders through voice

'Voice' becomes the key strategy in the fourth phase of the cycle for second-generation community leaders, when tensions between an existing (first) generation of leaders and a new (second) generation of community leaders result in challenges to established leaders. Challenges can also come from other members of the partnership to call for new voices to be welcomed into the partnership, and can lead to the recruitment of new leaders from new constituencies, such as minority ethnic groups in the inner cities.

In one case study, a black leader, now well established, had felt that black and minority ethnic communities had been excluded from the regeneration process in her city and poorly represented by the umbrella group originally charged with representing the voluntary and community sectors.

> 'Nobody in ____ had raised the issue of SRB with the voluntary sector let alone the black voluntary sector.... This is coming from my perspective as someone who had to fight her way into the partnership.'

It was not until she put in a rival bid against the local authority-led bid that regional Government Office intervention led to her entry into the existing regeneration partnership. In another inner-city case, the community representatives on a partnership board were all white and co-opted from a voluntary sector forum. A Bangladeshi business representative challenged the lack of representation of minority ethnic communities. As a result the forum held elections and replaced all three of the white representatives with minority ethnic representatives. In Chapter Eight in this volume, Beebeejaun and Grimshaw discuss further issues raised by leadership succession in relation to minority ethnic communities.

Leadership challenges also occurred on the peripheral estates but outcomes were less decisive. Here succession took the form of more persistent conflict over representation and accountability. In one case, new leaders had set up groups to oppose the existing community associations on three of the four constituent estates, with rival community associations mooted on two of the estates. On one of these estates, the steering group for the proposed community centre was drawn from the local neighbourhood watch and connected networks, while partnership representation came from the residents' association, with no communication between the two. The residents' association maintained a monopoly of representation and the steering group collapsed.

Some of the first generation of leaders in the study depended quite heavily on their role in the partnership to give them status, hence were not keen to let go of power, and prevented new voices from being heard.

Progression through exit and threatened exit

The SRB partnerships in the study were time limited and the final progression phase of the succession cycle consisted of the exit of community leaders from partnerships. Working with non-community-friendly partnerships is 'a full-time job' for many community leaders. They face conflicting claims on their time, energy and goodwill, particularly when caught between statutory and private partners neglectful of their needs on the one hand and on the other the community's widespread alienation from governance structures such as partnerships. Thus, many of the community leaders in this study were seeking an exit from participation one way or another. Hirschman's (1970) concept of 'exit' is based on choice: the decision to leave one organisation that is failing to meet the member's needs or demands and join another that will. The research identified three types of exit – threatened collective exit by a whole group of community leaders in a partnership; individual leaders moving on to other partnerships and roles within neighbourhood regeneration; and burnout, where the individual leader is lost to neighbourhood governance altogether.

Threatened collective exit is a hybrid of exit and voice (Hirschman, 1970). Collective exit, or the ability to realistically threaten exit, can sometimes be the most effective strategy for getting results that community leaders desire. Combining, as Hirschman points out, the qualities of exit with those of voice, the threat of exit has its limits too and must be credible to work (Harrison et al, 1995). While partnerships can easily survive the departure of individuals, block resignations, especially when followed up with rival bidding, are far more damaging to the statutory partners. Community representatives in one case study, who had been in protracted negotiations with the local authority planners, were able to get the local authority to complete the purchase of a building for a community centre when they threatened to leave the partnership and started to deal independently with the property owner.

'All of a sudden the council realised what we were doing, that if we pulled out of the SRB, the SRB money would be lost, wouldn't it, because they had to have it by certain dates. Well, if we had pulled out of it, they couldn't have done it and they would have lost all their money. We said: "You're messing us around, we've got to do this" … and then the council … pulled themselves together and it all suddenly happened.'

A second form of exit consisted of individual community leaders moving on to new leadership roles, to raise their voices in other more promising partnerships and projects. Here a community leader's departure from a particular partnership (or refusal to remain for its successor) was offset by the gain of them remaining in a wider circle of neighbourhood governance networks. Some local leaders gained the skills and experience from the SRB partnership to move on to new funding possibilities, which they felt would be less constraining, such as Healthy Living Centres and the Lottery Millennium Greens (grants), described as 'SRB in reverse' – that is, bottom up. Others found that their new skills led to qualifications and to paid jobs, often in the voluntary or community sectors. Some have also moved into managing the community centres and development projects that have sprung up through SRB funding. 'We needed SRB to understand our worth – almost like someone turned on the electric light.'

This form of exit can be a combination of weighing up the costs and benefits of working in a particular partnership on the one hand, while on the other hand using the contacts and experience of SRB partnership work for career development or to attract further funding for neighbourhood projects.

However, a common form of exit for leaders in the study was to give up community politics entirely due to burnout.

> 'My and J___'s energies are waning … we're finding it harder and harder to fight. If we get a knock it is upsetting us more, we can't just shrug it off quite so easily. We are both getting tired – we need new blood.'

In one focus group all the community representatives had been ill with overwork and stress during the first year. One person was considering leaving the partnership by the end of the first year and all the others felt burnt out. The physical and emotional cost to the individual leaders was so heavy that many felt that it was not worth the effort to continue to be involved. In another focus group neither of the two people present who had been on the partnership board said they would continue in the future. This sort of exit provides negative feedback about the sustainability of partnership working, but without presenting a more effective alternative model.

Burnout can create problems in leadership succession as it makes transferring skills from one generation of community leaders to the next difficult. Just as the first generation of community partners got to grips with the workings of SRB they were worn out by being asked to take on more and more work with little administrative help, leaving a gap in which another fresh face would have had to start the education process from scratch. In one area this affected some leaders to such an extent that they wished to 'retire' from these activities, even though there seemed to be no one willing to take on their positions, mainly because of the voluntary time commitment that the work entailed. Loyalty to the partnership was clearly a factor in delaying departure.

For the community leaders themselves, the cost of exit has a direct impact on individual identity as a leader, as a community activist or – more diffusely expressed – as a person who cares about their neighbourhood. Hence, community leaders try to balance voice and loyalty in attempting to influence partnerships, with exit only seen as an effective option *in extremis*.

Variations in community leadership cycles

Whereas a single community leadership cycle is outlined in Figure 7.1, this research on community leadership revealed two basic forms in which the leadership cycle played out, depending on the history of local community organisation and investment in the regeneration of the neighbourhood. The full cycle, going through all five phases from the emergence of new leaders to their progression, tended to occur in neighbourhoods that had little history of funding and few community organisations or visible community leaders. In the study sample, these were usually peripheral estates. On these estates, SRB offered substantial new opportunities, but a layer of community leadership needed to be created very quickly to support and champion the partnerships. While unpaid, this first tier of leaders quickly consolidated their positions to form a monopoly of access to the partnership. New leaders, who emerged from capacity building, challenged the legitimacy of the first generation of leaders in a number of ways. Some formed a second tier of leadership with more limited concerns and felt disconnected from the partnership and the official community representatives. Others felt open hostility to the established community leaders whom they saw as obstructive gatekeepers and even moved towards setting up new forms of representation in order to access the partnerships. Tensions arose because the management of SRB schemes was not in general keen on absorbing rival community groupings once a comfortable pattern of community representation had been established. Institutional partners tended to have little sense of these changes in community organisations during the lifetime of a partnership, choosing instead to concentrate on maintaining – with least inconvenience to the partnership – the existing community representatives in the partnership board.

A shorter community leadership cycle emerged most clearly from one of our inner-city case studies. This occurred where community leaders were well established and there was a long experience of dealing with funding streams. Here the partnership moved quickly from the consolidation phase to progression, with little embedding of the community leaders or challenge. High levels of need in the inner cities have meant that funding regimes have been coming in waves for some time (Fraser, 1996). Thus, local community leaders have been through several earlier cycles of succession and have coalesced into an established and professionalised voluntary sector, accustomed to assessing the new government initiatives in terms of their own role in service provision. Inner-city communities are extremely diverse and community leaders often see themselves as representing distinct constituencies and even acting as gatekeepers preventing direct access from partnership to community. These leaders are so well established that there is little scope for direct representation of local residents, with few new leaders appearing at all and then from a pool of experienced professionals. Capacity building, which is usually associated with developing new leaders, can become very contentious.

As community leaders move on to multiple partnerships in a neighbourhood, their familiarity with the other partners and their stock of relevant knowledge makes them increasingly difficult to replace. The leadership coalition begins to stabilise, with more enduring and more regulated relationships between community leaders and their statutory partners, although they may remain fraught. Thus, as a neighbourhood leadership coalition matures, it moves towards the 'kaleidoscope of recognisable faces' that Delbert Miller (1958) identified in Bristol in the 1950s.

Community influence in neighbourhood governance

The existence of partnerships does not automatically guarantee that community leaders are able to become influential members of a local leadership coalition. In the SRB case studies, local authorities were usually the authors of the bids for partnership funding and remained the leading partners and financial controllers of the SRB schemes. Thus, major power inequalities persisted between local authority and community leaders.

Local authorities were often perceived as having a secretive organisational culture. In one of our case studies, the community partners viewed the partnership as a 'one-way street', built on power, not trust. The community was obliged to trust the council, but the council did not trust the community. The community leaders felt undervalued; their time was used as if they had nothing else to do. They were not able to make any significant decisions but were merely informed of the decisions made by others. They felt manipulated into the partnership to serve the interests of the council rather than being properly consulted. In other cases community partners felt they had responsibility but no power or were 'just making up the numbers' on the board. Some partnerships seemed to be 'obsessed with hierarchical structures' and wanted to recreate these structures in the partnership; community partners often experienced partnership working as 'frustrating', 'a struggle' and as 'a constant battle'. Yet community leaders are not completely powerless and some were clearly able to capitalise on the opportunities that membership of a partnership provided, with community representatives chairing the partnerships in two case study areas.

The success of community leaders in gaining influence within a leadership coalition may be judged in terms of two types of outcomes – (a) their level of acceptance as social actors and (b) material or policy gains for their followers (Gamson, 1975). Between full success in achieving both of their aims and total failure, Gamson (1975) identifies two intermediary results – 'co-option' and 'pre-emption'. Co-option occurs when community leaders are accepted as players in the regeneration game but make no actual gains for their community; pre-emption occurs when the community receives tangible gains, but the community leaders receive no recognition for playing a part in the dispensation. In practice, community leaders are subjected to some degree of both co-option and pre-emption, in Gamson's terms.

On the one hand community leaders are co-opted in that they have nominal leadership positions, but are neither able to take decisions nor able to control partnership agendas. On the other hand communities may benefit from the distribution of resources through regeneration and other partnerships, but the role played by community leaders in acquiring these resources is frequently hidden from view by the way in which these dispensations are organised – what Gamson (1975) calls pre-emption. Where community leaders have succeeded in achieving clear and tangible benefits for their communities, eager press officers or inattentive local media may still attribute them to the council. Although central government programmes, such as SRB, have brought new faces into local leadership (Stewart, 1996), it remains a moot point whether community leaders have succeeded in winning material gains through control of funding or in achieving acceptance within the partnerships. While community leaders may have displayed the capacity to become part of local leadership coalitions (Miller, 1999), the roles open to them remained circumscribed by their more powerful partners. Much of the time community leaders find themselves locked in partnerships of dependency and conflict, where short bursts of dissenting voice alternate with grudging loyalty.

Voice can, however, also be used to engage in open-ended conversations to explore potential new shared discourses. Partnership working sometimes provides the fragile spaces of neighbourhood governance in which these collaborative conversations can take place across organisational and sectoral boundaries. Community leaders do sometimes find themselves able to engage in the partnership and wider leadership coalition discussions.

Conclusion

This chapter has been concerned with the formation of local patterns of leadership. It argues that these are most accurately represented in neighbourhoods by Miller's (1999) concept of 'leadership coalitions' and are of varying degrees of strength and stability. Its central claim is that community leaders engage with these coalitions through recurrent community leadership cycles. However, the path through the cycle depends on the previous experience of community leaders and organisations and their history of involvement with funding streams and partnerships in the neighbourhood. Community leadership cycles in neighbourhoods with a history of urban regeneration programmes tend to be curtailed in comparison with neighbourhoods that do not have such a history. This is because community leadership skills can be captured from earlier rounds of engagement in regeneration partnerships.

However, the construction and maintenance of neighbourhood-based leadership coalitions is seldom undertaken with an appreciation of the need to take these community leadership cycles into consideration. The new reliance on a more participative model of democracy within local governance is not, in general, matched by appropriate working methods in the partnerships. The accountability of the partnership to their local communities is best served where capacity-building activity cultivates new leaders, who are then brought into the decision-making process and not overloaded with work or subjected to resentment from their peer group. Yet, as this positive succession process is seldom followed through, negative forms of succession (burnout, holding on to power, submerged leadership selection) predominate and the legitimacy of partnership boards in general remains limited.

References

Bachrach, P. and Baratz, M. (1962) 'Two faces of power', *American Political Science Review*, vol 56, no 4, pp 947-52.

Banks, S. and Shenton, F. (2001) 'Regenerating neighbourhoods: a critical look at the role of community capacity building', *Local Economy*, vol 16, no 4, pp 286-98.

Bonjean, C. and Olsen, D. (1964) 'Community leadership: directions of research', *Administrative Science Quarterly*, vol 9, no 3, pp 278-300.

CLG (Communities and Local Government) (2006) *Strong and Prosperous Communities: The Local Government White Paper*, Cm 6939-I, London: The Stationery Office.

Dahl, R. (1957) 'The concept of power', *Behavioural Science*, vol 2, pp 201-15.

Diani, M., Lindsay, I. and Purdue, D. (2007) 'Weak ties, strong ties, and logics of collective action: insights from Britain', Paper submitted to the 102nd Annual Meeting of the American Sociological Association, New York, 11-14 August.

Fraser, P. (1996) 'Social and spatial relationships and the "problem" inner city: Moss-Side in Manchester', *Critical Social Policy*, vol 16, no 49, pp 43-65.

Gamson, W. (1975) *The Strategy of Protest*, Homewood, IL: Dorsey Press.

Harrison, L., Hoggett, P. and Jeffers, S. (1995) 'Race, ethnicity and community development', *Community Development Journal*, vol 30, no 2, pp 144-57.

Hirschman, A. (1970) *Exit, Voice and Loyalty*, Cambridge, MA: Harvard University Press.

HM Treasury (2002) *The Role of the Voluntary and Community Sector in Service Delivery: A Cross Cutting Review*, London: HM Treasury.

Home Office (2004) *Firm Foundations: The Government's Framework for Community Capacity Building*, London: Home Office.

Hunter, F. (1953) *Community Power Structure: A Study of Decision Makers*, Chapel Hill, NC: University of North Carolina Press.

Logan, J. and Molotch, H. (1987) *Urban Fortunes*, Berkeley, CA: University of California.

Lowery, D., de Hoog, R. and Lyons, W. (1992) 'Citizenship in the empowered locality', *Urban Affairs Quarterly*, vol 28, no 1, pp 69-103.

Miller, C. (1999) 'Partners in regeneration: constructing a local regime for urban management?', *Policy & Politics*, vol 27, no 3, pp 343-58.

Miller, D. (1958) 'Decision-making cliques in community power structures: a comparative study of an American and an English city', *American Journal of Sociology*, vol 63, no 3, pp 299-310.

Purdue, D. (2005) 'Community leadership cycles and the consolidation of neighbourhood coalitions in the new local governance', *Public Management Review*, vol 7, no 2, pp 247-66.

Purdue, D., Razzaque, K., Hambleton, R. and Stewart, M. with Huxham, C. and Vangen, S. (2000) *Community Leadership in Area Regeneration*, Bristol: The Policy Press.

Stewart, M. (1996) 'Too little, too late: the politics of complacency', *Urban Affairs Quarterly*, vol 18, no 2, pp 119-37.

Stewart, M. (2003) 'Towards collaborative capacity', in M. Boddy (ed) *Urban Transformation and Urban Governance: Shaping the Competitive City of the Future*, Bristol: The Policy Press.

Stewart, M. and Taylor, M. (1995) *Resident Empowerment in Estate Regeneration*, Bristol: The Policy Press.

Stone, C. (1989) *Regime Politics: Governing Atlanta, 1946-1988*, Kansas, KS: University Press of Kansas.

EIGHT

Neighbourhood governance and diversity: the diverse neighbourhood

Yasminah Beebeejaun and Lucy Grimshaw

The British, Indian and colonial people must face those problems together *as partners....* But if this is to be achieved, the British people will have to learn far more about the Empire than they consent to do now. (Campbell, 1945, p 8; emphasis in original)

Introduction

A widespread recognition of the diversity of the society in which we live has raised concerns, among politicians and professionals alike, that we are drifting towards becoming a divided nation. There are increasing anxieties surrounding 'multicultural' Britain (Cantle, 2001; Parekh and Commission on the Future of Multi-ethnic Britain, 2001; Blair, 2006). Such discussions and the concerns they raise are not new; nor is the exhortation to face problems 'together *as partners*' (Campbell, 1945, p 8; emphasis in original). Moreover, ethnic and gender-based inequalities within society continue to be documented (Macpherson, 1999; Morris et al, 2004). The neighbourhood is often seen as the place where diversity is experienced in everyday life (Amin, 2002). Given this, is neighbourhood governance a step in the right direction? This chapter asks if neighbourhood governance can be practised in a meaningful and potentially non-oppressive way. 'How can governance draw upon the richness of knowledge and understanding available to people in different cultural worlds without oppressively omitting richness through the dominance of particular ideas and power relations?' (Healey, 1997, p 49).

Insofar as governance is concerned, much of the current debate has focused on the necessity for underrepresented groups, including women and minority ethnic groups, to gain greater involvement. A key issue within neighbourhood governance is the sensitivity of institutional structures to the local population. The issues of representativeness and representation are a highly contested area in political theory (Young, 1990; Harvey, 1996; Parekh, 2000). However, there has been limited attention paid to how representation operates in practice. Understanding diversity is often seen to be a specialist area, with the interlocking but sometimes contradictory issues of gender, race and ethnicity grouped together. This chapter examines how ethnic difference and gender are addressed in governance and participatory structures within one New Deal for Communities (NDC) area.

Commitment to partnership working at local level is one of the key principles underpinning Labour's modernisation of local government (Sullivan and Skelcher, 2002; Stoker, 2004; Geddes, 2006). New Labour has also established a policy focus on neighbourhoods and in particular on the renewal of deprived neighbourhoods with an aim to reduce the gap between the poorest neighbourhoods and the rest of the country (SEU, 2001). A key strand in both policy areas has been an emphasis on engagement of civil society and community organisations as the means to achieve responsive and effective governance. Such partnerships are conceived as collaborations between public, private and civil society (more usually referred to as 'community') sectors. In particular there has been a policy turn towards involving 'hard-to-reach groups' and ensuring the representation of 'diversity' within the community through partnership working. It is this policy turn that we wish to focus attention on in the next section.

Governance and partnerships in diverse neighbourhoods

Neighbourhood-level governance offers the potential for the recognition of area-specific diversity. Discussions within the related fields of plan-making (Higgins et al, 2005; Reeves, 2005) and regeneration and renewal (Allen and Cars, 2001) all promise the possibility of engaging with the hitherto disengaged. It is argued that it is in neighbourhood-level collaboration that citizen participation is potentially widest and deepest since a wider range of stakeholders can be represented at a level nearer to the respective communities (Sullivan and Skelcher, 2002). Moreover, as we will discuss later in this chapter, it is often the level at which women engage in particular types of political activity. Government policy and guidance on community involvement and neighbourhood renewal has sought to capitalise on the potential within neighbourhoods to enable the inclusion of diverse communities, which in turn it is proposed will help to build cohesive communities (DETR, 1997, 2000; SEU, 2001; NRU, 2006).

The political debate around diversity has focused on the issues arising from attempting to recognise and represent different ethnic, cultural and faith communities at the local level. The neighbourhood is a key site of contestation, as academics' and politicians' attention continues to fall on the reasons for ethnic segregation and the issues that arise from this (Rex and Moore, 1967; Cantle, 2001; Johnston et al, 2002). The debate regarding segregation has previously focused on the segregation of all immigrant groups but more recently it has centred on Asian groups, identified through ethnicity, previous nationality and religion. This changing focus has arguably had considerable impact on the nature of neighbourhood governance and how groups become understood. Phillips (2006, p 28) argues that reports, including Cantle (2001),

> [c]onstructed the patterns of inner-city minority ethnic clustering observed in northern British towns as a 'problem'. This is consistent with earlier discourses of ethnic 'segregation' as signs of failure on the part of minorities to integrate socially, culturally, and economically.

It is possible, moreover, to argue that the physical expression of cultural differences, such as the mosque and temple, reinforces fear of lived differences (Gale and Naylor, 2002; Phillips, 2006). This chapter follows on from such research to suggest that neighbourhood governance structures may place particular emphasis on the need to develop cultural understandings of ethnic difference. Researchers have suggested that it is at the scale of the neighbourhood that we can 'begin to develop a nuanced view of multiculturalism which can be used to analyse the problems which (ethnic) cultural diversity raises for governance in socially excluded neighbourhoods' (Allen and Cars, 2001, p 2196). This chapter explores how such an assumption shapes the inclusion of ethnically different people in particular ways and the impact this has on women's involvement.

Allen and Cars (2001) base their analysis on an interpretation of Parekh's (2000) multiculturalism, which takes as a starting point the existence of discrete cultural groups. The work of neighbourhood governance is to provide opportunities for these discrete groups to engage in 'intercultural encounters' (Allen and Cars, 2001, p 2205) whereby groups' mistrust of each other can be broken down and intercultural understanding can begin to occur. This, it is argued, will form the basis for a cohesive neighbourhood that 'creates numerous opportunities for members of different cultural communities to meet and pursue common cultural, economic and other interests' (Allen and Cars, 2001, p 2205).

However, the outlook is not completely optimistic, as this case study illustrates. It is suggested here that the prioritisation of ethnic cultural difference over other identities raises a number of problems. If the focus is on different cultural communities this may allow space for some while excluding others or focusing attention on certain characteristics of a perceived group. This may act to create new stereotypes or reinforce existing ones. After all, how are decisions to be made about which are the most important differences to represent?

Representation and representatives

Inclusion, race, ethnicity and gender are not neutral terms but are discursive concepts, which frame groups and attempts to represent them. Race, ethnicity, black and minority ethnic (BME) are all contested concepts and there is not space here to discuss how such categories may become constructed (see Jenkins, 1997). Benhabib (2002, p 16) is suspicious of 'mosaic multiculturalism', warning that:

> The multiculturalist resistance to seeing cultures as internally riven and contested carries over to visions of selves, who are then construed as equally unified and harmonious beings with a unique cultural centre.

This chapter argues that the desire to find 'good' representation prioritises simplistic ideas of cultural identity over other possible identities and contributes to fixed notions of identifying groups for governance purposes. It explores some of the implications this may have for groups and individuals in tension with the overriding conceptualisations of cultures as coherent and discrete groupings.

Governance in diverse neighbourhoods is keenly concerned with achieving full representation. By this is meant the incorporation of the minority groups identified as significant. However, the reasons and presumed outcomes from such representation are under-explored, which is of interest as political theory continues to grapple with such debates (Young, 1990, 2000; Harvey, 1996; Benhabib, 2002). As Young (2000) notes, perfect representation is not achieved through ensuring that we represent everything or mirror society. There needs to be an understanding of the important differences and the reasons behind marginalised groups' lack of voice in the political sphere (O'Neill,

2001). More practically, there is importance attached to representatives as role models who may send out a signal to disenfranchised citizens who can gain confidence and aspire to this role (Squires, 1999; Sullivan and Skelcher, 2002).

Gaining a wider range of representatives is no easy task and requires willing participants. Barr et al (2001) identified common personal characteristics of people involved in regeneration partnerships – commitment, concern for justice and mutuality, perseverance, resilience, awareness of community perspectives and realism (see also Purdue et al, 2000). However, there are also structural inequalities in society that act as barriers, such as age, class, gender, disability and sexuality (Sullivan and Skelcher, 2002). Organisations face challenges in negotiating between gaining group representation and recognising the attributes that enable individuals to take this role. However, sadly, this can lead to a situation where groups can become perceived as a discrete whole, forming building blocks within a simplistic understanding of multiculturalism (Benhabib, 2002) – a retreat from the complexities of culture as well as individuals' multiple identities. Allen and Cars (2001) offer some pertinent insights into how neighbourhood governance structures could become realigned to recognise diversity. Their arguments reflect much of the literature, which is practically oriented towards the thorny issue of how to live fairly in difference. However, it is argued here that too little attention is given to working with concepts of race, ethnicity and gender as dynamic and socially constructed (Brownill and Darke, 1998).

Race, gender and governance

The current government has introduced a raft of initiatives around diversity, race and ethnicity. Developments in 2006 included the transfer of the remit for community cohesion and general equalities from the Home Office to the new Department for Communities and Local Government and the establishment by the Secretary of State for Communities and Local Government of a Commission on Integration and Cohesion. This has as its second term of reference '[s]uggesting how local community and political leadership can push further against perceived barriers to cohesion and integration' (CLG, 2006a). These developments are embedded within a turn towards 'community cohesion' within policy making, borne out of the Parekh (2000) and Cantle (2001) reports.

The Parekh and Cantle reports are the two most oft-discussed reports in recent debates about ethnically diverse Britain. The impetus for each report is quite different, with the Parekh report, commissioned by the Runnymede Trust, setting out a positive vision for a multi-ethnic Britain in the 21st century and the Cantle report being a response to the 'northern uprisings' of the early 21st century, set against a backdrop of ethnic segregation and shared social exclusion. Both reports have fed into understandings of how cultural differences are lived out in our neighbourhoods, particularly within socially excluded and economically marginalised areas. They have also had a significant impact on the Local Government White Paper (CLG, 2006b) and Tony Blair's (2006) speech on 'Our nation's future', which outlines a clear shift from regeneration based on multicultural communities towards clear imperatives to demonstrate integration within funding bids.

As a result of the previous neglect of race equality, since the late 1990s, neighbourhood renewal policy, backed by new race equality legislation, has sought to emphasise the importance of including and supporting people from minority ethnic groups. Specific race equality guidance was produced for the New Deal for Communities (NDC) programme (DETR, 2000). However, the national evaluation of the NDC programme states that more is being done in relation to BME issues within NDC partnerships than with regard to gender and disability (CRESR, 2005). Unlike race, gender has often been ignored or sidelined within policy documents (May, 1997; Brownill and Darke, 1998). The Neighbourhood Renewal Unit, as late as 2006, went some way to address this neglect, publishing a *Diversity and Neighbourhood Renewal Factsheet*, which identified key issues regarding the inclusion of communities of interest, including men and women and minority ethnic groups. In a side note it highlighted the possibility of multiple discrimination based, for example, on ethnicity and gender (NRU, 2006).

In the regeneration literature Brownill and Darke (1998) were among the first to highlight the contradictions in the emergence of new forms of governance such as local regeneration partnerships. Their research demonstrated that, while partnerships present barriers to inclusion along the lines of race and gender, they can also offer opportunities for inclusion and incorporation of different interests that might otherwise be excluded from regeneration processes.

However, the literature continues to state that men and women participate differently in governance processes (Newman, 2005); women tend to participate in more informal processes whereas men prefer more formal methods of organising (Lowndes, 2004; Furbey et al, 2006). Research has suggested that women tend to get involved at the community or 'grassroots' level in specific campaigns rather than in the formal decision-making processes (Furbey et al, 2006). Women's involvement is viewed as a means to an end, while for men it is an end in itself (Lowndes, 2004). Put more explicitly, Donnison (1988, p 13, quoted in McCulloch, 1997, p 55) notes that 'women often play leading roles in the early heroic days of the community projects, but then hierarchies, formality and bureaucracy reassert themselves and the men take over'.

However, others highlight the dangers of stereotyping women and their roles and emphasise the lack of involvement of men, in particular young men, in local partnerships (Scott et al, 2000).

> [T]he very idea of distinct styles and concerns for women's and men's community organising essentializes the contributions of women and men into dichotomies of 'masculine' – confrontational and competitive – and 'feminine' – nurturing and empowering. (Martin, 2002, p 334)

Case study

The following material in this chapter is based on empirical data from both the authors' doctoral research and from Grimshaw's involvement in the national evaluation of the NDC programme. The case study draws on semi-structured interviews with NDC and local authority staff and community representatives on the NDC board between 2001 and 2005. However, due to the sensitive nature of the issues to be discussed it has been decided to anonymise the case study.

The case study is set within an urban area marked by a legacy of industrial residualisation and containing a number of urban cores rather than one urban centre. The population has declined from nearly 375,000 in 1981 to around 280,000 in 2001. The area suffers from unemployment at above the national average, including a disproportionate number of both minority ethnic groups and young people (based on data from the 2001 Census of Population).

The 2004 Index of Deprivation ranked the case study area among the highest 10%. The Index, prepared by the former Department for the Environment, Transport and the Regions, measures multiple deprivation in sub-ward areas known as Super Output Areas and uses 37 indicators across seven domains (including income deprivation, employment deprivation, education, skills and training deprivation). Given the levels of relative deprivation within the area, part of three wards became eligible for additional government funding via the NDC, a 10-year regeneration programme launched in 1998, which established multi-sector partnerships in 39 of the most deprived neighbourhoods in England. The partnerships brought together public, private, voluntary and community sectors. Each partnership set out a 10-year delivery plan and then annual business plans for its local area. A key element within the NDC programme was a movement away from government to governance, with the partnership expected to involve, indeed be led by, the local community throughout the whole process, from developing plans to implementation (DETR, 1998).

This chapter now examines some of the ways in which people participated within governance structures on the basis of ethnicity and gender and draws out some implications this has for ideas about representation within neighbourhood governance.

Framing ethnicity?

The case study area has a minority ethnic population of approximately double the national average, predominantly from the Asian subcontinent (based on data from the 2001 Census of Population). Until 2003 the primary mechanism for the formal incorporation of the minority ethnic communities' voices in local authority practice was an overarching group – the Forum – with representatives from each of the 'main' BME populations. In practice, a number of pre-existing community organisations were used to fill places for each of these ethnic groups. The Forum was the overall mechanism through which views from BME groups about various local authority proposals were canvassed and it developed to support minority ethnic people in the area (Beebeejaun, 2004). The identification of the groups involved in the Forum became embedded into the structure of policy making within the local authority.

The Forum provided a route through which BME groups could have a voice within governance structures, although some officers acknowledged that this mechanism should not be expected to represent all minority ethnic people. The Chair of the Local Strategic Partnership expressed similar reservations:

> 'I have this idea that we possibly have made a mistake, that we rely too heavily on them ... and we are asking them to do a very difficult thing ... the problem is that we seem to be expecting it [the Forum] to somehow represent the ethnic minority communities and this is never going to be realistic...'

Nonetheless, this mechanism was to become embedded within practice. The Forum was renamed and reconstituted in 2003 in response to the 2003 Race Relations Amendment Act and following an evaluation that, according to one officer, 'highlighted, amongst other issues, the need to broaden representation, improve governance and strengthen accountability and resources'. One of the changes in governance was an increase in the number of members on the Forum management committee, which continued to include representatives from the six BME groups and also included public sector officers; the committee members continued to be predominantly men.

The Forum gave a focus to engagement and recognition of ethnic groups, emphasised the importance of inclusive governance and aimed to promote race equality and community cohesion. Nonetheless, there continued to be problems associated with identifying a number of homogeneous ethnic groups. Ethnicity was framed within the concept of a number of distinct communities but these categories are not unproblematic. The mode of representation for the Forum assumed some internal homogeneity but also assumed parity between each ethnic group. However, there were considerable disparities between them, which we will discuss briefly in the context of three of the groups. While this discussion focuses on Asian groups, it is emphasised here that the issues surrounding the tensions between gender and ethnicity are not limited to such groups; nor should they be assumed to be representative of Asian 'culture'.

A key aim of the NDC strategy was to engage with and build the capacity of the BME community groups. The most prominent pre-existing group was primarily a men's business interest group, which had negotiated a wider role in participation processes as representing the Indian community (Beebeejaun, 2004). This was the only minority ethnic group to engage with the statutory urban planning process and members spoke of the group as being 'formed to protect the rights of the Indian community who are the oldest and majority of the ethnic minority population'. Yet women's and young people's voices were not always heard in the NDC's formal processes, with the business group taking the opportunity presented by the local authority to gain influence based on the notion of cultural difference (Yuval-Davis, 1997). Within the NDC, the officers talked of 'hidden women' and of trying to change the culture within BME and faith organisations. One officer described how they were trying to influence the gender balance:

> '... eighteen months ago under our "this has to happen",
> [they] took a woman onto their management group.... But

if you look under the surface in all of those organisations there are women involved, look at the smaller groups that are attached, look at the ... Centre, the temple over the road, the women are there 12 hours a day cooking and no one recognises that, the fact that it's those women who keep that temple open all that time.'

Conversely, the Bangladeshi community, which is described as 'one of the fastest growing groups as a result of the relatively young profile of the community and the large size of the families' (unpublished case study document), did not hold such a privileged position. According to the 2001 Census there are approximately 3,500 Bangladeshis within the local authority area; however, officers thought this to be an underestimate. This community reportedly suffers 'social exclusion to a very considerable extent' (unpublished case study document) and, for a number of reasons, its members felt unable to engage fully with institutional structures. The presence of the NDC enhanced the development of the community and resulted in the establishment of a Bangladeshi Regeneration Steering Group and 'the community regarded the NDC programme as a window of opportunity to escape from disadvantages and poverty' (unpublished case study document). The Steering Group included young and female representatives, local mosque representatives and local residents.

There was also difficulty in getting a Pakistani representative on the NDC board due to divisions within the Pakistani community. NDC staff have worked with this community in recent years to increase their understanding of it. They took the view that the community was divided and needed to be brought together in order to create a Steering Group that might then receive NDC funds and provide representation on the partnership board. This has been a highly sensitive issue, further complicated by perceived gender issues leading to a separate Women's Steering Group and Men's Steering Group having been established, as 'the women weren't comfortable joining the men'.

A key NDC strategy has been to provide support and funds for the community organisations and groups represented on the board. This has been done through the development of local community organisations with a specific 'capacity-building programme' and through a Steering Group, which was established to foster collaboration and to build connections and support among the BME communities. The BME board members attended the Steering Group and they generally agreed that this was a useful tool for building links between the communities, leading to sharing of facilities and reducing tension. Black and minority ethnic representatives also saw this as a positive group where they could support each other and promote race equality. One representative highlighted the pragmatism of the group members, stating that 'we each have our own agendas' but that, after one group's bid for funds was rejected, there was a realisation that if they supported each other then they could all get what they wanted; as another commented, 'lots of people wised up'.

The perceived differential impacts of community engagement and subsequent influence through gaining funding led to perceptions of some ethnic groups losing out to others. A number of BME representatives within the NDC spoke about their levels of funding in comparison to others. Some saw NDC funding as setting communities against each other, to compete to deliver the same services but to different ethnic groups. Other community board members also expressed this view and were concerned that the NDC population was being split rather than brought together. Interviews with representatives and a focus group with young people from non-BME and BME communities questioned the need for separate community centres, separate youth workers, youth forums and activities.

Furthermore, BME communities were seen to be 'isolating themselves' and it was suggested that there should be more mixing between BME and white groups, in keeping with community cohesion agendas (Cantle, 2001). Yet such discourses have often placed the responsibility for this primarily on these groups themselves as being self-segregating rather than foregrounding contributing institutional factors (Cantle, 2001). Some argued that it was inevitable that people from similar cultures would want to meet and organise together and did not view this as problematic, as long as it was combined with a strategy for working across cultures where appropriate. As the NDC programme continued, most of the BME groups received funding for their own organisations for much-needed capacity building and the Steering Group aimed to operate at a strategic level and develop joint BME projects.

A diversity officer was employed to focus on community cohesion and embedding equalities issues within the NDC partnership as a whole, and it was also intended that a Diversity Group would be established to work alongside the Steering Group but cover other 'equalities issues' such as gender and disability. While there was some discussion of 'other' communities, such as asylum seekers, the NDC continued to focus in its governance structures on particular BME communities. The focus on race was dominant and the contested nature of gender was much more clearly articulated in reference to individual community representatives. It is to this that attention now turns.

Representation of the community

The NDC determined from the outset that the board would comprise no less than 51% community representation. The original community members of the board were all male and nominated themselves to the board but, since 2001, the community has been represented on the board by one BME representative elected from each group within the Forum and eight neighbourhood representatives elected through elections held in the NDC area. At the first elections for neighbourhood representatives seven women were elected, including a Bangladeshi and an African Caribbean woman. The second round of elections in 2004 resulted in eight neighbourhood representatives being elected, six women (four White British and two Bangladeshi women) and two men (one White British and one African Caribbean). The elected neighbourhood representatives have therefore been predominantly female while the non-elected BME representatives have been predominantly male – at the outset they were all men, but in 2005 a Bangladeshi woman was nominated to the board.

Who are the representatives expected to represent? Elected minority ethnic representatives always claimed to represent the *whole* of the geographical community, not just *their* ethnic group and to make decisions for the good of the community as a whole. The high number of elected women differs markedly from observed political representation and acts to raise questions about the nature of representation largely absent from male-dominated forums (Puwar, 2004). It is interesting that they gained positions as neighbourhood rather than BME representatives. Yet they existed in a dual space where they emphasised that they were representative of their neighbourhood but also because of their ethnicity. One woman stressed the importance of her ability to communicate in neighbourhood and other forums with other women from her own and other minority ethnic groups as a result of her ability to speak several languages. The elected women representatives also alluded to a potential to break down barriers for these women who might otherwise allow their husbands to participate on their behalf. This was important given that within some BME groups community engagement occurs through separate forums for men and women, for example as has been established for the Pakistani population.

Despite this potential, the women who had been elected to the board were aware that BME representatives might not be reaching out to all the community – for example one Bangladeshi female representative said (in 2003) that women within the Bangladeshi community still had 'nowhere to go' and as the key providers for childcare and their family's needs were 'isolated'. She highlighted the lack of venues for women and stated that mosques were not open to women in that area. However, she also said that there was a move towards focusing on women within the Bangladeshi and other communities with the consideration of projects targeted at women, such as one BME organisation providing a Women's Luncheon Club.

Power imbalances?

Community representatives expressed feelings of being marginalised and embedded within unequal power relations as a result of being part of the 'community sector'. Despite opportunities for pre-board discussions and meetings there was also a perceived lack of community solidarity and discussion at the board. Those community representatives who said they did speak out often said they felt they were ignored. Here the power differential between the community and the statutory agencies and the perceptions of women more generally were intertwined. A retired White British representative referred to her own and a colleague's perceived reputation – 'the two old fuddy-duddies they call us don't they?'. Another interviewee explained how she felt that gender played a role in the feeling of powerlessness of community representatives:

> 'As community representatives we've got three ladies that speak up. What I do feel is a gender bias, is the perception of these people, I don't feel that they are perceived as knowledgeable or as eloquent or as challenging as the men ... I think, I get that impression about other female members of the board that they are not taken as seriously as the men.'

An NDC officer reinforced this idea but said that the older women *allowed* the men (especially those in positions of authority) at the board to make decisions because of their traditional attitude of 'you know better', an old style of 'you men folk know better'.

Yet there were further tensions of representation for the women representatives from BME communities who, while nominally representing a 'disempowered' sector of the community, were also professional women working in statutory agencies. Although they had been elected through NDC processes their legitimacy was still questioned, ironically because of their education and professions. One NDC officer said:

> 'The BME representatives are generally professionals, they have a certain intellect, they are a benefit to the board but they don't necessarily represent the women in [the area]. They can argue the case, they can be assertive and I guess they're women and Asian women so they have some vulnerability, but the other women on the board don't see them as representing them, they're Asian and there is, there are those who have a problem with black people...'

These representatives were themselves aware of the difficulties for other minority ethnic women to participate and the isolation they may face. Yet they were criticised for not being representative as they were unable to meet the stereotype of the oppressed Asian woman. At the same time they were also marginalised for acting beyond the stereotype as well-educated and assertive professionals. They were better placed if they were seen to be breaking the mould of submissive women through their interactions within the board than through their own endeavours. Another female representative described one interaction:

> 'There is another female BME rep[resentative], a very smart, pretty girl, Indian, I think she represents the Hindu community.... She's now come on the board, she's quite nice, she came up to me after one meeting and said it's nice to see an Asian girl speaking up and getting a point across and I thought that's really lovely so she's the other one now. It's changing.'

Being pretty was also seen to be important enough to comment on! Here the presence, as well as the representativeness of women was scrutinised by others, arguably as they contradicted presumptions regarding gender roles within minority ethnic groups.

Discussion

The idea of incorporating the disempowered 'as partners' is not new to current society, having been put forward in progressive discussions regarding the former British Empire. This chapter has highlighted a range of issues of current concern for those interested in governance as a set of practices that can better engage with diversity. Given the changing nature of our society and the ongoing tensions between groups (Cantle, 2001) this is increasing in urgency. Recent government policy has seemingly prioritised recognising and incorporating diversity but what model of multicultural diversity is being created? There are a number of distinct issues to highlight in drawing this chapter to a close.

First, difference has a habit of becoming an unproblematic and homogenous entity whereby efforts are made to engage with people inhabiting different cultural spaces (Allen and Cars, 2001). Governance is reduced to a space to learn uncritically about other ways of knowing and being. The case study area's BME forum was established to try to reflect diversity more clearly but also reiterated the idea that there were distinct and separate minority ethnic communities. As ethnicity is centred on notions of different relativistic cultures and needs, self-regulating structures were probably seen to be the most appropriate means of gathering 'minority ethnic' views. Yet these acted in some cases to reinforce ethnicity as an unchanging constant. The present authors would question whether the establishment of the Steering Group within the NDC thus continues to reinforce this process and prevents further discussion and challenge about the ways in which ethnicity is incorporated into governance structures.

Second, in incorporating diversity, even when motivated by the desire to enhance equality, it is important to remain alert to the wider equalities agenda and not presume that the new inhabitants of white and male space bring with them a coherent and complementary set of progressive values. There are real dangers that mistaking race and ethnicity to mean equality can lead to uncritical acceptance of regressive views regarding gender (Benhabib, 2002). Moreover, focusing on important or numerous groups renders some invisible. In our case study, the Chinese, Irish and asylum seeker and refugee populations were invisible in policy making, as they were seen as too numerically small and as a result 'too difficult' to engage with and to be represented within governance structures.

Third, within our case study, women dominated community sector positions on the board, particularly where elected by their local community. They reversed perceptions that women are not interested in roles in the formal decision-making process. However, as a result of their position within the community sector and their gender they still faced considerable barriers in gaining power. The presence of women representatives, particularly from minority ethnic groups, became framed within a superficial 'mosaic multiculturalist' account of the role of women. As outlined earlier, women seemed to be scrutinised regarding the validity of their representativeness. They did not fit the stereotype of Asian women, which became a normative construct with which to contrast assertive professional Asian women. The BME male community representatives' statements about culture, in particular gender roles, were not directly questioned as they fitted in with stereotypes held regarding such cultures. Talking about culture as a discrete and unquestionable entity obfuscates the reproduction of sexist practices in society as a whole, but the lack of clear debate in policy terms is revealed when we consider that sexism is not seen to be an acceptable white or Christian practice, but continually challenged through societal debate and legislative measures.

There is a long-running debate regarding the intersections of race, ethnicity and gender (Okin, 1999; Young, 1990, 2000) and the need to guard against universalist prescriptions of right and wrong is recognised. However, there was an implicit assumption at work in the case study area that there was greater similarity both between and within minority ethnic groups as 'the other'. Such an approach to ethnicity, while seeing minority groups as different, leaves out the consideration of other types of difference. This is probably partly due to a pragmatic attitude and to awareness of the political sensitivities of race. Acting to shape the groups as a whole leaves potential conflicts within and between such groups. Although there may be arguments to say that it is in minority ethnic groups' best interests to work together to promote and lobby for their needs, it can sidestep difficult but meaningful debate. There is a need to think reflexively about simplistic explanations of culture and difference and, to paraphrase Campbell (1945), there is still much more for all British people (whatever their ethnic origin) to learn than they consent to do now.

References

Allen, J. and Cars, G. (2001) 'Multiculturalism and governing neighbourhoods', *Urban Studies*, vol 38, no 12, pp 2195-209.

Amin, A. (2002) 'Ethnicity and the multicultural city: living with diversity', *Environment and Planning A*, vol 34, no 6, pp 959-80.

Barr, A., Stenhouse, C. and Henderson, P. (2001) *Caring Communities: A Challenge for Social Inclusion*, York: York Publishing Services.

Beebeejaun, Y. (2004) 'What's in a nation? Constructing ethnicity in the British planning system', *Planning Theory and Practice*, vol 5, no 4, pp 437-51.

Benhabib, S. (2002) *The Claims of Culture: Equality and Diversity in the Global Era*, Princeton, NJ: Princeton University Press.

Blair, T. (2006) 'Our nation's future: multiculturalism and integration', Speech given on 8 December.

Brownill, S. and Darke, J. (1998) *'Rich Mix'*, Bristol: The Policy Press.

Campbell, A. (1945) *It's your Empire* (New Left Book Club Edition), Suffolk: Richard Clay and Company Ltd.

Cantle, T. (2001) *Community Cohesion: A Report of the Independent Review Team*, London: Home Office.

CLG (Communities and Local Government) (2006a) *Commission on Integration and Cohesion: Terms of Reference*, available at: www.integrationandcohesion.org.uk [URL correct as of May 2007].

CLG (2006b) *Strong and Prosperous Communities: The Local Government White Paper*, Cm 6939-I, London: The Stationery Office.

CRESR (Centre for Regional, Economic and Social Research) (2005) *New Deal for Communities 2001-2005: An Interim Evaluation*, Research Report 17, London: ODPM.

DETR (Department of the Environment, Transport and the Regions) (1997) *Involving Communities in Urban and Rural Regeneration*, London: DETR.

DETR (1998) *New Deal for Communities: Phase 1 Proposals: Guidance for Pathfinder Applicants*, London: DETR.

DETR (2000) *New Deal for Communities: Race Equality Guidance*, London: DETR.

Donnison, D. (1988) 'Secrets of success', *New Society*, 29 January, pp 11-13, cited in McCulloch, A. (1997) 'You've fucked up the estate and now you're carrying a briefcase!', in P. Hoggett (ed) *Contested Communities*, Bristol: The Policy Press, pp 51-67.

Furbey, R., Dinham, A., Farnell, R., Finneron, D. and Wilkinson, G., with Howarth, C., Hussain, D. and Palmer, S. (2006) *Faith as Social Capital: Connecting or Dividing*, Bristol/York: The Policy Press/Joseph Rowntree Foundation.

Gale, R. and Naylor, S. (2002) 'Religion, planning and the city: the spatial politics of ethnic minority expression in British cities and towns', *Ethnicities*, vol 2, no 3, pp 387-409.

Geddes, M. (2006) 'Partnerships and the limits to local governance in England: institutionalist analysis and neoliberalism', *International Journal of Urban and Regional Research*, vol 30, no 1, pp 76-97.

Harvey, D. (1996) *Justice, Geography and the Nature of Difference*, London: Blackwell Publishers.

Healey, P. (1997) *Collaborative Planning: Shaping Places in Fragmented Societies*, London: Macmillan.

Higgins, M., Hague, C., Prior, A., McIntosh, S., Satsangi, M., Warren, F., Smith, H. and Netto, G. (2005) *Diversity and Equality in Planning: A Good Practice Guide*, London: ODPM.

Jenkins, R. (1997) *Rethinking Ethnicity: Arguments and Explorations*, London: Sage Publications.

Johnston, R., Forrest, J. and Poulsen, M. (2002) 'Are there ethnic enclaves/ghettos in English cities?', *Urban Studies*, vol 39, no 4, pp 591-618.

Lowndes, V. (2004) 'Getting on or getting by? Women, social capital and political participation', *British Journal of Politics and International Relations*, vol 6, no 1, pp 45-64.

McCulloch, A. (1997) 'You've fucked up the estate and now you're carrying a briefcase!', in P. Hoggett (ed) *Contested Communities*, Bristol: The Policy Press, pp 51-67.

Macpherson of Cluny, Sir William (1999) *The Stephen Lawrence Inquiry*, Cm 4262-I, London: The Stationery Office.

Martin, D. (2002) 'Constructing the "neighbourhood sphere": gender and community organizing [1]', *Gender, Place and Culture*, vol 9, no 4, pp 333-50.

May, N. (1997) *Challenging Assumptions: Gender Issues in Urban Regeneration*, York: Joseph Rowntree Foundation.

Morris, Sir W., Burden, A. and Weekes, A. (2004) *The Case for Change: People in the Metropolitan Police Service*, London: Metropolitan Police Authority.

Newman, J. (2005) 'Regendering governance', in J. Newman (ed) *Remaking Governance: People, Politics and the Public Sphere*, Bristol: The Policy Press, pp 81-99.

NRU (Neighbourhood Renewal Unit) (2006) *Diversity and Neighbourhood Renewal Factsheet*, London: ODPM.

Okin, S. M. (1999) *Is Multiculturalism Bad for Women?*, Princeton, NJ: Princeton University Press.

O'Neill, J. (2001) 'Representing people, representing nature, representing the world', *Environment and Planning C*, vol 19, no 4, pp 483-500.

Parekh, B. (2000) *Rethinking Multiculturalism: Cultural Diversity and Political Theory*, Basingstoke and New York: Palgrave.

Parekh, B. (Chair) and Commission on the Future of Multi-ethnic Britain (2001) *The Future of Multi-ethnic Britain*, London: Profile Books.

Phillips, D. (2006) 'Parallel lives? Challenging discourses of British Muslim self-segregation', *Environment and Planning D*, vol 24, no 1, pp 25-40.

Purdue, D., Razzaque, K., Hambleton, R. and Stewart, M. with Huxham, C. and Vangen, S. (2000) *Community Leadership in Area Regeneration*, Bristol: The Policy Press.

Puwar, N. (2004) *Space Invaders: Race, Gender and Bodies Out of Place*, Oxford: Berg Publishers.

Reeves, D. (2005) *Planning for Diversity: Policy and Planning in a World of Difference*, London: Spon Press.

Rex, J. and Moore, R. (1967) *Race, Community and Conflict: A study of Sparkbrook*, Oxford: Oxford University Press.

Scott, G., Long, G., Brown, U. and MacKenzie, J. (2000) *Women's Issues in Local Partnership Working*, Edinburgh: Scottish Executive Central Research Unit.

SEU (Social Exclusion Unit) (2001) *A New Commitment to Neighbourhood Renewal: National Strategy Action Plan*, London: SEU.

Squires, J. (1999) *Gender in Political Theory*, Cambridge: Polity Press.

Stoker, G. (2004) *Transforming Local Governance: From Thatcherism to New Labour*, Basingstoke: Palgrave Macmillan.

Sullivan, H. and Skelcher, C. (2002) *Working across Boundaries: Collaboration in Public Services*, Basingstoke: Palgrave.

Young, I. M. (1990) *Justice and the Politics of Difference*, Princeton, NJ: Princeton University Press.

Young, I. M. (2000) *Inclusion and Democracy*, Oxford: Oxford University Press.

Yuval-Davis, N. (1997) *Gender and Nation*, London: Sage Publications.

NINE

Mainstreaming and neighbourhood governance: the importance of process, power and partnership

Ian Smith, Joanna Howard and Laura Evans

Introduction

One of the key themes of contemporary urban policy in England is that supplementary urban regeneration programmes such as the National Strategy for Neighbourhood Renewal (NSNR) cannot on their own tackle deeply ingrained and complex problems of area-based disadvantage. Disadvantage and exclusion must rather be addressed through existing 'core' (mainstream) expenditure on the public services that are already present in these neighbourhoods. From this perspective, mainstreaming, for contemporary policy makers, is a multifaceted transformation process that goes beyond merely spending more money in disadvantaged areas.

Key public services such as the police, education authorities and health trusts hold important resources of revenue, capital (such as buildings, property and vehicles) and the technical expertise embodied in their staff. During the financial year 2005/06 some £61 billion of extra public spending was being channelled into public services (over and above the previous year's spending) and the aim was to get some of this additional funding directed at disadvantaged areas (ODPM, 2004, p 3). By contrast, the Neighbourhood Renewal Fund directed only £400 million at disadvantaged neighbourhoods in the most deprived local authority areas. The transformation of existing public services in disadvantaged neighbourhoods becomes more urgent when it is argued that the poor quality of many of these services is linked to the spiral of neighbourhood decline (see SEU, 1998, or Johnson and Osborne, 2003). However, the idea of mainstream agencies responding more effectively to local issues and conditions sits more generally within the government's agenda of improving public services through the residents in neighbourhoods becoming 'more involved in the democratic life of their community' (ODPM/HO, 2005, p 3). This is an idea that applies to all neighbourhoods, not just the most disadvantaged.

In this chapter we will explore three questions:

- How do professionals and residents working in and around neighbourhood renewal make sense of 'mainstreaming' as a process of transformation in public services?
- Can we identify evidence of mainstream agencies changing either what they do or what they talk about as a response to the neighbourhood renewal agenda (that is, is there evidence of mainstreaming)?
- If so, what have been the conditions under which this mainstreaming has come about?

Neighbourhood partnerships need the resources held by core spending agencies but it is only through an examination of the evidence from neighbourhood renewal programmes that one can understand the limitations on neighbourhood partnerships to mobilise these resources.

Mainstreaming in current policy

The NSNR attempts to combine two broad approaches to funding regeneration activity. The first involves targeting exceptional pots of money in time-limited programmes; the second aims to transform existing public services and universal funding streams so that they can tackle particular problems as well as continuing to provide a general service. The NSNR provides exceptional funding to supplement, but also to change, key public services, with the intention that they will then use mainstream funding to continue to tackle area-based disadvantage once the specific initiatives of the NSNR have been wound up. The idea of using exceptional funding to transform ongoing core public services is an idea that New Labour administrations have applied to a wide range of area-based programmes that extend beyond the NSNR. For example, Health Action Zones focused on reducing health inequalities while also being required to consider wider issues and change the ways mainstream agencies delivered health and social care.

The concept of mainstreaming is picked out as important in two major initiatives of the NSNR: the New Deal for Communities (NDC) programme and the Neighbourhood Management Pathfinder (NMP) programme. Within each programme the role and expectations of core

Table 9.1: NSNR initiatives and mainstreaming

	NDC programme	NMP programme
Areas targeted	39 neighbourhoods	35 Pathfinders
Level of exceptional resources direct from central government	£50 million per partnership over 10 years (including running costs) Average £250-£1,000 per resident per year	£350-£500,000 per annum per Pathfinder over seven years (excluding running costs) Average £35-£50 per resident per year
Mainstream agency transformation through:	Experimentation with subsequent rolling out	Levering in funding from mainstream agencies

mainstreaming agencies differs slightly. Table 9.1 outlines some of the key characteristics of these programmes.

The levels of exceptional funding vary considerably between these programmes. The NDC programme has been described as one of the most intensively resourced comprehensive regeneration schemes ever launched in England (CRESR, 2005) whereas the NMP programme is more modestly resourced. One of the key aims of the NDC programme was to engage with partner agencies in order to help transform delivery of services, but the high level of funding allowed partnerships to attempt independent solutions if public service agencies chose not to engage. By contrast to NDC, neighbourhood management was to be a new approach to improving public services, building community capacity and promoting renewal in deprived areas. The central goal of neighbourhood management was to 'enable deprived communities and local services to improve local outcomes, by improving and joining up local services, and making them more responsive to local needs' (SQW, 2006, p 9).

Neighbourhood Management Pathfinders have partnership boards to regulate what they do, but the role of the neighbourhood manager is central. This manager is expected to 'manage' neighbourhood renewal in the designated area, first through bringing together residents and service providers to secure service improvements and second through levering in additional funding from mainstream partner agencies. In contrast to this, the resources available to NDC partnerships are intended to allow mainstream agencies to experiment at the behest of local communities. This was based on the assumption that the lessons learnt from project-based experiments would be rolled out to a wider area.

The NSNR clearly promotes the idea of neighbourhood-level working by 'core' mainstream public service agencies. However, the rising importance of neighbourhood-level working also comes from central government policy outside the neighbourhood renewal policy stream. The Local Government Modernisation Agenda has focused minds in the public sector on area working. There has been an increase in the number of area committees, area forums and neighbourhood management area working arrangements since the introduction of this agenda; this recent turn to decentralisation is also discussed in Chapter Five. This enthusiasm for area working has in some local authorities involved adopting a 'neighbourhood management approach' on a city-wide basis (better described as an 'area management approach'), to manage the decentralisation of some services to the area level, mainly for liveability-related services. The National Evaluation of Neighbourhood Management claims that by 2005, some 250 neighbourhood management initiatives had been set up, in addition to the NMPs, the majority of which were set up by either the local authority or the Local Strategic Partnership (LSP) for the local authority area (SQW, 2006).

Given that the mechanisms implicated in and the institutional arrangements associated with neighbourhood governance are varied, so too are the ways in which the mainstream agencies engage with neighbourhood-level interventions. It is this variety of themes that leads to some confusion as to what is specifically meant by mainstreaming in policy documents and on the ground within regeneration partnerships. This set of policies also sets up two potential spatial levels at which to achieve mainstreaming: through neighbourhood-level partnerships; or through LSPs that generally operate at the level of the local authority-wide area (see Chapter Four). However, the case for transforming public services goes beyond considerations of change and scale, since transformation through mainstreaming also stresses the importance of engaging with communities in neighbourhoods, both to secure sustainable improvements in public services, and to re-engage citizens with the institutions of government (ODPM/HO, 2005, p 7).

Policy-centred definitions of mainstreaming are a moving target but in this chapter four key interpretations of mainstreaming are used:

- recognition (focusing) on disadvantaged neighbourhoods and the reformulation of corporate policies in line with the implementation of mainstreaming;
- bending spending patterns within a wider area, often concentrating available budgets on the most needy;

- reshaping local services, involving the transformation of existing resources within a given area; and
- experimenting and learning from good or best practice followed by the rolling out of lessons learnt within regeneration initiatives to other areas.

The National Evaluation of Neighbourhood Management summarises how policy makers think about the process of transforming core public services to tackle disadvantaged neighbourhoods (adapted in Figure 9.1 from SQW, 2006). The key mainstream agencies within neighbourhood renewal are the local authority (including the local education authority), the police, the Primary Care Trust and associated agencies, the Learning and Skills Council and Jobcentre Plus. In addition, the LSP would be expected to facilitate the mainstream effort at neighbourhood level. The

Figure 9.1: Policy-based theory of change linking the transformation of core public services and improved floor target outcomes

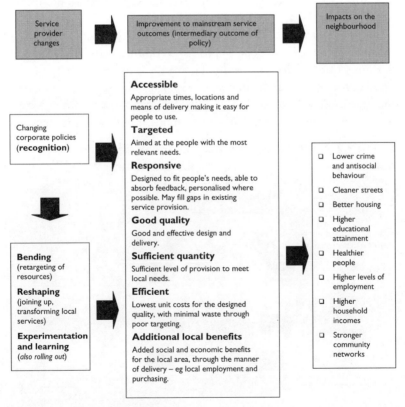

Source: Adapted from SQW (2006)

basic assumption is that the transformation of these public agencies and the services they provide in disadvantaged areas is a necessary step on the route to improving the everyday life and opportunities of people living in disadvantaged neighbourhoods.

Despite continuing uncertainty about definitions and interpretations, the level of dialogue about mainstreaming has risen. There is a growing realisation that the intensity of current exceptional funding is not sustainable and that there needs to be greater reliance on the transformation of mainstream services to tackle particular concentrations of area-based disadvantage. Over the coming spending rounds of central government, mainstreaming is likely to become more important, not less.

Mainstreaming and neighbourhood governance

There are two principal lenses through which the mainstreaming process is explored here. The first lens relates to the idea of mainstreaming being a transformational process while the second lens relates to the use of power in partnerships.

Figure 9.2 reformulates the 'theory of change' articulated in Figure 9.1 as a series of interlinked generic processes combining the four different interpretations of mainstreaming. The patterns of linkage suggest two possible forms of mainstreaming process over time: strategic or tactical mainstreaming (EIUA et al, 2006, p 9). 'Strategic mainstreaming' refers to refocusing the mainstream agency (both in terms of programmes

Figure 9.2: Mainstreaming processes and mainstreaming outcomes

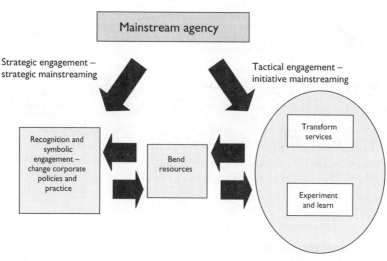

and funding) onto neighbourhood-level targets agreed with local partners, thus reflecting the needs of local communities (this top-down approach is often referred to as mainstream bending). Thus, one might expect strategic mainstreaming to be mediated either directly through neighbourhood governance or through engagement with LSPs and thus indirectly to neighbourhood governance.

Bottom-up, tactical or 'initiative mainstreaming' refers to a process that sees learning spread from localised, one-off pilots to mainstream programmes at a wider scale. Here, the link to neighbourhood-level projects is more tangible since many of these projects and pilots will be initiated in the neighbourhood often funded by neighbourhood renewal. Ultimately, strategic and tactical mainstreaming are linked since, for example, once mainstream transformation has been initiated through initiative mainstreaming one might expect changes in the symbolic language of the mainstream agency through its strategic documents.

At the neighbourhood level the process of transformation in mainstream public agencies has to be understood in terms of partnership working. However, the notion of partnership working has to be thought about both in relation to the relationships that are enacted within a neighbourhood-level partnership and the relationships that exist between territorial levels of governance (that is, within the context of multi-level governance – see Chapter Four). For the most part the examination of multi-level governance relates to the role of central government and of LSPs in shaping what goes on in neighbourhoods. Mainstreaming requires the core public agencies to mediate pressures emerging from neighbourhood governance and central government and is thus a barometer for measuring the relative influence of local governance over central government in the provision of public services. If mainstreaming was a vehicle for a substantive devolution of power and resources one would expect to see local mainstream agendas driven either by neighbourhood governance institutions or by LSPs rather than by central government (this is, governance without government – see Rhodes, 1997). However as Davies (2002) has pointed out, despite a rhetoric of local power in urban regeneration, in practice there has been a process of centralising power and control in urban regeneration over the past decade.

The tensions between different levels of governance and government lead us to the consideration of power. Power within governing can be thought of as demonstrating four forms: systemic power, command power, coalition power and finally pre-emptive power. Systemic power 'reflects the advantages and disadvantages conferred on certain groups in society based on their position within the socioeconomic structure'

(Stoker, 1995, p 64). Participants with systemic power need not be aware of the advantaged position they hold. By contrast, command power 'involves the active mobilisation of resources (information, finance, reputation, knowledge) to achieve domination over other interests' (Stoker, 1995, p 65). Coalition power is similar to command power in that it both has to be mobilised (unlike systemic power) and it is about making one partner comply with the wishes of the other (Stone, 1988). The difference between command and coalition power is that coalition power applies when both partners have a respective autonomous basis of strength. The fourth and final form of power (pre-emptive power) is based on the idea that power in a complex community is both fragmented and concentrated (Stone, 1988). For Stone, pre-emptive power is not about getting compliance but it is about the power to set an agenda and to maintain a position of influence through the creation of coalitions of partners. The assumption of pre-emptive power is that the parties will not have equal access to similar levels of resources but that it is through the manipulation of the policy agenda using pre-emptive power that corrects the imbalance.

In the case of mainstreaming it is possible to argue that, in the past, core public agencies (such as the police or education authorities) demonstrated either systemic power because the state mandates their domain of action or command power because of the level of resources (physical, human, budgets) they held in the provision of neighbourhood-level services. However, the move to forms of neighbourhood governance combined with the need for mainstream agencies to take on local needs and conditions in providing services implies that mainstream agencies must either mobilise coalition power with a neighbourhood partner or demonstrate pre-emptive power through working with a coalition of local groups in order to shape the local services agenda. It might be argued that the lens of power offers a parallel means of interpreting the emergence of mainstreaming to the notion of the path-dependent process indicated in Figure 9.2.

The evidence for mainstreaming

The empirical evidence for this chapter draws on evaluation research funded by the Neighbourhood Renewal Unit of the former Office of the Deputy Prime Minister. This evaluation work covered both the NDC and NMP programmes. At the time of the evaluation research (2005-06) both programmes were within their main delivery phase.

In order to make sense of mainstreaming on the ground there is a need to convert the abstract notions of mainstreaming presented earlier into concrete instances. For the five key public service providers at neighbourhood level and the LSP, Table 9.2 breaks our four categories down into observable activity and evidence across the NDC programme. Thus, mainstreaming as recognition is broken down into one or more of: expectations that the mainstream agency will have a representative on the partnership board; expectations that the partnership board will

Table 9.2: Percentage of NDC partnerships and claims of mainstreaming, 2003/04

Mainstream agency	Local authority	Police	Primary Care Trust	Learning and Skills Council	Jobcentre Plus
Floor target area of mainstreaming	Multiple themes	Crime	Health	Labour market	Labour market
Physical base or presence in area	82	79	85	13	74
Agency represented on NDC board (recognition)	69	85	95	21	64
NDC represented on agency body or working party (recognition)	72	56	67	33	49
NDC included in forward strategy (recognition)	87	59	77	28	67
Mapping spend in NDC area (bending)	41	33	31	5	31
Main programme spend on NDC activities (bending)	74	64	62	26	72
Increased resources (bending)	74	67	64	15	56
Changed patterns of delivery (reshaping)	82	85	64	10	74
Joint project funding (experimentation)	87	79	77	28	69

Source: CRESR (2005)

have reciprocal representation on some bodies of the agency; and, finally, that the NDC initiative is explicitly mentioned in the strategic documents of the agency.

In relation to mainstreaming as recognition, it is notable that 85% of partnerships have police representation and 95% of partnerships have representatives from Primary Care Trusts, indicating a level of symbolic and corporate engagement. Indeed, across the police, Primary Care Trusts, local authorities and job centres there is a consistent and reciprocal pattern of interaction between NDC partnerships and the mainstream agencies. The patterns of engagement by agency are not only consistent across mainstreaming as recognition but are consistent across all four aspects of mainstreaming.

Table 9.2 gives little indication of the quality of engagement but does indicate at least that there is lip service to recognising neighbourhood governance. Between 2002 and 2005 there was a reported rise in levels of mainstreaming consistent with the notion that 'being around' eventually attracts some interest from mainstream agencies. However, in probing the issue further through interviews and case study work, it was found that only nine respondents out of 112 could confirm a positive and practical move towards more mainstreaming across the NDC programme during the financial year 2004/05. This suggests that mainstreaming within the NDC programme may only remain at the level of superficial assertion.

As with the NDC programmes, within NMP programmes it was the police and Primary Care Trusts that were among the mainstream agencies most likely to engage in neighbourhood renewal and service transformation (see Table 9.3). Table 9.3 reveals intra-organisational differences in mainstream engagement in NMPs with local authority housing departments appearing as 'core supporters' of neighbourhood management while local authority social service departments are 'strangers' to it. The table also highlights some of the interorganisational complexity within policy sectors – for example, local schools are 'core supporters' while local education authorities are not mentioned at all. Taking all four interpretations of mainstreaming, the National Evaluation of Neighbourhood Management indicates a marked prevalence of tactical over strategic engagement by mainstream agencies. Thus, only one in six service changes to mainstream services related to changing corporate policy and practice (strategic engagement) whereas nearly 40% of changes related to bending resources and nearly half of changes related to either reshaping or joining up services (tactical engagement) (SQW, 2006).

Table 9.3: Assessment of mainstream service provider engagement with Round 1 NMPs

Level of involvement	Service provider	Change in 18 months 2004-06
Strong involvement – 'core supporters' (70% or more of Pathfinders with 'strong' involvement from the provider)	• Police	No change
	• Primary Care Trust	Stronger
	• Local schools	Stronger
	• Local authority housing services	Stronger
	• Local authority environmental services	No change
Good involvement –'friends, but not always close' (strong involvement in a few areas and at least 'some' involvement in most other areas)	• Jobcentre plus	Stronger
	• Local authority youth services	Stronger
	• Local authority leisure services	No change
	• Registered social landlord/housing associations	Stronger
Variable involvement – 'acquaintance' ('little or no' involvement in a third or more areas, but 'some' and occasionally 'strong' involvement in others)	• Local further education/higher education colleges	Weaker
	• Connexions	No change
	• Fire service	Stronger
Minimal involvement – 'strangers' (70% of Pathfinders with 'little or no' involvement from the provider and limited involvement in remaining areas)	• National offender management service	No change
	• Local Learning and Skills Councils	No change
	• Local public transport bodies	No change
	• Local authority social services	No change

Source: SQW (2006)

The evidence for bending service funding is difficult to find. Part of this is due to the difficulty of measuring public expenditure in small areas (see Bramley at al, 2005, for an outline of methodological problems). Nonetheless, despite the methodological difficulties, individual mainstream agencies claimed to have mapped neighbourhood-level expenditure (spend) in around one third of NDC areas (see Table 9.2). Match funding is the money pledged by regeneration partners from their own sources. Some of this money will be 'core' funding and some will be from other forms of 'additional' funding such as European Union structural funds, lottery money and so on. As such it can be taken as a crude and imperfect proxy for the promise of bending mainstream resources in relation to worklessness, education, health, housing and physical environment and community safety. Using match funding figures for 2003/04 from all sources additional to the NDC spend from central government across the programme as a whole, for each pound of NDC spend, there was some 39 pence added by mainstream match funding.

In terms of renewal themes, promises of mainstream resources varied from just 19 pence of match funding under the health theme to around 70 pence under housing and physical environment. Mainstream bending is particularly evident in policing. A number of NMP areas have achieved an increased level of beat policing through the addition of extra officers or police community safety officers, sometimes initially part funded by the Pathfinder and later funded by the police (that is, mainstreaming where experimentation leads to bending).

However, it must also be remembered that mainstream agencies can also withdraw funding as well as increase it. This is particularly difficult to prove given the problems of allocating spending to small areas (see earlier). Some NDC programmes have asserted the trend of 'bending backwards' where some mainstream agencies (mainly local authorities) have decreased resources dedicated to the NDC area as a result of the programme (see Stewart and Howard, 2004, p i). One NDC partnership, for example, reported that local authority youth services had been allowed to run down in the NDC area because the area had secured NDC funding.

Mainstreaming as a process over time

It is suggested in Figure 9.2 that the aspects of mainstreaming could be linked as a path-dependent process that might either be characterised as strategic or tactical. The evidence for any consistent pattern of relationships between the aspects of mainstreaming is difficult to establish. In NMP areas, mainstreaming as reshaping was more likely if there had been experimentation (such as joint-funded pilots) in the past. Both NDC and NMP programmes suggest that once a given agency has engaged (often early) it is likely to engage further but weakly engaged agencies do not appear to suddenly engage further down the line. In the case of the NMP programme, Table 9.3 shows the changing attitudes to mainstreaming by mainstreaming agencies over the period 2004-06. This would suggest that there are structural conditions that make mainstreaming a valued process for some agencies while negating its value for others.

Evaluation evidence would suggest that a key element of successful mainstreaming, or of setting off the chain of events that brings about mainstreaming, is when neighbourhood managers work with service providers to identify common agendas (SQW, 2006). This has been particularly fruitful where there is a shared philosophy of community engagement and partnership working and sufficient flexibility from the top to allow change in neighbourhood service provision by neighbourhood-level officers. Flexibility here is the capacity of local professionals to reconfigure how a service is provided on the ground with little interference from middle managers. This is the case with the police and both local authority housing and environmental services, where there is evidence of all four aspects of mainstreaming. Where there are shared objectives but limited flexibility, there is little evidence of bending or reshaping services but more evidence of using NDC and NMP initiatives to pilot new ways of working, which are often then mainstreamed. This is the case with health-related and education-related agencies as well as with Jobcentre Plus. However, this suggests that there is a path-dependent process but that the classification of strategic and tactical is not helpful since the process in any one locality may be complex. Progress is about the articulation of local conditions and for that one might expect the notion of power to offer insight into mainstreaming.

Mainstreaming and the deployment of power

There is evidence to indicate that mainstreaming takes place albeit unevenly across time, geographic areas and policy sectors. However, the next stage is to consider the conditions under which mainstreaming occurs and here the process of mainstreaming becomes associated with the concept of power. It is through looking at the relationship between mainstreaming and power that one can understand why mainstreaming had 'worked' in some places and not others.

Table 9.4 picks out three of the four interpretations of mainstreaming and considers a plausible explanation for why mainstreaming occurred under the conditions in the middle column. In relation to mainstreaming as bending, 'successful' mainstreaming examples included the use of increased neighbourhood policing that resulted in increased resident satisfaction. The plausible reason put forward for why this worked related to a consensus around common objectives between police and neighbourhood partnership that neighbourhood-level policing matters. The capacity for mainstream agencies to engage with these regeneration partnerships is thus related to the degree to which there is some common outlook between the agency and the partnership. One mainstream agency respondent within a NDC partnership noted:

> 'If you [represent the Primary Care Trust] then you have half of [the city] to take into consideration and the NDC neighbourhood is only a tiny bit of your area.... It is easier for the police because they have local beats and you can get them to tackle drugs and housing and the like.'

However, there is also some anecdotal evidence that some mainstream agencies had taken resources away from NDC areas (see earlier). This may be a function of the particularly intense level of funding directed at NDC areas (see Table 9.1) since this phenomenon was not reported in the NMP evaluation. It can be interpreted as the gamble of the NDC initiative where intense funding might have been the spur to the mobilisation of coalition power between neighbourhood partnerships and mainstream agencies. Such reports of bending backwards (Stewart and Howard, 2004, p 14) away from what is supposed to be a local flagship initiative illustrate the limited power of regeneration partnerships to persuade mainstream agencies to dedicate more resources to their areas.

Thus, in relation to bending it is clear that mainstream agencies retain some elements of command power. Where mainstream agencies consider bending resources to single NDC areas to be unfair to a wider constituency, they retain the unilateral power to allocate resources according to their sense of equity away from NDC neighbourhoods. Bending occurs where the neighbourhood body and the mainstream agency already have a common set of objectives. The capacity of neighbourhood partnerships to bring round mainstream agencies that do not support the principle of neighbourhood-level engagement with local interests appears weak.

Table 9.4: What works and why: mainstream service transformation and neighbourhood renewal, 2001-05

	Example of impact of mainstreaming on neighbourhoods	Reasons why mainstreaming worked, and with which agencies
Mainstreaming as bending	Increased neighbourhood policing and increased resident satisfaction with police presence	Commonality of objectives with police Neighbourhood policing policy of police *Agencies:* police and environment
Mainstreaming as reshaping • Joint working • Accessibility	Cleaner streets, increased resident satisfaction Increased take-up of health services Increased take-up of employment service	NMP/NDC as advocate for local community NMP funded needs assessment in Pathfinder area NDC/NMP pilot funding of outreach workers *Agencies:* police, environment, health, employment, housing
Mainstreaming as experimenting and learning	More inclusive and holistic services in schools	Effective funded pilots. Commitment/ representation on NMP/ NDC board of senior agency staff. *Agencies:* police, housing, environment, education, health

In relation to mainstreaming as the reshaping of services, Table 9.4 outlines examples of mainstreaming relating to the better joining up of existing services and making services more accessible. Based on the NMP programme experience, mainstreaming through reshaping implies the demonstration of pre-emptive power on the part of the NMP partnership. The source of pre-emptive power for the partnership emerges in three contexts: where the partnership acts as an advocate for the local community/communities with the mainstream agencies; where the NMP has funded a needs assessment identifying explicit service gaps; and where a successful pilot project has been funded in a related area. In each of these cases pre-emptive power emerges from the mobilisation of different assets such as resident support, knowledge of service delivery and knowledge of the expected benefits of changing the way services are produced. These allow the neighbourhood partnership to shape the agenda under which the mainstream agency engages in the reshaping of the mainstream service.

The final interpretation of mainstreaming in Table 9.4 is the aspect of mainstreaming as the opportunity for experimentation through the production of pilot projects and the potential learning and rolling out that might follow such pilots. The conditions under which this tends to happen suggest the need for appropriate funding and the presence of mainstream agency representation on the neighbourhood partnership. These are the conditions that most closely resemble coalition power because of neighbourhood programme resources to persuade mainstream agencies to change. In the same way that setting up a needs assessment boosts the pre-emptive power of a partnership, the funding of a pilot can also theoretically boost the capacity of neighbourhood management to engage with mainstream agencies. Transformation through rolling out can involve adopting a project more widely (project roll-out) or it might involve some aspect of the approach a particular project adopts (process roll-out). Either way, there is mainly roll-out in services that address crime and community safety, environmental and housing management and maintenance and the needs of young people, children and their families, because it is in these areas that neighbourhood management has been best able to demonstrate the benefits or potential benefits of its approach. However, these have also been the policy sectors that central government has most directed to look at neighbourhood-level working through neighbourhood policing, the 'In Business for Neighbourhoods' agenda for registered social landlords and the 'Every Child Matters' agenda for all agencies dealing with young people.

On the one hand this might appear to be simply a matter of resources. The two neighbourhood renewal programmes that form the basis of this chapter demonstrate the complexities of the situation. On the face of it the NDC 'model' of a well-resourced neighbourhood partnership engaging with core mainstream agencies on an 'equal' basis does not seem to work significantly better than the more lightly resourced NMP 'model' in promoting instances of mainstreaming. As noted earlier, there may be occasions where the resources associated with NDC initiatives create the conditions for mainstream agencies to withdraw resources from these disadvantaged areas. Thus, the capacity of an NDC partnership to deploy coalition power based on a relationship of 'equals' at the level of the neighbourhood can still be thwarted by the capacity of mainstream agencies to play on sufficient systemic and command power not to engage where this is not felt to be in the interests of the agency or a wider public. Under these conditions the NDC partnership at least retains a certain capacity to set up alternative services to those offered by mainstream agencies.

The NMP 'model' on the other hand has been widely taken up as an approach to joining up and improving service delivery at a spatial level below that of the local authority. NMP initiatives are relatively 'cheap' for mainstream agencies insofar as they only need to commit to transforming the services they already provide within an area but do not need to either commit to 'bending' additional resources into an area or commit to take on projects that NDC partnerships have been funding themselves. Despite this symbolic and strategic engagement, however, mainstream budgets have been influenced very little by neighbourhood partnerships. In the case of the NMP initiatives, limited direct funding forces the neighbourhood partnerships into the mobilisation of pre-emptive power. It is an issue for debate for mainstream agencies whether the risk of engaging is less where the 'stakes' only relate to money and resources that would be spent in an area anyway (the NMP model) or whether risk is less when they are dealing with an NDC partnership's exceptional funding of pilot projects (the NDC model).

Mainstreaming as process, power and partnership

This chapter has set out the evidence that mainstreaming does happen. The extent and impact of mainstreaming is patchy and it varies by area, over time and in relation to policy sector. It has not been possible to identify a consistent set of stages through which the mainstream relationship progresses, although it is clear from the evidence to hand that mainstream agencies that engage with neighbourhood programmes early tend to strengthen their engagement over time while those that fail to engage early are rarely resuscitated.

Understanding power in relation to command, coalition and pre-emptive forms and the way this relates to mainstreaming as bending, reshaping and experimenting is a useful way of conceptualising the process of mainstreaming. Using concepts of power there appear to be associations of command power with mainstreaming as bending, coalition power with mainstreaming as experimenting and pre-emptive power with mainstreaming as reshaping. Using this language it is clear that mainstream agencies retain some capacity to resist a neighbourhood agenda. Thus, mainstreaming tends to occur when the provision of dedicated resources and/or the explicit elaboration of a policy shift at national level promotes neighbourhood/outreach working by the mainstream agency. It is also important that the mainstream agency deems a neighbourhood partnership as having reached a level of maturity, developed sufficient trust and built enough effective links with other local and regional agencies to be considered seriously. Neighbourhood partnerships are not in a position to enforce compliance but need to work with local conditions.

The power of a neighbourhood partnership to deploy either coalition or pre-emptive forms rises where the partnership advocates a philosophy of community engagement and partnership working and where local agency officers have more flexibility with regards to budgets and targets. However, the flipside is that neighbourhood partnerships find their capacity to engage is sapped where:

- there are competing demands on core public service agencies by many different partnerships;
- there are differences in the geography of service provision between the agency and the neighbourhood; and
- mainstream agencies have to negotiate and mediate internal tensions between the 'vertical' accountabilities in a national organisation and the 'horizontal' opportunities to act effectively in partnership at a neighbourhood level.

It has to be remembered equally that mainstream service agencies are not always single homogenous organisations but are themselves coalitions of agencies combining local state actors and more arm's length agencies that provide services (the distinction between schools and local education authorities, GP surgeries and the Primary Care Trusts that fund them).

The success of neighbourhood management as a particular institutional form of neighbourhood governance often depends on the tactical abilities of the manager and their staff to identify the best point of entry with a particular agency or sub-division of an agency. This leads to the mobilisation of pre-emptive power in the case of the NMP programme and leads to the possibility of coalition power in the case of the NDC programme. Bargaining and dialogue are evident in all the examples of successful mainstreaming. The question is whether it is enough to try to influence the parts of agencies that you can reach, and the parts of their agendas where you can find common ground.

References

Bramley, G., Evans, M. and Noble, M. (2005) *Mainstream Public Services and their Impact on Neighbourhood Deprivation*, London: ODPM.

CRESR (Centre for Regional, Economic and Social Research) (2005) *New Deal for Communities 2001-2005: An Interim Evaluation*, Research Report 17, London: ODPM.

Davies, J. S. (2002) 'The governance of urban regeneration: a critique of the "governing without government" thesis', *Public Administration*, vol 80, no 2, pp 310-22.

EIUA (European Institute for Urban Affairs), OPM (Office for Public Management), University of Warwick and the University of the West of England, Bristol (2006) *National Evaluation of Local Strategic Partnerships: Formative Evaluation and Action Research Programme 2002-05: Executive Summary to Final Report*, London: ODPM.

Johnson, C. and Osborne, S.P. (2003) 'Local Strategic Partnerships, neighbourhood renewal, and the limits to co-governance', *Public Money and Management*, vol 23, no 3, pp 147-54.

ODPM (Office of the Deputy Prime Minister) (2004) *Mainstreaming and Neighbourhood Renewal*, Factsheet 18, London: ODPM.

ODPM/HO (Office of the Deputy Prime Minister/Home Office) (2005) *Citizen Engagement and Public Services: Why Neighbourhoods Matter*, London: ODPM.

Rhodes, R. A. W. (1997) 'The new governance: governing without government', *Political Studies*, vol 44, no 4, pp 652-67.

SEU (Social Exclusion Unit) (1998) *Bringing Britain Together: A National Strategy for Neighbourhood Renewal*, Cm 4045, London: The Stationery Office.

SQW (2006) *Neighbourhood Management: At the Turning Point? Programme Review 2005-06*, Research Report 23, London: ODPM.

Stewart, M. and Howard, J. (2004) *Mainstreaming in NDC Areas: Evidence from the National Evaluation 2003/04*, Research Report 25, Sheffield: Sheffield Hallam University.

Stoker, G. (1995) 'Regime theory and urban politics', in D. Judge, G. Stoker and H. Wolman (eds) *Theories of Urban Politics*, London: Sage Publications, pp 54-71.

Stone, C. (1988) 'Preemptive power: Floyd Hunter's "Community Power Structure" reconsidered', *American Journal of Political Science*, vol 32, no 1, pp 82-104.

TEN

Evaluation, knowledge and learning in neighbourhood governance: the case of the New Deal for Communities

Lucy Grimshaw and Ian Smith

Introduction

Knowledge is a vital resource within governance. One of the justifications given for neighbourhood governance in neighbourhood renewal is its capacity to incorporate the local knowledge of residents into local regeneration schemes. This chapter concentrates on the ways in which formalised explicit knowledge about the actual and likely outcomes of policy interventions within neighbourhood renewal is produced, managed and results in change.

New Labour administrations have promoted the learning of lessons, knowledge management and 'evidence-based' policy making and policy delivery. However, identifying the flows of knowledge within neighbourhood governance is not a simple story because it touches on the nature of knowledge, of knowledge management and of learning. The processes that regulate the flows of knowledge and frame questions about what works in neighbourhood renewal need to be understood in relation to issues of power and politics (see also Smith and Grimshaw, 2005; and Becker and Bryman, 2004, for a wider overview). Defining the terms under which knowledge is generated about a policy intervention constitutes an important source of power within governance institutions. Control of the terms under which knowledge is defined allows those with the capacity to define useful knowledge to set key priorities and marginalise alternative ways of defining success and what works. This can limit the capacity of neighbourhood governance to do what local stakeholders think is important where agencies outside of neighbourhood governance (such as central government departments) are in control of defining what counts as 'useful knowledge'.

This chapter discusses debates on the generation and flow of knowledge in neighbourhood renewal. It is in three parts. The first part will concentrate on the 'academic' debates on the use and value of evidence and in particular research-based evidence in policy processes while the second will set out the policy-centred debate. A third section concentrates on the New Deal for Communities (NDC) programme by first considering the programme as a whole and then considering how knowledge has impacted on the activities of two case study partnerships.

Exploring the processes by which knowledge is generated within the NDC programme captures some of the tensions inherent in the efficiency versus participation debate for local government more widely. Conventional wisdom suggests that participation follows empowerment but empowerment implies communities being able to define 'what works' on their terms. This multiplicity of definitions of success does not allow the easy comparison of different interventions across a national programme. An efficiency argument might suggest creating common definitions of success and impact. The development of performance management frameworks is consistent with the need for an effective instrument for looking across many local situations. The Local Government White Paper of October 2006 (CLG, 2006) acknowledges the tension between centralised performance frameworks and the need for locally defined solutions to difficult issues but emphasises the need to retain centralised performance management albeit in a radically simplified form.

Academic debates on generating knowledge

In the early 1970s academic researchers started to reflect on the question of why their carefully honed academic research was being commonly ignored by those who formulated and implemented public policy (see Weiss, 1998). The conclusion drawn from this questioning was that the evaluation evidence was not useful to those who formulated policy and put it into practice. It was not useful first because researchers had failed to consider the different ways policy people use evidence and the different political and social settings in which it is used, and second because they had not asked the questions that stakeholders needed to ask. Researchers had failed to appreciate that evaluation research only constituted one particular form of evidence in policy circles and that there was no simple link between evaluation evidence to policy or practice (Simons, 2004).

This utilisation debate threw up a number of useful categorisations for embracing the complex policy settings in which evaluation research was situated. It established a series of descriptive categories both for the ways in which evaluation research evidence was used in policy circles and for the ways in which evaluation research (both in terms of findings and the process of doing research) is used as evidence. Weiss (1998) developed three types of use: instrumental use, symbolic or political use and finally conceptual or enlightenment use. Instrumental use implies that there is a direct relationship between the findings of a piece of research and the policy under scrutiny – thus a policy might be changed as a result of evaluation. Symbolic use implies that evaluation research is used to bolster policy decisions that are already taken whereas conceptual or enlightenment use is where policy actors use conceptual frameworks developed within evaluation work to reframe the way they think about policy making and practice.

The utility of evaluation research to policy people goes beyond the research findings alone. Evaluation research can provide, for example, new knowledge frameworks (such as conceptual models or definitions) and also gives time to participants to reflect on their roles and practice because they were part of an evaluation (Weiss, 1998). Thus, evaluation can be used in a variety of ways and its usefulness extends beyond the simple reading of key findings and recommendations.

The utilisation debate has traditionally been about making research more 'user-friendly' and hence more likely to be used through changing research methods. However, more recent work has focused on understanding how different stakeholders see the world differently consequently leading to differences: in what counts as useful knowledge (questions of competing epistemology or world-views); in who decides what knowledge counts as evidence; and in how knowledge is used in practice (Sanderson, 2000; Boaz and Hayden, 2002; Simons, 2004). The different dimensions of the debate about the nature of the knowledge within neighbourhood renewal can be understood in terms of the competing professionalised world-views held by researchers and policy makers, the relationship between professionalised knowledge and other ways of knowing and the relationship between tacit and explicit knowledge.

Those trained in the social sciences, whether social researchers doing evaluation work or those commissioning it, commonly adopt one of three epistemological world-views: positivist, constructionist or realist. Each of these ways of thinking adopts a different view on the nature of evidence and the degree to which social researchers can explain things that happen in the social world. Positivism is a theory of knowledge put forward to explain natural sciences in which the search for causation is essential as is the separation between facts and values. Researchers working with the constructionist framework state that knowledge is socially constructed and grounded in the socio-historical context in which it is based. Here facts are viewed as interpretations and competing perspectives can make valid judgements about the same phenomena (Fischer, 2003). Finally, scientific realists try to construct a third way between positivism and constructionism (see Pawson and Tilley, 1997), adopting the capacity to objectively measure phenomena but accepting that there are different perspectives on measuring the social world.

The key characteristic of these world-views is that they are explicitly held by professional actors and can be considered as frameworks for 'expert' knowledge. There is more to knowing than just these three particular and abstract world-views. As Fraser and Lepofsky (2004) have noted, there is a tension between 'expert' knowledge held by regeneration professionals and 'local' knowledge held by residents. For Habermas (see Healey, 1997, p 50) the world can be understood in terms of abstract systems and life-worlds. The world-views of evaluation researchers and policy people outlined earlier (positivist, constructionist or realist) can be seen as abstract systems of knowing. However, these abstract systems are unable to capture the full diversity and richness of personal experience (life-worlds) and framing all of what we know about life-worlds in abstract system terms will constrain what we can know. Thus, in order to know more about life-worlds (and on a pragmatic level about neighbourhood problems) a more composite way of knowing is required whereby abstract systems and life-worlds can talk to each other.

The issue raised here is how to achieve communication between those who see the world in terms of abstract systems (agencies and those trained in the social sciences) and those who see the world in terms of holistic life-worlds (generally residents thinking about life in their neighbourhood). This touches on ways in which knowledge becomes formalised or explicit, and is then communicated and whether there is learning and change as a result. Accepting that learning is one possible outcome of communicating knowledge, learning can be conceptualised at two different levels – the individual and the social. Our concerns here are less with the learning of individuals in isolation since it is relatively simple to demonstrate that individuals within neighbourhood renewal learn from their experiences. Rather, our concerns focus on issues of social learning and the development of a collective memory about how to 'do' neighbourhood renewal or area-based regeneration.

This raises the question of who is talking, who is listening and (by implication) who is learning.

Learning in neighbourhood renewal programmes is complicated because stakeholders hold different epistemological positions (relating to both abstract systems and life-worlds) and have varying resources for evidence building. However, within this complexity there are two basic ways of analysing how different stakeholders 'rub along' with each other when it comes to making use of evidence: the first perspective is based on communicative theory (also known as the collaborative approach); the second is based on the idea of 'governmentality' theory. These two frameworks for analysing the interactions between social actors are summarised in Table 10.1.

The collaborative approach is underpinned by the work of Healey (1997) and Kooiman (2003) among others. It assumes a co-production of knowledge in policy making and problem solving that extends

Table 10.1: Alternative frameworks for analysing communication and learning in neighbourhood renewal

Understanding of knowledge generation based on:	Communicative theory	Governmentality theory
Views on relationships between different ways of seeing the world	Powerful stakeholders are under moral duty to empower all stakeholders (although not necessarily equally) and come to a consensus	Powerful stakeholders attempt to frame the ways in which neighbourhood renewal is understood and to dominate other ways of seeing the world
Who is 'learning'/ changing their point of view?	All parties	Those who hold ways of seeing the world that are different from the dominant view
Typical abstract system views from dominant stakeholders	Constructionist/realist	Positivist/realist
What are typical knowledge-generation strategies for underpinning dialogue?	Deliberative and participative evaluation methods	Performance management and audit, centrally controlled evaluations

beyond the assessment of the technical efficiency of policy options. This would include assessments of political interest and the needs of the larger political community (including citizens). By establishing a wider pluralist base for the deliberative process the collaborative approach brings in a wider range of world-views and hence a wider evidence base. Collaborative approaches assume that the communication process is a two-way dialogue and hence are said to promote favourable conditions for learning based on finding common ground, the explicit acknowledgement of differences (Kooiman, 2003) and the need to address imbalances in power between participants. It is through the two-way dialogue bringing together professionals and other experts within 'local forums' that the bridge between the abstract systems and life-worlds of all stakeholders is made.

The promoters of the collaborative approach would accept that the description of the local forum set out earlier is an idealised situation and that the suspension of politics and power in such a forum is unlikely (Sanderson, 2000, p 451) but this does not detract from the pragmatic application of the approach. The collaborative approach demands a reflective approach from enlightened and moral practitioners in positions of power to policy analysis, evaluation and learning. There is an assumption that all stakeholders learn from talking to each other and that there is an examination of how all can then cooperate and create, sustain or change their ideas through dialogue (Kooiman, 2003). The challenge for those constructing knowledge from such interactions is to play a 'facilitation' role (Yanow, 2000; Fischer, 2003) to capture and challenge the diverse sets of assumptions and value systems that are likely to be deployed.

By contrast, governmentality theory offers a rather different insight for analysing interactions. Instead of assuming a normative position where all parties are striving for consensus and thus sharing a normative position, governmentality theory offers up the normative positions of the participants for analysis. Under this framework one can make sense of policy making in which dominant stakeholders with particular ways of seeing the world attempt to reinforce their position of power through the dominance of their normative position. This might also be labelled the hegemonic approach, in which powerful stakeholders expect those who hold different world-views to bend them to the dominant interpretation of the world and learning is seen as restricted to the weaker partners. The logic of this approach leads to knowledge-generating strategies such as performance management and auditing that tend to stress 'compliance to a national standard rather than local learning' (Hartley and Benington, 2006, p 102). One would expect to see a centrally controlled evaluation research agenda with a strong emphasis on accountability and measurement in relation to a dominant concept of 'good' governance. In this way national evaluation exercises can become instruments of governance (see Segerholm, 2001).

Policy debates on learning in neighbourhood renewal

The *Modernising Government* White Paper published in March 1999 (Cabinet Office, 1999) placed a strong emphasis on the importance of evidence-based policy and on finding out 'what works'. 'Evidence-based' policy was to be a model of professional policy making that not only stressed funding evaluation as evidence for policy but also included systematic evaluation, ongoing reviews and the learning of lessons (from Nutley and Webb, 2000, p 22). It was to be a model that was embraced in particular by policy makers working on health and policing issues but it was also to be applied to urban policy.

Thirty years of urban policy did not seem to have had much sustainable impact on disadvantaged areas and New Labour also came to power pledging to tackle area-based disadvantage. The House of Commons Select Committee (2003, p 10), scrutinising the Office of the Deputy Prime Minister (now the Department for Communities and Local Government) concluded that rolling evaluation and the sharing of best practice was the basis of developing longer-term initiatives that would better insert the idea of learning into the development and implementation of urban policy initiatives. This had been an idea that the first Labour administration had embraced in 1998. The report of the Social Exclusion Unit *Bringing Britain Together* (SEU, 1998) identified the need to set up 18 Policy Action Teams (PATs). Within each PAT, acknowledged experts and people working in deprived areas were to gather the available evidence on different aspects of social exclusion and the policy instruments to deal with social exclusion. As a general principle, these working groups were to be paragons of the evidence-based approach and the bedrock of the emerging National Strategy for Neighbourhood Renewal (NSNR).

Two of these teams (PAT16 and PAT18) were specifically tasked with themes that directly touched on the development of evidence in neighbourhood renewal: PAT16 dealt with *Learning Lessons* (PAT16, 2000) and PAT18 explored *Better Information* (PAT18, 2000). The PAT16 report recommended that the government develop a strategy for learning and this emerged as the *Learning Curve* in 2002 (NRU, 2002a). This strategy set out both the approach of central government to learning in neighbourhood renewal and a form of action plan to build knowledge and skills. The keystones of this strategy were the development of the skills and knowledge of residents, regeneration professionals and civil servants (NRU, 2002a) and the recognition that people learn in different ways (NRU, 2002a, p 15). It clearly indicated that funded evaluation research (in particular within the NDC programme) was to be made available as a learning resource across the neighbourhood renewal theme. On the face of it, the Learning Curve Strategy appears to promote a collaborative approach of social learning where all stakeholders from residents to central government should learn collectively from what they are doing. At the local level the strategy expected local agencies, Local Strategic Partnerships and NDC partnerships among others to develop local learning plans to deliver the nationally drafted strategy. *The Learning Curve* therefore had and has a key role in building a knowledge base of activities and projects that are judged to 'have worked' and learning from solutions that have been 'tried and tested' through setting up information resources (expert practitioners or neighbourhood renewal advisors and online information), supporting dissemination and underpinning the development of resident consultancies and expertise.

For critics, evidence-based policy and the 'what works' agenda place too great an emphasis on issues of effectiveness and the measurement of outcomes. They make too many simplistic assumptions about how evidence is used within the policy process (see Weiss, 1998). Critics note that the very concept of drawing up an evidence base assumes the rationality of scientific knowledge, ignoring the context and politics of setting up evidence (since it is assumed to be based on rational criteria) (Sanderson, 2000; Simons, 2004). Implicit within the evidence-based agenda is either a positivist or realist world-view that leads to a preference for empirical observation as a means of testing hypotheses and a 'reluctance to adopt collaborative, community-based approaches to urban policy evaluation' (Wilks-Heeg, 2003, p 216). Harrison (2000, p 208) has argued that urban policy is too political and the interventions are set in contexts that are too complex to be able to isolate individual measures and thereby measure what works. Hence, for Harrison, urban policy interventions are just too complex to be able to assemble within a comprehensive and coherent evidence base.

Generating evidence about neighbourhood programmes

As the most intensively resourced initiative within the NSNR, the NDC programme was expected to be both an example of good (if not best) practice of learning (NRU, 2002b) and a valuable source of evidence for what worked in neighbourhood renewal. Local NDC partnerships were expected to engage with the National Learning Plan either through supporting the development of the learning actions (such as supporting resident consultancies or creating a local knowledge base) or through the use of the resources that the Learning Plan made available (such as the online knowledge management system, 'renewal. net' or neighbourhood renewal advisors).

As the programme has developed, four principal processes of generating explicit formalised knowledge about what works have emerged (see Table 10.2): the performance management scheme, the national evaluation of the NDC programme, the evaluation research activities undertaken through the local NDC partnerships and the project-monitoring activities of the individual partnerships. Table 10.2 distinguishes between these activities in relation to the key audience of each knowledge-generating activity, the key questions to be addressed, ways in which evidence was gathered, the types of evidence collected and the degree of control local NDC partnerships had over the process of knowledge-generating activities.

The first knowledge-generating activity is performance management which has developed from a general process of review to a structured process of enquiry. This has reflected a broader set of changes within central government since 1998. During the Comprehensive Spending Review negotiations of 1998, the Treasury had pushed the idea of linking spending to performance targets for central government departments with a shift to outcome-related targets (that is, targets directed at the impact of public services) in 2000. Of the 250 Public Service Agreement (PSA) targets identified in 2000/01, 12 were specifically linked to neighbourhood renewal and became known as 'floor targets'. These floor target indicators (subsequently 'refined' to 15 indicators in 2004) related to the five main themes of the NSNR programme: worklessness, education, health, crime and housing.

The initial delivery plans of NDC partnerships (plans that were to structure and prioritise activities over the 10 years) were formulated and agreed in the period immediately prior to the emergence of PSA floor targets. The partnerships knew the five key themes and had been offered guidance as to what indicators to include in their initial area profile (the 'core statistical baseline information' – see DETR, 2000a). For most partnerships the indicators within baseline studies did not readily line up with the central government floor targets and often covered a wider range of themes, but over the life of the programme, local partnerships have been expected to align targets within a common

Table 10.2: Knowledge-generating activities within the NDC programme

	Performance management framework	National Evaluation	Local Evaluation	Monitoring (project and scheme)
Key audience	Central government via government offices	'All those with an interest in the programme'	Local NDC partnerships (agencies and residents)	NDC partnerships and local accountable body
Key questions	Effectiveness in delivering programmes/ outcomes?	What is impact of national programme?	How effective were projects? Progress on local targets?	Have projects/ programmes delivered outputs promised?
Evaluation process (data gathering)	Local partnerships then validated by Government Office	External researchers commissioned by central government	Local partnerships commissioning evaluation research	Project managers fill in quarterly returns
Type of evidence gathered	Progress towards delivery of impacts – structured around floor targets	Process assessment by case study work (mixed data) and impact through secondary data and household survey	Mixed and variable quality	Counting outputs – quantitative measures (some qualitative milestones)
Degree of local control	NDC partnerships consulted on process	NDC partnerships consulted on process	NDC partnerships in control of process	NDC partnerships mandated to deliver information to central government

comparable structure dictated by the Neighbourhood Renewal Unit (NRU).

The performance management process as it stood in 2006 had two elements: the first element was about the agenda to be discussed (the framework); the second element was about the process of scoring partnerships within the framework. This is a process that was developed over the period 2001-06 in consultation with local NDC partnerships. The framework directs the annual review process between Government Offices and the NDC partnerships. It focuses the review meeting onto six process-related issues covering the whole scheme (such as the robustness of the partnership and the degree to which the programme is well managed and coherent) and onto outcomes achieved and plausibility of interventions in the five floor target themes. The basis of the framework is the set of floor target indicators set by central government.

There has been an element of innovation in the process of scoring against issues defined by the framework that has become a self-assessment process. Local partnerships score themselves against the framework, sometimes advised by neighbourhood renewal advisors funded by the NRU. During the annual review meeting this score is discussed with and verified by regional Government Offices, on behalf of central government, to become a validated score that is then moderated across different Government Offices.

The second knowledge-generating activity is the National Evaluation of the NDC programme which has been described as 'one of the most comprehensive regeneration evaluations ever undertaken in this country' (NRU, 2002b, p 3). It was expected to be a key driver of the learning from the programme. The National Evaluation was divided into two phases: the first from 2001 to 2005 and the second from 2005 to 2010. A consortium of 14 university research centres and consultancy firms was awarded the contract to carry out the first phase of evaluation work. In addition to the consortium, MORI was contracted to undertake two resident surveys (in 2002 and 2004). The evaluation considered a wide range of issues touching on the delivery process as well as assessing early impacts of the programme. The structure of the evaluation employed both generalist teams working with local partnerships and specialist teams to consider programme impacts under the 'floor target' headings. In addition there was a floating set of resources to take on cross-cutting and emerging issues such as mainstreaming and liveability issues. Despite early recommendations that the evaluation should track the scheme as it emerged (House of Commons Select Committee, 2003, p 11), the initial national evaluation was commissioned three years after the scheme was announced and one to two years after local delivery plans had been agreed.

The third knowledge-generating activity is local evaluation work carried out by individual partnerships. Central government guidance covering monitoring, review and evaluation emphasised the importance of local evaluation activities (DETR, 2000b). Local partnerships were responsible for evaluating projects and the local scheme overall but the DETR reserved the task of checking 'the development of appropriate outcome and output measures and the progress towards outputs and outcomes for each partnership' (DETR, 2000b, p 7). These guidelines indicated the need for two tiers of evaluation: project evaluation that would be done on completion of projects; and scheme-wide evaluation based on analysing impacts against a baseline of locally defined outcomes indicators. However, no guidance was given as to how much money was to be dedicated to the activity.

Local partnerships have found doing local evaluation problematic. Evidence from the national evaluation showed that less than a third of local partnerships had developed an evaluation plan by November 2002 and only a handful had monitoring systems in place that could precisely indicate the total project expenditure, outputs, beneficiaries and planned outcomes (Lawless, 2004). By 2004 'virtually all' partnerships were undertaking the evaluation of projects within their overall programme. Such 'local' evaluation also included assessing the impact on beneficiaries and just over half of the 39 partnerships had formally agreed an evaluation plan (CRESR, 2005). The National Evaluation also reported that most NDC partnerships believed that local evaluation had resulted in project- or programme-level changes (CRESR, 2005). Despite the overall increase in local evaluation activity only 18 partnerships had undertaken cross-cutting evaluation work and only 15 had established a programme-wide dissemination strategy through which any lessons might be passed on. The National Evaluation concluded that local evaluation is an area where there is 'huge variation' and the process of using the results to change policy is still problematic. Changes in projects were not being appropriately evaluated and recorded. The result is that the lessons to be learnt remained 'in the heads of project leaders' (CRESR, 2005, p 279).

In practice, at their halfway point NDC partnerships were still exploring how they might evaluate their respective programmes with two basic institutional 'models' emerging for the task. The first model has local NDC partnerships evaluating themselves, using in-house teams to interpret, commission or carry out evaluation work. The second model has partnerships subcontracting the complete evaluation task to external consultants, often with the idea that the consultants will train partnership staff to take on the evaluation role in the future.

The final knowledge-generating activity is monitoring which is defined as 'the activity of checking the progress of individual projects' (DETR, 2000b, p 7), was something that all partnerships were expected to do as part of everyday project management activities. Unlike earlier schemes NDC partnerships were not expected to monitor against standardised output measures but were supposed to define their own output measures (in the same way as they were to define their own outcome measures). Again, over the first half of the scheme, these measures came to be standardised in an attempt to monitor the programme as a whole, relative to value for money measures.

Combined, these four knowledge-generating exercises constitute the means by which knowledge of and lessons from the programme either have been or are due to be formally recorded. The activities are resourced to very different levels and are influenced equally to very different levels by actors embedded within the structures of neighbourhood governance. For the most part, performance management and the National Evaluation, despite their starting points as self-assessed reviews and formative evaluative models, have come to be symptomatic of a hegemonic approach. Within performance management, local partnerships report being happy with the self-assessment process on the whole. Some partnerships have used it as a means of opening up a debate within their area as to the performance of the partnership. However, there is a question as to what happens through the moderation process between Government Offices since this phase has not been transparent. The framework of performance management has been set by central government, and regeneration officers working outside the five floor target themes report feeling unsupported. The direction of travel appears to be one of concentrating on a common core set of outcome measures set by central government. Equally, the national evaluation that was initially described in NDC guidelines as formative (learning-centred) based on elements of 'action research' and 'a genuine partnership between all those who have an interest in the success of the programme' (DETR 2000b, p 14) has come to be more centrally directed. This central direction has given a greater importance to value for money assessments and a core of neighbourhood change indicators that are different from the floor target indicators.

Case studies: the impact of knowledge generation at neighbourhood level

When looking at the ways in which local partnerships use the knowledge produced through the four knowledge-generating processes, it is evidence generated through performance management that has come to dominate the minds of central government and local partnerships. The national evaluation has come to be less interesting and less useful to local partnerships and it appears that learning from local evaluation has also been very limited.

Table 10.3 outlines, for two partnerships, an assessment of the relative impact of performance management, the national evaluation and local evaluation on the activities of local partnerships. It is the performance management framework that has had the greatest impact on the two local programmes. In both partnerships the overall design of the schemes had been altered to better fit the conceptual schema of the performance management framework. Thus, within the floor target areas, local outcomes had been redefined to fit with centrally defined outcomes. In the case of Partnership A this reorganisation extended beyond the baseline to the reorganisation of teams within the partnership to work to the framework agenda. In Partnership B, while the organisation of partnership staff was not changed, there was a clear increase in emphasis on the five floor target areas at the expense of theme work associated with locally defined priority themes. Both the redefining of outcome targets and the reorientation of working teams can be seen as the conceptual use of the performance management scheme.

Local partnerships made little use of the national evaluation as a whole. Both partnerships were able to make instrumental use of the household survey data but use of secondary administrative data was variable. Partnership B found this data to be out of date for their purposes and was suspicious of its reliability but Partnership A used the data to update their baseline. The main evaluation reports were found to be of little use because of a range of reasons: they were not timely enough, they did not offer a view of what other partnerships were doing and they gave no idea of what constituted best practice. Partnership B reported using the findings politically to lever extra funding from a mainstream agency (they had already been agitating for more funding). Equally, Government Office officers had used the partnership report politically to secure higher levels of cross-theme working. For the most part the annual partnership reports were open to political use because they tended to gather the stories of the different partners. Where the final report was politically useful it could be used, but where the partnership did not agree with the thrust of the findings,

Table 10.3: Assessing the impact of knowledge-generating activities in two local NDC initiatives, 2000-05

Changes in local programme resulting from:	Partnership A	Partnership B
Performance management framework	Conceptual use in restructured delivery plan focusing on measurable outcomes and restructuring thematic teams to be more strategic (and theme centred)	Conceptual use in restructured delivery plan focusing on measurable outcomes
National Evaluation of NDC	Little evidence of impact overall Instrumental use of household survey and administrative data for baseline update Some instrumental use of findings in performance management self-assessment	Little evidence of impact overall Instrumental use of household survey Political use (by Government Office) in joined-up working and political use (by partnership) in negotiating levered mainstream funding with one partner
Local evaluation work	Instrumental use to refine some major projects as a result of project evaluation work Instrumental use of evaluation to justify continuation or termination of projects	Little evidence of change across initiative – evaluations too patchy and late in project review process However, instrumental use where two major projects forced to modify service provided based on evaluation evidence of first round of funding

the annual evaluation reports could be criticised as out of date and based on too few, 'subjective', interviews. There was little evidence that change resulted directly from these annual reports, again, perhaps, because of the failure to disseminate them to a wider audience than the senior management team.

Given the variable coverage and quality of local evaluation on top of the current concentration on project evaluation it is little surprise that the impact of local evaluation has been limited. Partnership A had used locally commissioned evaluation work to make changes to the projects it funds and, in the case of health, encourage the local health agency to mainstream NDC activities. Partnership B had used an evaluation at the end of Phase One funding to redesign a project on tackling worklessness for a second phase of funding, although this rethink had been initiated by the Government Office. On the whole, local project evaluations were completed too late in the project management cycle to be useful in redesigning projects. The absence of a programme-wide evaluation in either partnership up to the end of 2005 meant that neither had an 'independent' evidenced view of how they were doing overall to counterweight the views expressed through either the performance management framework or the National Evaluation.

Knowledge and social learning in neighbourhood renewal

It is possible to identify activities within the NDC programme where knowledge is being generated and formalised. But it is clear that different stakeholders have both different understandings and expectations of activities such as performance management, national evaluation and local programmes of evaluation. At the local NDC level, evaluation is often very low down on the list of priorities since the priority is to be seen to be delivering and implementing the programme. This means that in terms of providing an evidence base that can be used to learn about 'what works', formal evaluation is often neglected. The National Evaluation's role became less important to the local partnerships as the performance management process emerged, with direct lines of accountability and reporting to central government via their regional Government Office.

The performance management framework has come to be viewed as being more essential to the NDC management processes and it can be seen as a means of regulating some of the diversity of local partnerships in theme areas strategically important to central government. Although the performance management process and national evaluation fed into each other the two differed in approach, and partnerships in the case study areas, ironically perhaps, felt more 'in control' of the former. The process of performance scoring has been based on self-assessment and group discussions about progress and it also produced direct feedback on performance from government. However, the national evaluation has had some instrumental value through the production of quantitative data that partnerships have used to demonstrate change in their area. Yet under a perceived pressure from central government and always being in a position of 'catch-up' given the late commissioning of the research, the national evaluation has gradually turned into a more summative piece of work.

Whereas it is always possible to identify individuals who learn from this activity, it is difficult to demonstrate that social learning as part of a collaborative approach has taken place. Social learning needs to take place in a context of cooperation that in turn enables the creation of common ground or consensus that enables the mutual adjustment of strategies and joint action (Koppenjan and Klijn, 2004). Learning is not only about having strategies and plans in place but about the quality of interactions between actors and the facilitation of open dialogue between actors at all stages and in all decision-making arenas (Koppenjan and Klijn, 2004). We would argue that there is little evidence for such social learning in the context of the knowledge-generating activities set out in the discussion of the NDC programme earlier. Local partnership officers in the case study areas report that the response of the NRU has not demonstrated that NRU officers have learnt by adjusting the strategies of central government to the conditions local partnerships have met on the ground.

The argument here is that without the collaborative approach and the social learning implied within it, the formal generation of explicit knowledge of what works will always be open to being an instrument of control that limits the possibilities of neighbourhood governance. Consistent with the hegemonic framework, central government control can, through its ability to resource the generation of knowledge, prevent actors from challenging policy direction by establishing rules and systems that produce conformity rather than local diversity. The introduction of floor targets and the performance management framework shifted the attention of local partnerships to concentrate on meeting centrally dictated criteria rather than community-based objectives albeit that the process was gilded by an element of consultation with local partnerships. Local partnerships have attempted to circumvent some of the central control over what gets included in the evidence base through running national conferences and by having a seat on the advisory board of the National Evaluation, but it is not clear how these strategies have influenced the National Evaluation.

Within this context Geddes (2006, p 85) reports how local neighbourhood renewal strategies 'do not project differing local values and priorities but conformist allegiance to government policy and guidance' and also refers to the 'sameness of local NDC strategies' as a result of the lack of experience of local residents who sit on the partnership boards and the 'powerful control and "guidance" exercised by government over local NDC [partnership's] plans', which in turn fail to analyse or challenge the roots of deprivation. In this way the capacity of neighbourhood governance is severely constrained by the ability of central government to frame the ways in which neighbourhood renewal is considered to be successful.

There is an inherent contradiction within the evaluation of NDC and urban policy evaluation in general between the desire for communities to take a lead and government-led policy making, implementation and evaluation (Wilks-Heeg, 2003). There is a need to rethink the relationships between researchers, evaluators, citizens and decision makers (Healey, 1997; Fischer, 2003) and to promote more open and democratic exchange in order to establish collaborative and participatory interactions. This may well provide more opportunities for public learning and political empowerment.

References

Becker, S. and Bryman, A. (eds) (2004) *Understanding Research for Social Policy and Practice*, Bristol: The Policy Press.

Boaz, A. and Hayden, C. (2002) 'Pro-active evaluators: enabling research to be useful, usable and used', *Evaluation*, vol 8, no 4, pp 440-53.

Cabinet Office (1999) *Modernising Government*, White Paper, Cm 4310, London: The Stationery Office.

CLG (Communities and Local Government) (2006) *Strong and Prosperous Communities: The Local Government White Paper*, Cm 6939-I, London: The Stationery Office.

CRESR (Centre for Regional, Economic and Social Research) (2005) *New Deal for Communities 2001-2005: An Interim Evaluation*, Reserach Report 17, London: ODPM.

DETR (Department for the Environment, Transport and the Regions) (2000a) *New Deal for Communities: Gathering Baseline Information*, London: DETR.

DETR (2000b) *New Deal for Communities: Monitoring, Review and Evaluation*, London: DETR.

Fischer, F. (2003) 'Beyond empiricism: policy analysis as deliberative practice', in M. A. Hajer and H. Wagenaar (eds) *Deliberative Policy Analysis*, Cambridge: Cambridge University Press, pp 209-27.

Fraser, J. and Lepofsky, J. (2004) 'The uses of knowledge in neighbourhood revitalisation', *Community Development Journal*, vol 39, no 1, pp 4–12.

Geddes, M. (2006) 'Partnership and the limits to local governance in England: institutionalist analysis and neoliberalism', *International Journal of Urban and Regional Research*, vol 30, no 1, pp 76–97.

Harrison, T. (2000) 'Urban policy: addressing wicked problems', in H. T. O. Davies, S. M. Nutley and P. C. Smith (eds) *What Works? Evidence-based Policy and Practice in Public Services*, Bristol: The Policy Press, pp 207–28.

Hartley, J. and Benington, J. (2006) 'Copy and paste, or graft and transplant? Knowledge sharing through inter-organisational networks', *Public Money and Management*, vol 26, no 2, pp 101–8.

Healey, P. (1997) *Collaborative Planning: Shaping Places in Fragmented Societies*, London: Macmillan.

House of Commons Select Committee, Housing, Planning, Local Government and the Regions (2003) *The Effectiveness of Government Regeneration Initiatives*, Seventh report of session 2002-03, volume 1, London: The Stationery Office.

Kooiman, J. (2003) *Governing as Governance*, London: Sage Publications.

Koppenjan, J. and Klijn, E.-H. (2004) *Managing Uncertainties in Networks*, London: Routledge.

Lawless, P. (2004) 'Locating and explaining area-based urban initiatives: New Deal for Communities in England', *Environment and Planning C*, vol 22, no 3, pp 383–98.

NRU (Neighbourhood Renewal Unit) (2002a) *The Learning Curve: Developing Skills and Knowledge for Neighbourhood Renewal: Summary*, London: ODPM.

NRU (2002b) *Evidence into Practice: New Deal for Communities National Evaluation*, London: DTLR.

Nutley, S. and Webb, J. (2000) 'Evidence and the policy process', in H. T. O. Davies, S. M. Nutley and P. C. Smith (eds) *What Works? Evidence-based Policy and Practice in Public Services*, Bristol: The Policy Press, pp 13–42.

PAT 16 (2000) *Report of Policy Action Team 16: Learning Lessons*, London: Social Exclusion Unit.

PAT 18 (2000) *Report of Policy Action Team 18: Better Information*, London: Social Exclusion Unit.

Pawson, R. and Tilley, N. (1997) *Realistic Evaluation*, London: Sage Publications.

Sanderson, I. (2000) 'Evaluation in complex policy systems', *Evaluation*, vol 6, no 4, pp 433-54.

Segerholm, C. (2001) 'National evaluations as governing instruments: how do they govern?', *Evaluation*, vol 7, no 4, pp 427-36.

SEU (Social Exclusion Unit) (1998) *Bringing Britain Together: A National Strategy for Neighbourhood Renewal*, London: The Stationery Office.

Simons, H. (2004) 'Utilizing evaluation evidence to enhance professional practice', *Evaluation*, vol 10, no 4, pp 410-29.

Smith, I and Grimshaw, L. (2005) 'Evaluation and the New Deal for Communities: learning what for whom?', in D. Taylor and S. Balloch (eds) *The Politics of Evaluation*, Bristol: The Policy Press, pp 189-204.

Weiss, C. H. (1998) 'Have we learned anything new about the use of evaluation?', *American Journal of Evaluation*, vol 19, no 1, pp 21-33.

Wilks-Heeg, S. (2003) 'Economy, equity or empowerment? New Labour, communities and urban policy evaluation', in R. Imrie and M. Raco (eds) *Urban Renaissance? New Labour, Community and Urban Policy*, Bristol: The Policy Press, pp 205-20.

Yanow, D. (2000) *Conducting Interpretative Policy Analysis*, Thousand Oaks, CA: Sage Publications.

ELEVEN

The future of neighbourhoods in urban policy

Eileen Lepine, Ian Smith and Marilyn Taylor

The significance of neighbourhood

Neighbourhoods matter to all of us, and they matter most to those whose choices (about where and how they live) are most restricted. It is in the neighbourhood that global forces and government policy intersect with everyday life. Although for many of us neighbourhoods may not be at the centre of our existence, nonetheless, those of us who can afford to choose select the neighbourhoods where we live with care, looking for somewhere that offers us safety, good neighbours and access to good local schools and other services. As the 2006 Local Government White Paper puts it, '[w]e all want to be able to send our children to a good school; to live in a safe, attractive and environmentally sustainable neighbourhood' (CLG, 2006a, p 15). As Sullivan and Taylor suggest in Chapter Two, neighbourhood offers a source of identity and connection, a place where basic needs may be met and predictable encounters occur. However, despite the rosy glow that often accompanies notions of neighbourhood, identities forged in the neighbourhood may be negative rather than positive, connections may be limited, services poor and encounters fraught with danger. Indeed, the poor quality of public services and perceived absence of social capital in the most disadvantaged neighbourhoods in the UK are among the features that have driven New Labour neighbourhood renewal policy.

Neighbourhood is a slippery concept, as many contributors in this volume have made plain; this is discussed in some depth in Chapter Two. It is a term that brings with it complex associations with community, social capital, inclusion and exclusion, cohesion and diversity. The statistics of disadvantage are an important element in setting the boundaries of the areas or sites that are to be the subject of policy intervention. However, concern with place-based disadvantage has not been accompanied by clarity or consistency in what is meant by neighbourhood either in the UK or in the wider European context discussed by Atkinson and Carmichael in Chapter Three. Nonetheless, – even in a centralised country like England – the drive to improve service delivery, re-engage citizens with democracy and build a safer, more cohesive society has repeatedly focused on this level. Both here and in the wider European context, therefore, while the detail of policies and arrangements may vary, the promotion of neighbourhood governance has been a common response to area-based disadvantage.

This volume has been concerned with the place of neighbourhood governance in the delivery of public policy and public services and with its potential for engagement with the imagined and real communities that reside in the neighbourhood. The move from government to governance may be seen as one response to a recognition that in today's complex society, the state no longer has the resources, legitimacy or knowledge to govern alone. At neighbourhood level, it offers the opportunity to coordinate and reshape public services, draw in other partners and engage directly with citizens, communities and consumers. More broadly, following the argument of Kearns and Parkinson cited in Chapter One, it can also be seen as an essential building block for a democratic society, 'on which the other levels of governance must depend' (Kearns and Parkinson, 2001, p 2108).

As work on this volume began, government in England was exploring the potential to devolve power, resources and responsibility downwards. Its proposals have since taken shape in the Local Government White Paper published in October 2006 (CLG, 2006a), whose stated aims are:

> to enable effective local services and to create better places, through new relationships and better governance, by:
>
> • promoting more responsive services and empowered communities;
> • advocating a stronger role for local authorities as leaders and place-shapers;
> • promoting stronger and more stable local authority leadership;
> • supporting councillors in their role as democratic champions;
> • fundamentally rebalancing the central–local relationship;
> • promoting community cohesion; and,
> • developing the economic prosperity of our towns, cities and regions. (CLG, 2007, p 2)

The implementation plan for the 2006 White Paper refers to it as 'a clear vote of confidence in councils and councillors as the leaders of their communities' (CLG, 2007, p 2). As several chapters in this volume describe, new forms of neighbourhood governance are broadly encouraged as well as triggers for citizens to hold local government to account through their ward councillor. But it is not yet clear what emphasis will be given to neighbourhood governance in the course of implementation. Nonetheless, regardless of current developments, it is part of the argument of this volume that interest in the neighbourhood transcends the interests of particular governments or parties and will continue to be a periodic feature of future policy.

Chapter One suggested that the emergence of neighbourhood governance can be understood in terms of *sites*, *spaces* and *spheres*. Thus, neighbourhoods can be seen as *sites* of intervention – the spatial territory in which policy is enacted and services delivered while the levers of power remain elsewhere. However, with the move from government to governance, new *spaces* for action have opened up, in which state and non-state actors are involved in new practices or institutions. These actors, however, remain separate, driven by distinct interests and having different perspectives on the spaces they inhabit. Were things to move beyond this, then a *sphere* of governance might be created, characterised by new relationships between actors in which devolution and collective decision making and well-understood connections to other levels of governance would be significant. Only in the third case – the *sphere* – is it suggested that there is a genuinely new settlement between different players implying, among other things, agreements freely entered into, a shift in the quality of partnership, a rebalancing of power relationships, and ways of working that transcend sectoral boundaries (without losing any distinctive strengths and expertise). This chapter now draws on these concepts to examine the realities of neighbourhood governance.

The contributions to this volume have drawn on an evidence base of research on developments in neighbourhood governance in the past decade, the ideas that underpin it and what it can achieve. This chapter brings together key issues raised by contributing authors in order to examine the potential place of neighbourhood governance in a new settlement between central and local government, community and citizen. In doing so, it does not claim that neighbourhood governance is the answer to all the challenges of a complex society – it also addresses the limitations of neighbourhood governance – but it argues for an understanding of its proper place in a complex polity (Hood and Jackson, 1991). Hence this chapter examines the importance of context in shaping developments in neighbourhood governance, the place of the neighbourhood within multi-level governance and the assumptions about democracy that underpin these new forms of governance. It also revisits the discussion that began in Chapter Two of the persistent tensions and dilemmas that characterise attempts to establish a new approach to governance at neighbourhood level. What are the implications for democracy and citizenship of such developments? What is gained and lost, in terms of efficiency and equity? Is neighbourhood governance particularly useful as a response to diversity and a means to promote community cohesion? Does it have the capacity to deliver what is asked of it?

Developments in neighbourhood governance – site, space or sphere?

Some of the policy initiatives outlined in Chapter One have begun to move beyond the targeting of the neighbourhood merely as a site for externally driven action – the detailed examination of these initiatives by a number of contributors here makes this plain. Opportunities have clearly been created for involvement in new spaces, some with significant spending capacity, all facing complex challenges. But how far do these represent new spheres of governance?

Atkinson and Carmichael (in Chapter Three) set the discussion of neighbourhood governance in a European context. In doing so they offer insights into the influence of social, cultural and historic context on the capacity of neighbourhood governance in different countries, its room for manoeuvre, and its place in a wider set of multi-level governance relations. Thus, the authors' examination of governance and participation in area-based programmes in three European countries (England, Denmark and France) finds that concern with disadvantaged neighbourhoods has had similar socioeconomic and political drivers across Europe. However, the resulting developments in governance have varied, as new arrangements have formed around particular programmes, alongside and sometimes in conflict with existing governance arrangements and with differing expectations of the role of the state and the citizen.

In none of the cases examined do Atkinson and Carmichael find clear examples of co-management and co-decision-making processes at a local level; nor is there evidence that a coherent sphere of neighbourhood governance is developing in any of these cases. Their analysis suggests that, while developments in participation may, perhaps, be most 'advanced' in England (at least in the sense of how far non-state players are engaged), the tensions inherent in neighbourhood governance are certainly not resolved in the English case. Indeed, the authors suggest that the scope for local decision making has often been limited and the role of community participants in new partnerships has been diluted rather than increased as those partnerships have developed.

Atkinson's discussion of the English city-region and the neighbourhood (in Chapter Four) also sets developments in neighbourhood governance in a wider context – that of multi-level governance within England. Atkinson argues that in spite of their significance in policy debates neither city-region nor neighbourhood have a clear form or function, comparable with that of the local authority or region – again, it appears that evolving governance arrangements fall short of the development of effective spheres of governance. He suggests that multi-level governance is characterised by more or less ad-hoc partnerships and that connections between the neighbourhood and other levels of governance remain poor. As a result, the necessary framework is lacking for effective action at neighbourhood level and beyond.

Smith et al's discussion of mainstreaming in Chapter Nine focuses attention on the use of partnerships to tackle disadvantage through changes in mainstream service delivery – this has been a key and increasingly important feature of the National Strategy for Neighbourhood Renewal (NSNR). They suggest that, while developments in neighbourhood governance have created new spaces and opportunities for action, the capacity of neighbourhood partnerships to affect mainstream delivery has also faced significant difficulties and limitations. This examination of agency involvement in neighbourhood programmes finds, unsurprisingly, that change in mainstream provision is more likely where there is a good fit between neighbourhood and agency interests but that this fit certainly cannot be taken for granted. On the contrary, agencies urged to join neighbourhood partnerships frequently lack a neighbourhood focus and are driven mainly by a different remit or constituency, including the demands of conflicting sets of targets issued by the different parts of central government. While new spaces have been created at neighbourhood level, therefore, there is no guarantee that agencies will enter, let alone commit to, that space.

The opportunities for agencies working at a neighbourhood level are also shaped by 'what counts' in terms of performance and who defines this. In Chapter Ten, Grimshaw and Smith suggest that dominant trends in evaluation, performance management and monitoring in the New Deal for Communities (NDC) programme have limited the potential for learning about 'what works', shaping the work of partnerships at neighbourhood level, even while encouraging them to define their own priorities with local residents. This has resulted in a reinforcement of policy silos rather than the new, more holistic formulations of neighbourhood problems and solutions that are a fundamental aspect of neighbourhood governance and that might constitute a governance sphere.

In Chapter Nine, Smith et al argue that if limitations to mainstreaming are to be overcome, neighbourhood interests must be pursued not only within the neighbourhood but also at a more strategic level. As Atkinson argues in Chapter Four, one appropriate means of making connections beyond the neighbourhood would appear to be via the Local Strategic Partnerships (LSPs) that are now widely established at local authority level. With a remit now extending beyond an initial focus on neighbourhood renewal funding and disadvantaged areas, they offer a persuasive framework for developments in governance. However, Atkinson suggests that connections between the neighbourhood and LSPs are not yet well developed. Other research has also suggested that the 'evidence of effective links between neighbourhood arrangements and LSPs is patchy' but that stronger links may be associated with 'experience with local regeneration and renewal, mainly in urban areas' (CLG, 2006b, p 6; see also Sullivan and Howard, 2005).

It is not yet clear how far this important issue of connections within multi-level governance will be addressed as the White Paper's proposals are implemented. There are signs, however, that this is the 'direction of travel'. The White Paper does reinforce the role of LSPs and particularly of Local Area Agreements as the delivery mechanism for community strategies. The new duty to work in partnership at this level may demand more of horizontal connections between agencies. However, the effective operation of different levels of governance also requires good vertical connections between them and it remains unclear how sub-local authority and regional levels of governance will develop as the White Paper is implemented. The permissive nature of its proposals sits well with the necessary recognition that one size does not fit all at a local level, but the risk therefore remains of governance structures and relationships that are ad hoc, inconsistent and not fully able to address the key issues of competitiveness and cohesion that are the persistent concerns of urban policy.

In recent debates about the 'new localism' (which is discussed in Chapters One and Five), an interest in neighbourhood governance has clearly been connected with the changing relationship between central and local government. The 'double devolution' debate that preceded the recent White Paper suggested that change in local government was to be secured in part through devolution beyond it. The price local government was to pay for greater freedom from central drivers of its performance was a strengthening of community or citizen power. The White Paper has clearly been informed by these debates, but its dominant concern appears to be the relationship between central and local government. In the 'rebalancing' of that relationship, an intended shift away from central control is to be accompanied by greater responsiveness to other levers, but it is not yet clear what individual or collective forms these levers will take. A significant reduction in central performance management targets is promised but a streamlined framework for the delivery of a central agenda does not imply the creation of an effective sphere of neighbourhood governance.

The chapters of this volume describe a complex, evolving, dynamic situation in which it is possible to see signs that neighbourhood may be moving beyond its traditional place as a *site* of policy intervention in disadvantaged neighbourhoods and a 'supple scale within which ... state interventions can be legitimated and realised' (Whitehead, 2003, p 280). However, there are limitations within the new *spaces* that have undoubtedly been created, with respect to agency commitment, its place within multi-level governance and the continued shaping of these spaces by central government performance measures that limit the potential for neighbourhood governance to emerge as a new *sphere*. There are also many tensions that face the actors in these spaces, if its potential to become a new sphere is to be realised.

Commentators have been critical of the normative use of the term 'governance', its imprecision and the tendency of its advocates to treat it as unproblematic (Newman, 2001). There are inherent tensions in any form of governing and neighbourhood governance – as any other form of governance – will ultimately be judged for the opportunities it provides to find new ways of addressing those tensions. These issues are discussed further in the following sections.

Inherent tensions within neighbourhood governance
Democracy and citizenship

Concern with revitalising citizenship and democracy has been a recurrent aspect of neighbourhood policy. Chapter Five discusses the part such concern has played in varied decentralisation initiatives over more than 30 years as well as the associations generally made between small-scale governance, participation and responsiveness (Dahl and Tufte, 1973). However, attempts to encourage active citizen involvement at a local level have always raised complex issues about how new forms of engagement fit with traditional democratic arrangements and about just what is being asked of citizens.

The White Paper implementation plan (CLG, 2007), with its already noted reference to a vote of confidence in local government, appears concerned with extending or revitalising forms of representative democracy, but there are also appeals to more direct citizen involvement, whether individual or collective. Ideas about extending citizen engagement are taken forward in the White Paper's proposals for community or parish councils and in the Community Call for Action, in which councillors are to have an important championing – and gate-keeping – role.

In Chapter Six, Howard and Sweeting discuss the forms of representative, participatory and market democracy at work in the complex partnerships that have developed in spaces created by the NDC and Neighbourhood Management Pathfinder initiatives. Howard and Sweeting conclude that since different understandings of democracy and citizenship are inevitably at work in neighbourhood governance, what is needed is coherence and compatibility between these different understandings and in the strategies and arrangements developed in order to pursue them. Their analysis highlights the problems that can arise from muddled thinking about these issues and the resulting lack of clarity about what is being asked of people and why. In local partnerships, forms of representative, participative and market-based democracy combine, and at times clash, to the discomfort and confusion of participants who may face challenges to their capacity, their leadership or their right to represent a community.

Targeting, efficiency and equity

There is a traditional association of large-scale governance with efficiency (Dahl and Tufte, 1973; Gershon, 2004) but it may also be argued that targeted, local responses can offer both an equitable distribution and the efficient use of resources. Should the neighbourhood therefore be seen as an efficient, effective level at which to act, targeting limited resources on the worst off and creating a capacity to respond to needs that can be best understood and met at this level? Or is neighbourhood governance likely to involve demands for differentiated, responsive, local delivery that are too expensive to be acceptable? As Chapter Five's examination of decentralisation over several decades illustrates, these are perennial questions. They are likely to be significant again in the debate following the 2006 White Paper, particularly since the context for its implementation includes challenging efficiency savings to be sought in the Comprehensive Spending Review.

A more universal approach to neighbourhood working may perhaps emerge from the White Paper, which does seem to move away from the NSNR's focus on 'closing the gap' between the most deprived neighbourhoods and the rest. Indeed, as Chapter Two argues, it might be argued that sustaining a long-term focus on disadvantage has limited political appeal, given that policies to tackle social exclusion have to be paid for and mandated by the 'included'.

There is also a tension between the targeting of specific areas and the requirements of equity. Criticisms of area-based initiatives frequently refer to the fact that there is a great deal of deprivation outside these areas. As noted in the earlier discussion of mainstreaming, local authorities and other agencies have a role in balancing need and provision across their whole constituency and this may conflict with the need to respond to the demands of particular neighbourhoods. Current policy interest in roll-out of initiatives, for example in relation to neighbourhood management, acknowledges the need to ensure that all priority neighbourhoods at least reap the benefits claimed for this approach. However, such developments do not begin to address the needs of small pockets of deprivation in more affluent areas nor the needs of the neighbourhoods that have not been the casualties of economic change. Nor do they meet all concerns about the fundamental importance of universal standards and the unfairness of postcode lotteries. These issues are also raised in the following discussion of the neighbourhood response to diversity.

Cohesion and diversity

As we have seen, the appeal to neighbourhood is often made precisely on the basis that it allows a reformulation of the relationship between the state and the diversity that is embedded in civil society. The incorporation of diversity within governance is a significant challenge and Atkinson and Carmichael's examination of developments in Europe (Chapter Three) indicates the role social unrest has played in the development of a neighbourhood focus in England and the other European cases examined here. Their suggestion that in Denmark, for example, the problems of disadvantaged areas have recently been redefined primarily in terms of their inhabitants' non-integration into society goes to the heart of some of the most complex and difficult issues in neighbourhood governance.

The recent White Paper calls for '[s]tronger local leadership, greater resident participation in decisions and an enhanced role for community groups [which] can all help local areas to promote community cohesion' (CLG, 2006a, p 6). While it assumes that its overall aims and approach will serve to bring benefits in terms of community cohesion, it also expects that, in some areas in particular, specific, targeted action will be necessary – through Local Area Agreements, LSPs and Community Strategies and in line with further proposals expected to come from the Commission for Integration and Cohesion. Local government's role as a 'place-shaper' is called on here, as it suggested both that problems are best understood at a local level and that 'only local authorities have the democratic mandate to offer and develop a shared vision' (CLG, 2006a, p 156).

In Chapter Eight, Beebeejaun and Grimshaw make an important contribution to debates about neighbourhood, cohesion and diversity and argue for a willingness to engage with considerable complexity in dealing with these issues. However, as Lepine and Sullivan suggest in Chapter Five, in this field as in others, talk of the neighbourhood serves partly rhetorical purposes as ideas about neighbourhood summon up images of a 'cosy inclusivity' (Fraser, 1996, p 100), which may belie the reality and direct attention away from who is excluded by such images.

Assumptions about the dislocation of some individuals and areas from the norms of wider society and a sense of blame attaching to those in deviant neighbourhoods are often in the air when neighbourhood is called on. As Sullivan and Taylor point out in Chapter Two, neighbourhood then appears as 'an appropriate site within which to recreate ... [lost] ... ties and associated moral responsibilities'. In Chapter Three, Atkinson and Carmichael argue that this can be seen at present in 'responsibilisation' – the inculcation of people, particularly in deprived neighbourhoods, with new (individual) citizen rights and responsibilities in order to make them responsible for their future and bring about changes in their behaviour (that is, to make them active and responsible citizens).

The evidence examined by Beebeejaun and Grimshaw makes it plain that an appropriate response to diversity cannot be made simply by going to the neighbourhood level, nor is it easy to respond at that level. The homogenous neighbourhoods of the 1950s, which exist at least in the popular imagination, certainly do not exist now and the authors take as their starting point that the neighbourhood *is* a place for the everyday, lived experience of diversity. They see some potential for neighbourhood governance to respond to that diversity but reject easy assumptions about its capacity to do so. Their examination of attempts to deal with these issues within an NDC partnership suggests that action based on views of ethnicity as an unchanging constant, from which more complex, shifting, multiple identities are absent, will be quite inadequate to the challenges posed by diversity.

Beebeejaun and Grimshaw also reject overly simplistic ideas about the development of a cohesive society and of mutual understanding through intercultural encounters. Instead they emphasise the importance of seeing concepts of race, ethnicity and gender as dynamic and socially constructed. Such arguments are concerned with the need to work with complexity and not with oversimplified notions of communities of any kind. As Taylor argues elsewhere, 'debates on whether action on exclusion should be targeted at territorial or interest communities should no longer be an "either-or" debate, but should explore ways in which the two approaches can be integrated' (2003, p 183).

According to Cantle (2005) neighbourhoods do have the potential to encourage cross-cultural contact but this requires deliberate interventions and the addressing of structural barriers that support and perpetuate communities' leading 'parallel lives', including segregated schools, housing and labour markets. Understanding how different individuals and groups make use of the neighbourhood and of wider connections would also be helpful here (see, for example, Vaiou and Lykogianni, 2006, on the ways in which different women interact with the neighbourhood and Forrest and Kearns' (1999) research (cited in Chapter Two) on the interplay between neighbourhood and wider support mechanisms for minority ethnic groups).

Leadership and capacity

Beebeejaun and Grimshaw also raise issues of leadership and representativeness in their chapter. The issue of leadership is of particular significance since community participation is generally mediated through the formal participation of relatively committed individuals or community leaders and expects much of those leaders and of often fragile community groups. In Chapter Seven, Purdue examines tensions between leadership, representation and participation and considers how community leaders relate to their wider constituency, how far they become part of local leadership coalitions, rather than being left on the margin and how issues of succession are dealt with. His analysis suggests that failure to address such issues is likely to result in burnout and periodic crises of leadership, with detrimental consequences for the individuals, of course, but also for the capacity of local organisations and partnerships. The significance of past history to cycles of leadership is also highlighted by Purdue and in recent research on 'exemplars of neighbourhood governance', which suggests that residents' 'effective engagement at neighbourhood level is most likely where there is a tradition of community group activity' (CLG, 2006b, p 6).

Chapters One and Two draw attention to debates about the demands of neighbourhood governance on the most disadvantaged and about whether concern with re-engaging citizens with the institutions of governance should lead to more wholesale changes, involving not only the poor but all citizens. What emerges clearly from the contributions here is that for local citizens, and particularly those in poor or marginalised communities, considerable investment may be needed in order to help generate sufficient confidence and competence to support developments in governance. There are also, of course, issues of capacity within the agencies with whom they interact.

The future potential of neighbourhood governance

For policy makers, the notion of neighbourhood governance appeals because of the infinite variety of real places with which the term neighbourhood connects. There is some evidence that the neighbourhood focus in regeneration is having some, albeit mixed, impact. Neighbourhood governance is not a 'silver bullet' for urban problems of all types but can be an appropriate ingredient in the mix of public policy approaches to complex social problems. The neighbourhood connection does offer opportunities to understand and to respond to such problems and to engage people through the day-to-day experiences and connections that matter to them. The analysis here suggests, however, that while the tensions that surround neighbourhood governance are perennial, they are played out differently in different times and places – a focus on disadvantage has been at the forefront over the past decade and at the moment the closely connected issues of cohesion and diversity appear to be moving to the foreground of these debates.

The discussion so far suggests that the NSNR programmes and other developments in the past decade have moved beyond the use of neighbourhoods as *sites* of intervention and opened up new *spaces* for neighbourhood governance, particularly in the most disadvantaged areas. However, it has questioned how far these developments have created a new *sphere* of governance. Significant uncertainties also remain about the forms that local governance might take and the development of coherence in the connections between different levels of governance. The White Paper is considered here as the most recent development in policy – as to its lasting effects, one can only say that it is too soon to tell.

As noted earlier, recent debates have focused on the rebalancing of the central and local government relationship and continue to have a strong focus on performance management. The evidence offered by contributors suggests that there is a role for central government (possibly through its regional Government Offices) as a 'meta-governor', focusing on the maintenance of key national standards – including standards of community engagement – that may need to be met (in full or in part) by action within neighbourhoods, and on the overall direction of neighbourhood policy. Finding the right balance between this role and the flexibility that the White Paper offers will not be easy, but a supportive steer is likely to be needed given the scale of the challenges involved in developing the capacity of neighbourhood governance.

The contributions here demonstrate that it is possible to learn important lessons from careful examination of the ways in which the inevitable tensions of governance are at work in the neighbourhood. It is even possible to develop our understanding of 'what works' – the 'Holy Grail' of evidence-based policy. However, there have been important challenges to government's claims of an evidence-based approach (see, for example, Coote et al, 2004). In Chapter Ten, Grimshaw and Smith question the rational and linear models of the policy process that underpin the 'what works' approach. They reflect on the evaluations that might be expected to provide the evidence base about 'what works', suggesting that, in practice, central direction has come to dominate processes of both national and local evaluation. This places limits on the knowledge generated and used at local level and, in turn, makes social learning by policy makers – in which policy and practice are reframed as a result of evaluation – most unlikely. In Chapter Five, Lepine and Sullivan highlight the further limitations placed on learning if lessons from the past are rejected by appeals to 'newism' (Hood and Jackson, 1991) or if talk of neighbourhood governance has more to do with its rhetorical appeal than a realistic examination of what it can offer in a particular context.

While the Cities Research Centre's involvement in evaluation makes it plain that the neighbourhood offers opportunities for learning, it is therefore clear that if such learning is to take place, research will need to rise to these challenges, as it gathers the evidence that is needed both on how existing tensions are playing out and on the impact of new developments. Effective evaluation involves major methodological challenges as well as convincing policy makers of the value of multiple 'ways of knowing'. Methodologies and approaches are needed both to generate convincing evidence on which to build new approaches to governance and to generate the kinds of knowledge exchange that can really transform the nature of governance in the way that the idea of a sphere suggests.

In relation to the particular tensions considered here, there is still much to be learnt, especially about developments within the formal representative system, including the changing role of councillors and about the relationship between that system and the range of participatory developments that government has been encouraging. Research is needed, both at the level of evaluating new practice and in understanding the factors that trigger the kinds of cultural change that will be needed if neighbourhood governance is to become a new sphere. As new demands are made of citizens, more evidence is also needed on the way that leadership emerges and is renewed in communities and how it can connect realistically with the diversity of communities in any one neighbourhood; as Beebeejaun and Grimshaw remind us, many overlapping identities influence people's engagement and exclusion. How will neighbourhood governance create cohesion while still respecting diversity and allowing individual expression? What will be the interplay between inter-generational, inter-gender and inter-faith tensions, for example?

The focus of this volume has been on disadvantaged neighbourhoods. But, if as suggested here, the future of neighbourhood governance relies on its value to the other 90% of neighbourhoods, evidence is needed as to how it plays out across the country. Other European countries may have smaller units of local governance but Atkinson and Carmichael suggest that the English experience has advanced furthest in relation to citizen participation. Are there ways of sharing the learning more effectively across countries?

For the future, developments in technology are likely to have a significant impact on neighbourhood governance, both in relation to issues of scale and service delivery and in relation to new technologies for decision making. What will e-enabled neighbourhood governance look like? Will contemporary forms of expertise such as Wikipedia challenge the position of regeneration and agency experts in the delivery of public services in neighbourhoods? And will the new technology really usher in a new era of connected citizens?

As this volume has been put together, the issue of climate change and broader issues of sustainability have moved to the centre of the global agenda. The mantra of 'Think Global, Act Local' suggests that action at the neighbourhood level is relevant to the global agenda.

This book has been critical of current connections within multi-level governance but tackling big cross-cutting issues such as climate change and environmentally sustainable forms of urban life will require new ways of joining up policy areas – could neighbourhood be a 'sphere' within reworked policy arenas? And if so, what are the governance mechanisms that could make this a reality?

Neighbourhood governance is dealing with complexity. There are no simple solutions or right answers. Nor is it possible to frame discussions of governance in purely technical or managerial terms. Rhetoric and reality are at work in the policy process, and essentially political choices are not reducible to a technical or value-neutral discourse. Addressing these tensions requires dialogue and a willingness to take risks. A willingness to learn would lessen risk and a contribution to learning and the processes of long-term change is offered here. However, such learning – like neighbourhood governance – requires a capacity on the part of government to exercise its meta-governance role in a way that allows the development of other effective spheres of power and action.

References

Cantle, T. (2005) *Community Cohesion: A New Framework for Race and Diversity*, Basingstoke: Palgrave.

CLG (Communities and Local Government) (2006a) *Strong and Prosperous Communities: The Local Government White Paper*, Cm 6939-I, London: The Stationery Office.

CLG (2006b) *Exemplars of Neighbourhood Governance*, London: The Stationery Office.

CLG (2007) *Strong and Prosperous Communities: The Local Government White Paper. Making it Happen: The Implementation Plan*, London: The Stationery Office.

Coote, A., Allen, J. and Woodhead, D. (2004) *Finding Out What Works*, London: King's Fund.

Dahl, R. A. and Tufte, E. R. (1973) *Size and Democracy*, Stanford, CA: Stanford University Press.

Forrest, R. and Kearns, A. (1999) *Joined-up Places? Social Cohesion and Neighbourhood Regeneration*, York: Joseph Rowntree Foundation.

Fraser, E. (1996) 'The value of locality', in D. King and G. Stoker (eds) *Rethinking Local Democracy*, Basingstoke and London: Macmillan, pp 89-110.

Gershon, P. (2004) *Releasing Resources to the Front Line: Independent Review of Public Sector Efficiency*, London: HM Treasury.

Hood, C. and Jackson, M. (1991) *Administrative Argument*, Aldershot: Dartmouth.

Kearns, A. and Parkinson, M. (2001) 'The significance of neighbourhood', *Urban Studies*, vol 38, no 12, pp 2103-10.

Newman, J. (2001) *Modernising Governance: New Labour, Policy and Society*, London: Sage Publications.

Sullivan, H. and Howard, J. (2005) *Below the Local Strategic Partnership*, Issues Paper, National Evaluation of Local Strategic Partnerships, London: ODPM.

Taylor, M. (2003) *Public Policy in the Community*, Basingstoke: Palgrave Macmillan.

Vaiou, D. and Lykogianni, R. (2006) 'Women, neighbourhoods and everyday life', *Urban Studies*, vol 43, no 4, pp 731-43.

Whitehead, M. (2003) 'Love thy neighbourhood: rethinking the politics of scale and Walsall's struggle for neighbourhood democracy', *Environment and Planning A*, vol 35, no 2, pp 277-300.

Glossary

A

Active Community Unit: a unit within the Home Office until May 2006. The aim of the unit was to promote the development of the voluntary and community sector and to encourage people to become actively involved in their communities especially in disadvantaged areas. Since May 2006, this unit has formed part of the *CLG*.

ACU: *see Active Community Unit.*

Area-based initiative: a popular form of spatial targeting associated with social policy. It is a policy intervention targeted at specific disadvantaged areas that are generally smaller than a local authority area.

Area committee: a body set up by a local authority that operates at a sub-local authority level and to which executive decision-makers' powers might be assigned.

Area forum: a consultative body with an advisory role set up by a local authority to cover an area smaller than the whole local authority area.

B

Best Value: a performance management framework associated with the *Local Government Modernisation Agenda.*

C

City Challenge: a five-year government regeneration programme initiated in the early 1990s whose objective was to transform targeted areas in run-down inner-city areas and improve the quality of life for local residents within the targeted area.

Civil Renewal agenda: a political programme initiated in 2003 by the then Home Secretary and based on his vision of a society that enables and supports individuals to take greater control of their lives and the decision making that shapes their communities. The agenda is about reforms to empower communities and boost active citizenship.

CLG: the preferred acronym in 2007 for the *Department for Communities and Local Government*.

Commission for Integration and Cohesion: a fixed-term advisory body that was set up in the summer of 2006 with the aim of considering how local areas can make the most of the benefits delivered by increasing diversity – and how they can respond to the tensions it can sometimes cause. It will develop practical approaches that build communities' own capacity to prevent problems, including those caused by segregation and the dissemination of extremist ideologies.

Communities First Programme: a neighbourhood-focused regeneration programme funded by the Welsh National Assembly Government and is based on the notions of a comprehensive approach and the involvement of the local community.

Community Chest: a funding stream that was set up in 2001 as one of the *Community Participation Programmes* to offer small grants to community groups to renew their neighbourhoods. It applied to the 88 most disadvantaged local authority areas and was administered by voluntary sector 'lead' organisations.

Community Development Projects: an initiative of 12 action research projects that ran between 1969 and 1977 involving partnerships between the Home Office, local government and local universities/polytechnics. Their focus on local self help was called into question by workers in many of the projects who raised wider issues of inequality.

Community Empowerment Fund: one of the *Community Participation Programmes* set up in 2001. The aim of the fund was to empower community and voluntary groups to participate within *Local Strategic Partnerships* (*LSPs*) and neighbourhood renewal.

Community Forum: *see National Community Forum.*

Community Learning Chest: one of the *Community Participation Programmes* that comprised small grants of between £50 and £5,000 to help both individuals and groups play an active role in neighbourhood renewal through learning.

Community Participation Programme: the umbrella title for a series of funds designed to build community capacity to engage in policy making and implementation at the local level. It incorporated the *Community Chest*, the *Community Learning Chest* and the *Community Empowerment Fund* and was applicable to the 88 most disadvantaged local authority areas in England. It ran from 2001 to 2004 when it was amalgamated into the *Single Community Programme*.

Community partnership: a generic term for any governance arrangement bringing together stakeholders including residents within an area.

Community Planning: a process whereby a local authority and partner agencies come together to plan for the well-being of their communities, implying the active engagement of communities in decisions on the services that impact on people's lives. It is a concept that is used in Scotland to apply to the Scottish approach to neighbourhood renewal.

Community Strategy: under the 2000 Local Government Act all local authorities in England have a duty to prepare a strategy for promoting or improving the economic, social and environmental well-being of their area.

Comprehensive Spending Review: a Treasury-led exercise where the aims and objectives of central government targets are completely reviewed. This exercise was carried out in 1998 and the second Comprehensive Spending Review is due to report in the summer 2007.

Contrats de ville: An agreement within French urban policy between either a single lower-tier local authority or a group of lower-tier local authorities to deliver on targets contained within the regional '*contrat de plan*'. There have been two phases of implementing '*contrats de ville*' – the first ran from 1994 to 2000 and the second ran from 2000 to

2006. *Contrats de ville* for the period 2000 and 2006 were the policy framework for *Grands Projets de Villes*. Since 2007 *contrats de ville* were superceded by *contrats urbain de cohésion sociale*.

D

Department for Communities and Local Government: the government department set up in May 2006 with responsibility for urban policy in general, neighbourhood renewal, sustainable communities and local government among other issues.

Department of the Environment, Transport and the Regions: the government department that had responsibility for urban policy in general, urban regeneration, planning and local government among other issues between 1997 and 2000.

Department for Transport, Local Government and the Regions: the government department that was responsible for urban policy, urban regeneration, planning and local government among other issues from 2000 until 2002.

DETR: *see Department of the Environment, Transport and the Regions.*

Double devolution: a policy debate floated in 2005/06 by the then Minister for Communities and Local Government that sought to explore the idea that power and resources might be decentralised to local government and from local government to community/neighbourhood bodies.

DTLR: *see Department for Transport, Local Government and the Regions.*

E, F

Floor target: a generic term that was first used in the Spending Review of 2000 to describe a target that set a minimum standard for disadvantaged groups or areas or a target that aimed at narrowing the gap between these disadvantaged groups or areas and the rest of the country.

G

Gershon Review: an independent review carried out by Sir Peter Gershon as part of the Treasury's Spending Review in 2004. Its theme was the review of public sector efficiency and, in particular, it set out the scope for efficiencies associated with the public sector's back office, procurement, transaction service and policy-making functions.

GO: *see Government Offices for the Regions.*

Government Offices for the Regions: set up in 1994, these regionally based Government Offices represent central government departments and are the primary means by which a wide range of government policies are delivered in the English regions. Their responsibility for the *Single Regeneration Budget* (SRB) was passed to the *Regional Development Agencies* (RDAs), but they are responsible for maintaining a regional overview on the *National Strategy for Neighbourhood Renewal* (NSNR).

GPV: *see Grands Projets de Ville.*

Grand Projects de Ville: an area-based initiative that has been implemented since 2001 in France.

I

IMD: *see Indices of Multiple Deprivation.*

Indices of Multiple Deprivation: a statistical instrument to measure levels of disadvantage in small areas that is used to target urban renewal spending. Area-based disadvantage is measured in terms of a range of different themes such as educational, health-related, worklessness, income-related and housing-related disadvantage (among others) of the people living in the areas and individual indices are combined using a form of weighting. Central government has periodically revisited the calculation of these indices – in 1998, 2000 and 2004. Due to changes in method, geographic areas and data used, these indices cannot be used to understand changes in deprivation over time.

J

Jobcentre Plus: a government agency supporting people of working age from welfare into work, and helping employers to fill their vacancies. It is part of the Department for Work and Pensions. The agency was created in April 2002 from the amalgamation of the Employment Service and the Benefits Agency.

K

Kvarterløft: a Danish urban regeneration programme (translated as 'neighbourhood uplift') based on *area-based initiatives*. Alternative anglicised spellings include *Kvarterloft* and *Kvarterloeft*.

L

LAA: *see Local Area Agreement.*

Learning and Skills Council: established in April 2001, the Learning and Skills Council largely took over the functions of the former Training and Enterprise Councils. It is concerned with further education, work-based training and young people, workforce development, adult and community learning, information, advice and guidance for adults and education and business.

Learning Curve: a strategic document published in 2005 by the *Neighbourhood Renewal Unit* dealing with the skills issues associated with the delivery of neighbourhood renewal in England.

LGMA: *see Local Government Modernisation Agenda.*

LNRS: *see Local Neighbourhood Renewal Strategy.*

Local Area Agreement: a three-year agreement based on a *Sustainable Communities Strategy* that sets out the priorities for action between central government (represented by the *GO*) and a local area represented by the local authority/authorities and the *LSP* (among others). The priorities are shaped with regards to specific central government targets. The Local Area Agreement includes the notion of freedom and flexibilities for local authorities to join up budgets and services to meet local needs. These were initially piloted in 2004 with a decision (taken in 2005) to roll out Local Area Agreements to all upper-tier local authorities in England by 2007.

Local Government Modernisation Agenda: the name given to the New Labour programme to modernise local government. It is generally considered to have been initiated with the Local Government White Paper in 1998.

Local Neighbourhood Renewal Strategy: a strategic document elaborated by an *LSP* indicating how the *LSP* sees its priorities for meeting neighbourhood renewal *floor targets*.

Local Public Service Agreement: an agreement between an individual local authority and the government setting out the authority's commitment to deliver specific improvements sought by the government and the rewards gained by the local authority for achieving the targets set out in the agreement.

Local Strategic Partnership: a cross-sectoral, umbrella partnership generally coterminous with a local authority area bringing together the public, private, voluntary and community sectors (generally including local government, local health and education authorities, the police and community representation) to provide a single overarching local coordination framework within which other, more specific partnerships can work. They were originally associated and specified for the 88 most disadvantaged local authority areas in the *NSNR* action of 2001 (LSPs allocate and oversee the use of the *Neighbourhood Renewal Fund*: NRF). However, they have also been set up in many local authority areas outside of these 88 local authorities.

LPSA: *see Local Public Service Agreement.*

LSC: *see Learning and Skills Council.*

LSP: *see Local Strategic Partnership.*

M

MAA: *see Multi-area Agreement.*

Multi-area Agreement: a mechanism defined in the Local Government White Paper of 2006 akin to a *Local Area Agreement* but applicable to groups of local authorities cooperating together.

Multi-level governance: a concept that captures the idea that governing and governance occur at many different territorial levels and that there are linkages between these territorial levels. The reality of this proposition is not universally accepted.

N

National Community Forum: a body set up in January 2002 made up of 24 community activists. The setting up of such a body was a commitment under the *NSNR*. Its original remit was to inform the government's *Neighbourhood Renewal* agenda but since January 2005 its remit has been extended to inform the *CLG*'s broader agenda of tackling disadvantage.

National Strategy for Neighbourhood Renewal: A New Commitment to Neighbourhood Renewal: A National Strategy Action Plan, launched in 2001, following a period of consultation and policy development, in part through *Policy Action Teams*.

NDC: *see New Deal for Communities.*

Neighbourhood Council: an early attempt in the early 1970s to tap into a local community's concerns on how their neighbourhood should be developed.

Neighbourhood governance: arrangements for collective decision making and/or public service delivery at the sub local authority level.

Neighbourhood management: a particular form of intervention at the level of the neighbourhood. This is a term that is coming to be used generically as well as being used in specific reference to the *Neighbourhood Management Pathfinder Programme.* The approach can be summarised as the local organisation, coordination and delivery of core civic and community services within a neighbourhood generally based on the ideas of community participation, a partnership with key public service providers and a neighbourhood manager. Different 'models' of neighbourhood management include *NDC, Neighbourhood Management Pathfinder* (NMP) and *NRF* interventions.

Neighbourhood Management Pathfinder: a neighbourhood-level intervention in one of 35 neighbourhoods (in two 'waves' of Pathfinders) where the model of '*neighbourhood management*' is currently being promoted under the Neighbourhood Management Pathfinder Programme.

Neighbourhood Renewal Advisor: an expert retained by the *CLG* that can be assigned to assist neighbourhood partnerships with their implementation of the *NSNR*.

Neighbourhood Renewal Fund: a fund allocated to the 88 most disadvantaged local authority areas in England to be directed at the most disadvantaged neighbourhoods within these areas over the period 2002-08. This fund was to be allocated by an *LSP* through the elaboration of an *LNRS*.

Neighbourhood Renewal Unit: a unit originally set up as part of the *Office of the Deputy Prime Minister* (ODPM) and charged with implementing the vision for neighbourhood renewal set out in the *NSNR*. It is responsible for the *NDC* programme, the *NRF* and *NMPs*.

New Deal for Communities: an innovative programme for the regeneration of the most deprived neighbourhoods in England initiated in 1999. Its aim is to reduce deprivation and inequality through intensive, focused help to the most deprived neighbourhoods. It brings together regeneration and housing programmes at the local level, enhancing economic and employment opportunities and offering better neighbourhood management with increased community decision making.

New localism: taken to refer broadly to a political agenda that promotes active participation by citizens in local democracy and decision making in particular in relation to the involvement of citizens in shaping public services. For New Labour this is part of the need to create a 'new settlement' between the state, citizens and public services.

NMP: *see Neighbourhood Management Pathfinder.*

NRA: *see Neighbourhood renewal advisor.*

NRF: *see Neighbourhood Renewal Fund.*

NRF area: one of the most disadvantaged local authority areas identified within the *NSNR.*

NRU: *see Neighbourhood Renewal Unit.*

NSNR: *see National Strategy for Neighbourhood Renewal.*

O

Objective 1 funding: relates to funding available through the *Structural Funds* of the European Commission. Objective 1 funding is available to particular regions for the period 2000-06 for promoting the development and structural adjustment of regions whose development is lagging behind.

ODPM: *see Office of the Deputy Prime Minister.*

Office of the Deputy Prime Minister: the department that was responsible for urban policy, urban regeneration, planning and local government between 2002 and 2006.

P

PAT: *see Policy Action Team.*

PCT: *see Primary Care Trust.*

Policy Action Team: one of 18 teams set up in 1998 as a result of the *Social Exclusion Unit* (SEU) report *Bringing Britain Together.* They were made up of civil servants from a range of departments and outside experts including residents and worked on the 18 themes that informed the elaboration of the *NSNR* Action Plan in 2001.

Primary Care Trust: locally managed freestanding NHS organisations responsible for improving health, commissioning and delivering healthcare for local residents relating to primary care (that is, the first stage of treatment such as GPs and community clinics). The concept of the Primary Care Trust was as an independent Primary Care Group that was in turn established in April 1999 as the NHS internal market and GP fundholding was abolished. Primary Care Trusts were reorganised to create larger trust areas in October 2006.

PSA: *see Public Service Agreement.*

PSA target: a performance measure included within a *Public Service Agreement* (PSA). Where PSA targets relate to disadvantaged groups and areas, they are also known as *floor targets.*

Public Service Agreement: a form of three-year agreement between government departments and the Treasury that sets out the key improvements that the public can expect from government expenditure as part of the Spending Review process. Each PSA sets out a department's high-level aim, priority objectives and key outcome-based performance targets. While they are commonly associated with specific departments, they can also be cross-departmental in nature.

Q, R

RDA: *see Regional Development Agency.*

Regional Assembly: a body that was set up in 1999 to scrutinise the work of the country's eight *Regional Development Agencies* outside of London. With the reforms of the land-use planning system, Regional Assemblies have acquired the responsibility to elaborate a *Regional Spatial Strategy* for their region. The assemblies or chambers comprise councillors and representatives from the private and voluntary sectors.

Regional Development Agency: Regional Development Agencies were set up in 1999 in the English regions and in London. They are non-departmental public bodies and their main role is as strategic drivers of regional economic development. They aim to coordinate regional economic development and regeneration, enable the regions to improve their relative competitiveness and reduce the imbalance that exists within and between regions. These regional agencies took over responsibility for the *SRB* from *GOs*; later, from 2002 to 2003, their funding was brought together into a single, cross-departmental budget, referred to as the Single Pot.

Regional Economic Strategy: a document prepared by *Regional Development Agencies* to shape economic development in their respective regions.

Regional Spatial Strategy: a document prepared by *Regional Assemblies* to shape land use (or spatial) planning in their respective regions.

S

Safer and Stronger Communities Fund: a fund that brought together the *Single Community Programme* and funding streams from the *Home Office* to enable local partners to work more closely together with the local community to tackle crime, antisocial behaviour and the poor quality of public spaces, and in disadvantaged neighbourhoods to make services more responsive to local needs.

SEU: *see Social Exclusion Unit.*

Single Community Programme: the renamed and amalgamated *Community Participation Programmes*. It ran from 2004 to 2006 when it was to be further amalgamated into the *Safer and Stronger Communities Fund* that was administered by local authorities. Applicable to the 88 most disadvantaged local authority areas in England.

Single Regeneration Budget: a funding programme that was launched in 1994 to encourage local communities to develop local regeneration initiatives to improve the quality of life in their area. It brought together 20 separate programmes from five government departments. Six annual rounds of SRB funding were made available via a competitive bidding process.

Social Exclusion Unit: a unit set up in the Cabinet Office in 1997 tasked with the responsibility of considering how best to tackle social exclusion. In 2006 it was disbanded although a Social Exclusion

Taskforce was established under a Minister for Social Exclusion, again as part of the Cabinet Office.

Social Exclusion: often synonymous with poverty, but in practice a wider concept of deprivation and disadvantage reflecting marginality in labour and housing markets and lack of access to the rights, benefits and services enjoyed by mainstream society.

SRB: *see Single Regeneration Budget.*

SSCF: *see Safer and Stronger Communities Fund.*

Structural Funds: European Union funds to remedy structural economic disparities. Structural Fund actions for the period 2000-06 were guided by three Objectives (see *also Objective 1 funding*).

Sustainable Communities agenda: a set of policy ideas initially elaborated in the document *Sustainable Communities: Building for the Future* in February 2003. This plan attempts to locate the need for more affordable housing (particularly in the South East) and improving the quality of urban neighbourhoods, within the parameters of sustainable development.

Sustainable Communities Strategy: an alternative name for a *Community Strategy* since the emergence of the *Sustainable Communities agenda*; these embrace a wider understanding of the concept of sustainability than deployed within the *Sustainable Communities agenda*.

T, U, V

URBAN: a neighbourhood-focused urban regeneration programme funded by the European Union concerned with the economic and social conversion of towns, cities and urban areas in crisis. URBAN I ran between 1994 and 1999 while URBAN II was a European Community Initiative that ran between 2000 and 2006.

Urban Programme: a central government programme introduced in 1968 to grant-aid regeneration projects in local authorities with high levels of urban deprivation. Although subject to several reviews over the years, it remained in operation until the advent of the Single Regeneration Budget in 1994.

VCO: voluntary and community sector organisation.

W, X, Y, Z

–

Index